The Assessment Debate

A Reference Handbook

CONTEMPORARY EDUCATION ISSUES

The Assessment Debate

A REFERENCE HANDBOOK

Valerie J. Janesick

A B C CLIO

Santa Barbara, California • Denver, Colorado • Oxford, England

Library of Congress Cataloging-in-Publication Data
Janesick, Valerie J.
  The assessment debate : a reference handbook / Valerie J. Janesick.
    p. cm. — (Contemporary education issues)
Includes bibliographical references (p.) and index.
  ISBN 1-57607-279-7 (hardcover : alk. paper); ISBN 1-57607-567-2 (e-book)
  1. Students—Rating of—United States. 2. Educational tests and measurements—United States. 3. Educational evaluation—United States.
I. Title. II. Series.
  LB3051 .S66   2002
  371.26´0973—dc21
                                                        2001005350

06 05 04 03 02 01   10 9 8 7 6 5 4 3 2 1

This book is also available on the World Wide Web as an e-book.
Visit www.abc-clio.com for details.

ABC-CLIO, Inc.
130 Cremona Drive, P.O. Box 1911
Santa Barbara, California 93116-1911

This book is printed on acid-free paper.
Manufactured in the United States of America

◆ Contents

Series Editor's Preface   *ix*
Dedication and Acknowlegdments   *xi*

Chapter One: Introduction and Overview   *1*

What Is Authentic Assessment?   *1*
The Assessment Debate and Discussion   *3*
Some History of Assessment   *4*
Examples of Authentic Assessment   *7*
  Writing Rubric A: Evaluation of Your Writing   *8*
  Rubric B: Analytic Rubric for a Question on
    an Essay Exam   *10*
  Rubric C: Holistic Rubric for a Question on
    an Essay Exam   *11*
  Do's and Don'ts for Essay Exams   *11*
Portfolios and Assessment   *12*
  Types of Portfolios   *13*
    The Working Portfolio   *13*
    The Record-Keeping Portfolio   *13*
    The Showcase Portfolio   *14*
  How the Electronic Portfolio Works   *14*
  Portfolio Contents   *16*
  Portfolio Assessment Examples   *16*
    Example A: Sample Teacher Portfolio   *17*
    Example B: Sample Doctoral Student Portfolio   *36*
    Example C: Sample Middle School Student Portfolio   *54*
    Example D: Sample University Undergraduate Portfolio   *58*
Educational Autobiography   *71*
Authentic Assessment and Today's World   *79*
Current Research on Assessment   *81*
  Theme One: The Value of Assessment   *83*
  Theme Two: Examples of Authentic Assessment   *85*
Summary   *87*
References   *87*

Chapter Two: Chronology   *89*

Introduction   *89*
Postmodernism   *89*
Postmodernism and Applications for Assessment   *90*
Chronology of the Assessment Movement   *91*

Chapter Three: The Standards Movement and Assessment   *95*

Standards and Assessment   *95*
Ethical Problems with the Standards Movement   *96*
   The Texas School Reform Case   *97*
   Teaching for the Test   *100*
   The New Discrimination   *101*
Continuing Ethical Questions Regarding
Norm-Referenced Tests   *102*
   Is the Test Score Accurate?   *103*
   Race, Class, and Gender Bias in Testing   *103*
Ethical Questions Arising from Work on
Multiple Intelligences   *106*
Easy Answers to Complex Questions:
The Manufactured Crisis   *108*
The Importance of Educational Assessment   *110*
Why "Standards" and "Testing" Are Important Words   *112*
Problems with High-Stakes Testing   *112*
What FairTest Is Teaching Us   *113*
The Major Problems   *115*
Hope for the Future   *115*
References   *116*

Chapter Four: Pulling this All Together   *119*

Summary   *119*
Remembering Key Aspects of Assessment   *120*

Chapter Five: Selected Resources   *125*

Print Resources   *125*
   Books   *125*
   Articles   *136*
Videotapes on Performance Assessment   *146*
Web Sites with Performance Assessments   *149*

Web Sites about Performance Assessments *150*
Summary *153*

*Chapter Six: Organizations Supporting
Performance Assessment* *155*

**Organizations that Provide Information
on Assessment** *155*
Related Key Organizations *168*
Related Educational Groups *170*

*Appendix A: A List of State Coordinators for
Testing Reform* *179*
*Appendix B: State-by-State Report on Assessment
among States that Replied to the Survey* *181*
Appendix C: A Glossary of Assessment Terms *223*
*Appendix D: Sample Letter for Exercising Your Right
to Information on Testing in Your State* *225*
Index *227*
About the Author *233*

⬤‑◆ Series Editor's Preface

The Contemporary Education Issues series is dedicated to providing readers with an up-to-date exploration of the central issues in education today. Books in the series will examine such controversial topics as home schooling, charter schools, privatization of public schools, Native American education, African American education, literacy, curriculum development, and many others. The series is national in scope and is intended to encourage research by anyone interested in the field.

Because education is undergoing radical if not revolutionary change, the series is particularly concerned with how contemporary controversies in education affect both the organization of schools and the content and delivery of curriculum. Authors will endeavor to provide a balanced understanding of the issues and their effects on teachers, students, parents, administrators, and policymakers. The aim of the Contemporary Education Issues series is to publish excellent research on today's educational concerns by some of the finest scholar/practitioners in the field while pointing to new directions. The series promises to offer important analyses of some of the most controversial issues facing society today.

—*Danny Weil*
Series Editor

⚫► Dedication and Acknowledgments

I want to dedicate this book to my students who work every day to develop, refine, and implement authentic assessment for their students. Their dedication, interest, and commitment to their students, preschool–adult, is an inspiration for me. Special thanks to Christie Ahrens, Beth Demarest, Michele Galecka, Jamie O'Brien, Carolyn Stevenson, Saul Sztam, Heather Van Vooren, Grant Wiggins, and that hardworking, authentic organization, FairTest.

—Valerie J. Janesick
March 1, 2001

Chapter One

•❖ Introduction and Overview

In the 1980s a movement began to reform testing procedures in schools. That movement is called the assessment movement. Many professionals, researchers, and educators were dissatisfied with typical standardized tests, which in general measured only correct responses without determining the methods test subjects used to arrive at them. These concerned individuals relentlessly began to concentrate on assessment to see whether students could explain, apply, and critique their own responses and justify the answers they provided. Thus, a new movement was born. This movement looked at what students should be able to do and continually learn, and how students progress through their studies. The term most often used to describe assessment is authentic assessment. It stands in contrast to typical tests. Typical tests are known by the following general characteristics:

1. Require one and only one correct response
2. Are disconnected from the learner's environment
3. Are designed by a bureaucrat removed from the learner's environment
4. Are designed by someone who may not be knowledgeable about the field in which the questions are asked
5. Are simplified for ease in scoring
6. Provide a score.

Many educators were dissatisfied with this approach to testing and evaluating students. Thus, a new way of defining and viewing assessment took shape. This new approach was called authentic assessment.

WHAT IS AUTHENTIC ASSESSMENT?

Numerous books and articles are available on authentic assessment. Grant Wiggins (1998) has devoted his life's work to describing and explaining authentic assessment. He suggests the following standards for authentic assessment. An assessment task is authentic when:

1. It is realistic. He means by this that the assessment task should follow closely the ways in which a person's abilities are "tested" in the real world. For example, the *plies, releves,* turns, and other moves that ballet dancers practice in dance class are merely exercises. As a former dancer, in ballet class we practiced dance exercises such as plies, releves, turns, etc. But these are merely exercises. The realistic assessment task would be found in the actual performance of the ballet.
2. It requires judgment and innovation. Here the student must use knowledge and skills to solve problems.
3. It asks the student to "do" the subject. In the case of the ballet dancer, he or she must put all the steps together and perform a role in an actual ballet.
4. It replicates or simulates actual "tests" in the workplace, personal life, and civic life.
5. It assesses the student's ability and skills to effectively and efficiently use a repertoire of many skills to complete a problem or task.
6. It allows many opportunities to practice, rehearse, consult, get feedback, and refine actual performances and productions. Thus we have performance, feedback, performance revision, feedback, performance, etc. In other words, students must learn something and get better at doing the task at hand.

The reason authentic assessment is important is obvious. Every teacher is forced to assess the achievement and progress of students. Because teachers deal with assessment issues constantly, educators in every arena want to find a realistic, workable, authentic system of assessment. Likewise, the reader can clearly see the difference between typical tests and authentic tasks as listed below.

Thus, an authentic assessment task is designed to provide a richer, stronger, more complex approach to understanding student progress. The actual performance or production not only tells us about what the student has been learning, it also provides a way for students and teachers to keep track of the student's progress. When authentic assessment is used, the student must provide evidence of some growth and improvement. It is an approach to assessment whose time has come. It stands in contrast to typical tests. In typical testing, one cannot

Characteristics of Typical Tests and Authentic Tasks

Typical Test	*Authentic Task*
Requires correct answer	Requires quality performance or product
Is disconnected from the learner's environment	Is connected to the learner's world
Is simplified	Is complex and multilayered
Is one shot	Is continuing with multiple tasks
Provides one score	Provides complex feedback continually recurring, and the learner self-adjusts, performance is improved
Looks for one level of thinking	Looks for higher-order skills with a demonstration of knowledge

always be sure that growth has taken place. If a student crams and memorizes facts to be recalled one time on a one-shot test, how can we know exactly what was learned? Because the typical test usually tests knowledge of some facts devoid of the learner's actual experiences in a social context, how can we assume the learner learned?

THE ASSESSMENT DEBATE AND DISCUSSION

The "debate" among practitioners in the field of assessment is more like a series of dialogues and discussions on the following matters:

1. The nature of the use of assessment
2. The need for displaying how students think, learn, and solve problems
3. The need to focus on student achievements
4. The correct balance, case by case, school by school, between performance-based and authentic assessment and the use of standardized testing
5. Delineating the concerns and problems with standardized tests.

The concerns at issue in Number 5, above, include:

1. Schools and districts may not be reporting data accurately. The literature is filled with examples on the way some school

        test reporters get around accurate reporting. Consequently, the data reported is used deceptively.

2. Some teachers are pressured into teaching for the test only. Consequently, the regular curriculum is abandoned for drilling for the test.
3. Pressure to report test scores publicly in newspapers, for example, divides communities and individuals. Most often poor, underfunded schools have lower test scores on standardized tests.
4. Test bias exists against various ethnic groups, females, students with limited English proficiency, and low-income students.
5. Testing is extremely costly. Considerable school district resources go into the high cost of standardized testing. This takes money from other worthy budget categories like teacher development or classroom materials. The testing industry has become a multibillion dollar affair, which profits test makers.

Thus, the discussions raised and that continue on these critical points are the heart and soul of the assessment debate. Throughout this text, you may be the judge on the status of this debate by looking at the sources for evidence listed in this text.

SOME HISTORY OF ASSESSMENT

Public schools in the United States have always been under scrutiny. However, since the 1950s a number of writers have been concerned with learning and the measurement of what is learned. Calls for reform in education began in the 1980s when it appeared that students were illiterate. David Berliner, Dean of the School of Education at Arizona State University, and teacher education scholar Bruce Biddle (1995, 5–10) describe how the 1980s were filled with reports attacking teachers and schools. According to Berliner and Biddle, these attacks were unjustified and based on inaccurate information. They uncovered several myths, which sparked the assessment movement. The myths they exposed include:

1. Student achievement in American primary schools has recently declined. In fact the authors found no evidence for their claim.
2. The performance of American college students has recently

fallen. Again, the authors found no evidence to support this claim.

3. The intellectual, abstract-thinking, and problem-solving skills of our youth have declined. Once again, the writers found no evidence to support this and in fact found evidence to the contrary.

It is critical to remember that the public perception of American schools is affected by newspaper and popular media reports, whether or not there is evidence to support the negative press. Educators consequently have gone on the offensive and taken up the reform agenda. They want to seriously:

1. Make schools better for students
2. Provide meaningful and appropriate instruction for each grade level
3. Design authentic assessment tasks, which truly show what students can do and what they learned from their studies
4. Respond to critics of public schools with solid demonstrable results.

We are at an exciting time in this era of educational reform. Researchers are making great strides in finding out how the mind operates. For example, particularly interesting is the work of Howard Gardner (1993, 17–32), faculty member of Harvard Medical School and author of numerous books on multiple intelligences, who has done more than anyone in this area. His documentation of multiple intelligences illuminates our understanding of how the mind works. He argues that the mind is complex. How we learn is complex. Up to now, we have been relying on tests that are narrow, limited, and one-shot ordeals to evaluate learning. He argues that we must try to understand the full range of human intelligence to evaluate how we learn in order to survive on this planet. He describes intelligence as something more than ability to provide correct answers on a test. He claims intelligence entails the ability to solve problems or fashion products that are important in a particular cultural setting. In fact, he describes eight intelligences:

1. Musical Intelligence
2. Bodily kinesthetic intelligence
3. Logical mathematical intelligence
4. Linguistic intelligence
5. Spatial intelligence

6. Interpersonal intelligence
7. Intrapersonal intelligence
8. Naturalist intelligence.

If we look at each of these, it is clear that what we have been doing for years in testing and assessment is inadequate. Thus, the authentic assessment movement naturally evolved and continues to gain strength and momentum. It provides educators with a space to truly address the issue of what a student knows and how the student can apply knowledge in an actual performance-based assessment. That knowledge can more easily document what was learned, as well as monitor the student's progress.

Put simply, authentic assessment goes beyond what a student knows to what a student can do. Let's examine this more closely and contrast this to typical texts. David E. Tanner (1997), an educator, suggests that the reform movement of the 1990s began the serious questioning of testing as we know it. The basic issue on the minds of reformers was, "Do the traditional tests we administer to children actually test for the information the children learned in school?" Needless to say, the answer in many cases was a resounding "No!" Consequently, authentic assessment offered teachers a valuable tool. This tool was used to evaluate learning in the settings that were closely related to the real world. Furthermore, students had to give reasons for their answers. They had to provide evidence that they fully understood concepts. It allowed for active learning on the students' part. Multiple indicators were used to show that students actually understood the content under study. Students had to use their judgment and powers of reason. At the same time, they had to explain and evaluate their work and responses to the problems. They had to actually demonstrate what they learned.

Throughout the 1990s many writers suggested that typical tests offered very poor content coverage and emphasized a narrow range of cognitive skills. In addition, many of the tests were removed from the children's actual experience. It is not surprising then that Wiggins's (1998, 45–50) work was a powerful beacon of light. He and others saw the value of how assessment had been traditionally used in the arts, music, and many vocational education classes. In these disciplines, students almost always use authentic assessment procedures. The student of music, for example, must ultimately play the concerto on the piano or compose the musical piece. The student of drawing must deliver samples of drawings for review. The student studying mechanics must perform a mechanical task for evaluation. Thus, to be authentic, assessments must have meaning in themselves, and whatever learning they measure must be meaningful to the learner. As Lauren Resnick (1990, 63–80), an reknowned educator, pointed out, two key assumptions of conventional test design are false and problematic. First the notion that we can decompose elements of knowledge, and second, the idea that we can decontextualize knowledge both send a noneducative message. We simply cannot continue to make false assumptions about learning given what we know through research and practice. These two assumptions only punctuate Wiggins's warning that we are not preparing our students for the messy real world. He often has stated in quoting a teacher: "The trouble with kids today is that they don't know what to do when they don't know what to do."

EXAMPLES OF AUTHENTIC ASSESSMENT

The reader may more fully come to know the importance of authentic assessment by looking at the following examples of authentic assessment. Here are some of the most common authentic assessment techniques:

1. Essays and writing samples
2. Performances
3. Demonstrations
4 Simulations
5. Oral presentations
6. Progress interviews
7. Formal observations
8. Self-assessment
9. Evaluations of case studies
10. Recordings on audio- or videotape of readings or performances
11. Journal writing
12. Writing folders that chronicle a student's development through a course of study
13. Role plays
14. Portfolios.

For the moment, let us focus on the authentic assessment task of portfolio development. The portfolio is often the most recognized of authentic assessment techniques. Portfolio assessment is widely used to review the progress of a learner's work over time. The learner *selects* which artifacts go into the portfolio. For example, a learner may include research papers, book reports, reflective writing and/or journal reflections, group projects, videotapes, photographs, drawings, software, slides, holograms, and even test results such as report cards. Most often there is some standard, or learning objective, that guides the learner to select examples of the best practices for the portfolio. Again, one can see that this is a technique borrowed from artists and designers, who always have kept portfolios. In a way, the portfolio is a learner's historical record. It is an information-gathering process for the purpose of reflection and growth. Likewise, the portfolio uses multiple indicators and evidence sources to demonstrate a person's learning. This is a technique borrowed from the arts and humanities that provides educators with the historical documentary progress of a learner's understanding of a given subject or knowledge base. It also puts responsibility on the learner to actively select the best examples of his or her work. It is meant to be an active process. It is not a one-shot procedure but a work in progress. The portfolio is constantly changed and upgraded.

I mention portfolios here to illustrate their value as an authentic task. All the techniques listed share the characteristics described earlier: They require a performance and product; they are connected to the learner's world and experience; they are complex; they require multiple tasks and problem-solving skills; and they provide feedback on a continual basis. The learner adjusts to the feedback and performance is improved. The reader may be asking, if portfolios are so valuable, how are the contents of the portfolio reviewed and assessed? What rubrics are used in the process? A rubric is a set of categories with a value assigned for each category in order for a teacher to evaluate a student's work. Think of it as a scoring matrix, if you will. For example, here is a rubric I use in all my classes when I ask students to do a writing assignment. This was developed after adapting it from several different rubrics.

Writing Rubric A: Evaluation of Your Writing

Comprehensiveness and Accuracy

5. The topic is addressed creatively, as well as thoroughly and accurately. All pertinent information about the topic is included.
4. The topic is addressed thoroughly and accurately. All pertinent information is included.
3. The topic is addressed, but some minor information is omitted. All information is accurate.
2. The topic is addressed superficially. Important information is omitted or inaccurate.

1. The topic is addressed superficially and so much information is in-accurate or omitted that the paper is misleading about the topic.

Conventions of Grammar and Writing

5. The organization of the paper enhances the reader's understanding of the topic, and there are no errors in grammar, punctuation, or spelling
4. The organization of the paper is appropriate for the topic, and there are no errors in grammar, punctuation, or spelling
3. The organization of the paper is appropriate for the topic, and there are a few minor errors in grammar, punctuation, and/or spelling
2. The organization of the paper is unclear, or there are several errors in grammar, punctuation, and spelling
1. The organization of the paper interferes with the reader's under-standing, and/or there are major errors in grammar, punctuation, and/or spelling.

Use of Sources

5. More than five sources are cited correctly in the paper and included in the reference list
4. At least five sources are cited correctly and included in the reference list
3. At least three sources are cited correctly and included in the refer-ence list
2. At least four sources are cited and included in the reference list but their form is incorrect
1. Fewer than four sources are cited or referenced.

Use of Appropriate Topical Examples

5. Examples appropriate to this topic are used creatively and appropri-ately and are explained in a way that the meaning of the paper is en-hanced
4. Examples are used appropriately and are explained so as to add to the meaning of the paper
3. Examples are used but do not add to the meaning of the paper
2. Examples are used but are not explained
1. Examples are used inappropriately or none are included.

Note: In the final grade for this paper, the score for comprehensiveness and accuracy will be weighted double the score for each of the other traits.

Here are two other rubrics found in Brookhart's (1999, 47–48) text.

Rubric B: Analytic Rubric for a Question on an Essay Exam

4. Thesis is defensible and stated explicitly; appropriate facts and concepts are used in a logical manner to support the argument
3. Thesis is defensible and stated explicitly; appropriate facts and concepts are used in a logical manner to support the argument, although support may be thin in places and/or logic may not be made clear
2. Thesis is not clearly stated; some attempt at support is made
1. No thesis or indefensible thesis; support is missing or illogical.

Content Knowledge

4. All relevant facts and concepts included; all accurate
3. All or most relevant facts and concepts included; inaccuracies are minor
2. Some relevant facts and concepts included; some inaccuracies
1. No facts or concepts included, or irrelevant facts and concepts included.

Writing Style and Mechanics

4. Writing is clear and smooth. Word choice and style are appropriate for the topic. No errors in grammar or usage.
3. Writing is generally clear. Word choice and style are appropriate for the topic. Few errors in grammar or usage, and they do not interfere with meaning.
2. Writing is not clear. Style is poor. Some errors in grammar and usage interfere with meaning.
1. Writing is not clear. Style is poor; many errors in grammar and usage.

Another example is:

Rubric C: Holistic Rubric for a Question on an Essay Exam

4. Thesis is defensible and stated explicitly; appropriate facts and concepts are used in a logical manner to support the argument. All relevant facts and concepts are included; all accurate. Writing is clear and smooth. Word choice and style are appropriate for the topic. No errors in grammar or usage.

3. Thesis is defensible and stated explicitly; appropriate facts and concepts are used in a logical manner to support the argument, although support may be thin in places and/or logic may not be made clear. All or most relevant facts and concepts are included; inaccuracies are minor. Writing is generally clear. Word choice and style are appropriate for the topic. Few errors in grammar or usage, and they do not interfere with meaning.

2. Thesis is not clearly stated; some attempt at support is made. All or most relevant facts and concepts included; inaccuracies are minor. Writing is not clear. Style is poor. Some errors in grammar and usage interfere with meaning.

1. No thesis or indefensible thesis; support is missing or illogical. No facts or concepts included or irrelevant facts and concepts included. Writing is not clear. Style is poor. Many errors in grammar and usage.

Many educators would find such rubrics helpful, particularly after paying attention to some of the following "do's" and "don'ts" for writing essay exams.

Do's and Don'ts for Essay Exams

Short Essays

1. Do use several short essay questions to give a student a choice to illustrate the student's levels of thinking.
2. Do state the thought-provoking question clearly.
3. Do require critical thinking. For example, require the learner to:
   a. explain cause and effect
   b. explain assumptions
   c. explain arguments
   d. state and defend a position with evidence

> > e. compare and contrast evidence and idea
> > f. apply a principle
> 4. Do use clear scoring criteria.
> 5. Don't ask simple recall questions.

Extended Essays

1. Do test a deep understanding of the topic
2. Do ask students to express multiple ideas in an organized way
3. Do allow time for the work either in class or in a take-home exam format
4. Don't rush students once they begin earnestly working.

The reader may already be asking, if authentic assessment makes so much sense, why aren't more educators using authentic assessment? Are there any drawbacks that bureaucrats or teachers may find problematic?

PORTFOLIOS AND ASSESSMENT

Portfolios have long been a key method for presenting what a student has learned. A portfolio is a multifaceted and complex product. It may have a theme and surely will be judged against a set of criteria, usually evidenced in a given rubric. A rubric shows the viewer of the portfolio levels of performance. Constructing portfolios and assessing them takes time, effort, and dedication to the task. Many practitioners define portfolios as a historical record of student work. It is more than a collection of papers in a folder. It is evidence of a student's work over time and may include accomplishments, capability records, a history of a person's development, and critique of one's work by both student and teacher. Of course, the items included can be many, however, whatever is included should authentically reflect what the student learned. Usually the tasks the student performs show evidence of learning and may fall in the following major areas:

1. The tasks performed were done in multiple ways and for a variety of purposes over time
2. The tasks provide evidence of learning and growth and sample a wide spectrum of cognitive tasks

3. The tasks show evidence of work at many levels of understanding
4. The tasks are tailored to the individual learner and offer the
learner to show what is known.

Types of Portfolios

There is no one sacred model or type of portfolio. Depending on the discipline of study—for example, reading, math, physical education, art, or
music—the portfolio construction varies. However, in looking over the
body of literature on portfolios, there seem to be at least three categories
of type of portfolios:

1. The working portfolio
2. The record-keeping portfolio
3. The showcase portfolio.

Note that often parents are involved in looking over the portfolio, giving
some feedback on its contents, and even rating the student's work. Let
us review what these three major types might look like.

The Working Portfolio

This type of portfolio is mostly the work of the student on a daily basis
and gives evidence of ongoing learning in one or more areas of study.
Teachers, students, and parents freely comment on all aspects of the
work. The samples for the portfolio are most often selected by the student, described fully, and critiqued by the student. Teachers and parents, of course, comment as well. However, this type of portfolio offers
the learner the opportunity to be self-aware and more articulate about
learning and the learner's own growth process. Many schools begin
portfolios at the elementary level and carry through to high school. One
example of this is the San Diego School District, which has continuously
worked on the use of portfolios for its students and which provides resources to train teachers in the use of portfolios.

The Record-Keeping Portfolio

This type of portfolio may be used along with, or even integrated into,
the working portfolio or the showcase portfolio. As the name implies, it
is a history of records. It may contain samples of report cards, results of
tests, and other such records. It is also monitored and devised by the
learner with input from teachers, parents, or administrators.

The Showcase Portfolio

This is the most well-known and used type of portfolio assessment. Here, the learner constructs a showcase of samples that best illustrate the learner's progress to date in a given area or multiple areas. It is something like the portfolio a photographer or artist might put together. Usually this includes completed works that are excellent or outstanding. It is meant to be the record of the student's best work.

Thus, we see at least three types of portfolios that provide a record of authentic tasks and learning. Many states have encouraged the use of the showcase portfolio and, in fact, some use the portfolio in electronic format.

How the Electronic Portfolio Works

Portfolio assessment is well in place in most of the fifty states. In the past decade, with the growth of technology and computers in the classroom, electronic portfolios have become a valuable method of assessment. Electronic portfolios allow for easier storage and retrieval of information and also allow for easier inclusion of parental input and feedback. Portfolios are kept on diskettes or CD-ROMs. A big bonus with the use of the electronic portfolio is the ability to store material that a traditional notebook portfolio cannot. For example, songs, poetry, musical performances, and dramatic readings are more easily stored in digital form and more accurately and visually capture the activity. Furthermore, with an electronic portfolio, a new dimension may be introduced—that of interactivity. With the wonderful software available for electronic portfolios, students can be more creative and use digital means to verify and adjust their portfolio contents. Some of the current software available includes:

1. ClarisWorks
2. Microsoft Works
3. HyperCard
4. SuperCard
5. HyperStudio

Many ask, Why use an electronic portfolio? The benefits are obvious:

1. Work can be stored digitally more efficiently and allow for more student options.

2. If students happen to stay in the same school district, they may have a true historical record of their work from kindergarten through twelfth grade. If they leave a district, they may more easily carry the digital portfolio reflective of their work over time than any other portfolio format.
3. Display of the best samples of students' work may be represented more elegantly and more often with the flexibility of the digital format.

To use just one example, the Wilson Academy for International Studies in the San Diego Unified School District is currently piloting a computer software application that provides for collecting, organizing, and presenting student portfolio information. This will eventually be used by the entire district. Educators, of course, see the value of this.

Students love it because it allows them to edit, cut, paste, and play back what they have entered. Parents are delighted with the ability to take part and learn about computers and their child's work at the same time. The state of California has supported authentic assessment and the use of electronic portfolios as well, as evidenced by the state's Senate Bill 662. This bill actually mandates authentic assessment measures for all students in reading, mathematics, writing, science, and social science. Thus, the outlook is very good for portfolio assessment, and states are getting behind educators to support these endeavors.

Although teachers, parents, and students are well into the computer age and all that it requires, one can imagine that the transition to electronic portfolios is gradual and not necessarily easy. Yet the benefits of the electronic portfolio can surely be persuasive as teachers move to the electronic record. If we ask the reason for using an electronic format, many benefits may be listed. For example, consider the following:

1. Electronic portfolios foster engaged learning, active learning, and student ownership of ideas. Parents also become part of the process.
2. Electronic portfolios are repositories of feedback in a medium familiar to many of today's students.
3. Electronic portfolios are the basis for student discussion of their own progress and a record of their reflections on what they learn.
4. Electronic portfolios are easily accessible, portable, and able to store vast amounts of data and information.
5. Electronic portfolios are set up to cross-reference student work in a way that is remarkable, efficient, and effective.

Portfolio Contents

The creative activity of constructing a portfolio rests on the learner. Any system may be used. For example, some portfolios are displayed in binders, boxes, display cases, or any combination of the above. Currently, electronic portfolios on disk or CD-ROM are used in some schools. Whatever method of display is used, reason dictates that it should be manageable, accessible, and portable. Samples are created, selected, and self-evaluated by the learner. The contents of the portfolio may include:

1. Works in progress, such as writing samples in various drafts and revisions that show evidence of learning
2. Outstanding products, such as poetry, short stories, photographs, artwork, descriptions of activities, audiotapes, videotapes, compact disks, book reports, math problem-solving work, etc.
3. Evaluative comments by the student, teacher, or parent.

Remember that the portfolio is at the end of the process chain. Prior to the portfolio development, the teacher already had a series of goals, plans, and objectives for students to enable them to take charge of learning. Teachers work to make each activity relevant and meaningful to the learner, focusing on complex skills and with respect for the learner. In other words, portfolios remind us of the authentic tasks that students performed and critiqued. Portfolios widen the repertoire of assessment strategies and provide solid evidence that students can "do" something. It is a testament to what the learner accomplished and learned. Thus, portfolios are a critical element in the process of assessment.

Portfolio Assessment Examples

Review the following example of one way to assess a sample for a portfolio entry as suggested by Silver, Strong, and Perini (2000). Imagine this for a verbal-linguistic assessment menu:

1. Mastery = the ability to use language to describe events and sequence activities
   a. Write an article
   b. Develop a plan
   c. Put together a magazine

        d. Develop a newscast

        e. Describe a complex procedure

2. Interpersonal Ability = the ability to use language to build trust and rapport

        a. Write a letter

        b. Make a pitch

        c. Conduct an interview

3. Understanding = the ability to develop logical arguments and use rhetoric

        a. Make a case

        b. Make or defend a decision

        c. Advance a theory

        d. Interpret a text

4. Self-Expressive Ability = the ability to use metaphoric and expressive language

        a. Develop a plan to direct

        b. Tell a story

        c. Develop an advertising campaign.

This is only one example of a matrix for assessing a sample in a learner's portfolio.

Now you will see several examples of sample portfolios listed below:

1. A sample teacher portfolio
2. A sample doctoral student portfolio
3. A sample middle school student portfolio
4. A sample undergraduate student portfolio.

Example A: Sample Teacher Portfolio

As a teacher/professor for nearly twenty-five years, I began to keep a portfolio of teaching evaluations, students letters, and awards for teaching as part of an ongoing life portfolio of teaching. I was inspired by the words of Bertrand Russell and others who often said something to the effect that one never knows when the influence of a teacher ends. The implication was that teachers have a profound effect on students and although immediate results may not be seen, students write letters of gratitude many years after a given class is completed. I originally put this portfolio together in notebook format, although now, after writing this book, I am going to switch to an electronic format. It is organized with:

1. A statement of beliefs about teaching
2. A sample course syllabus
3. A self-assessment about the teaching of the course
4. Sample student evaluations
5. Sample letters from students.

I try to do a self-assessment with every course I teach at the university level. I also change my syllabus every year. I do this partly to keep up with the reading in my field, but also so I don't get boring or repetitive. Here is the first element, a statement of belief about teaching. I am including only the belief statement and evaluations.

Statement of Belief about Teaching

Teaching has always been enjoyable and profoundly meaningful to me. My history as a teacher begins during high school when I inadvertently became the ballet and modern dance instructor for my gym class. I liked it so well, I continued to teach dance throughout college and graduate school while pursuing my formal education. Once I became a professor of educational research and curriculum I knew I had found my niche. Teaching is forever creative. It has become an outlet for my creativity and keeps me thinking. It brings me new ideas from students who continually challenge the readings in class and are part of deep and inspiring discussions. Teaching is always with me and I never stop thinking of what might be useful in the next class. I am inspired, of course, by the work of John Dewey, Howard Gardner, Grant Wiggins, Maxine Green, and Henry Giroux. These writers always sustain me through any difficult times in teaching for when I return to these texts, I find what is needed at that particular moment.

Here now is a sample of my course syllabus, to familiarize the reader with what is involved in a course. It is one of my most recent syllabi and that is why it is selected.

ELOC 535 Research Methods II- Qualitative Research Methods
Spring 2001 4:30–9:30 P.M. every other Wednesday beginning January 24, 2001. Classes are on the following dates: Jan. 24, Feb.7, Feb.21, Mar. 7, Mar. 28, and April 25.

We will have some time to work in the library after the first class night and, if all agree, can begin class at 4:00 after the first class night.

THEMES: *Some set great value on method, while others pride themselves on dispensing with method. To be without method is deplorable, but to depend on method entirely is worse. You must first learn to observe the rules faithfully; afterward, modify them according to your intelligence and capacity. The end of all method is to seem to have no method.*

—Lu Ch'ai

From *The Tao of Painting* (1701)

Life was meant to be lived, and curiosity must be kept alive.
One must never, for whatever reason, turn his back on life.

—Eleanor Roosevelt

From the *Autobiography* (1961)

COURSE DESCRIPTION: This course emphasizes qualitative research methods, design, data collection, analysis, and interpretation. Participants will practice observation and interview techniques as well as document analysis, archival techniques, and multimethods integration. In analysis of date, learners are encouraged to analyze implications regarding race, class, gender, and ethical issues.

Goals: In this course you will be expected to:

- complete all readings and in-class assignments
- master library research and archival skills
- practice interview and observation skills
- practice writing analytical vignettes based on field work
- discuss in small groups and the groups as a whole, problems related to field work including ethical issues that arise in research
- become aware of major writers in the field and learn how to read research articles as a reflective, critical, active agent
- understand the knowledge base underlying various approaches to research
- understand which questions are suited to qualitative research techniques
- practice using tape recorders and video recorders as data collection tools
- understand how the review of literature is essential to the methodology portion of the dissertation
- read, write, discuss, and reflect upon key issues in qualitative research methods including issues of race, class, and gender.

INSTRUCTIONAL METHODS: Small group discussion and groups work, computer lab and library work, projects in and out of the classroom.

Some guest speakers to be announced, some lecture/demonstration/ discussion, Socratic methods of questioning, minilectures as needed.

REQUIRED READING:

Creswell, John W. (1998) Qualitative Inquiry and Research Design: Choosing Among Five Traditions. Thousand Oaks, CA: Sage.

Janesick, Valerie J. (1998) Stretching Exercises for Qualitative Researchers. Thousand Oaks, CA. Sage. Note: This text has a complete description of our assignments.

Rubin, Herbert J., and Irene S. Rubin. (1995) Qualitative Interviewing: The Art of Hearing Data. Thousand Oaks, CA: Sage.

Various articles distributed in class.

RECOMMENDED READING:

Smulyan, Lisa. (2000) Balancing Acts: Women Principals at Work. Albany, New York: SUNY Press. OR

Salkind, Neil. (2000) Statistics for People Who Think They Hate Statistics. Thousand Oaks, CA: Sage.

ASSIGNMENTS:

There will be two major written assignments:

1. Nonparticipant observation assignment due the fourth class, March 7, 2001. This is 25 percent of your grade.
2. Interview project assignment due the final class, April 25, 2001. This is 50 percent of your grade. There will be two in-class assignments including an observation exercise and an interview exercise, Pass/Fail grading.
3. Attendance and class participation is 25 percent of your grade.

GRADING: Students must inform the instructor before the due date if an assignment will not be ready on time. Students who are absent must find someone to take notes and pick up any in-class handouts for them.

1. Students must inform the instructor before class when and if they will be late or absent from any class.
2. If a student is late with a written assignment a penalty will be included in the grading process of a flat 10 percent off the given grade.
3. Each project is worth:
    a. Nonparticipant observation assignment 25 percent
    b. Interview assignment 50 percent
    c. In-class participation 25 percent

4. Grading is based on the following scale:
   % Mastery Grade
   1. A
   2. B
   3. C
   4. D
   Below 58 F

Note: The grade of "C" is unacceptable in graduate studies. You will be put on academic warning if you earn a C or less in any of your graduate work. If you earn more than one C during your studies, you will be expelled from the program and from the university. Be sure to get a copy of the university's graduate catalogue which spells out this policy. A grade of "D" is totally unacceptable in graduate school. You must complete all requirements in this class. There are no Incomplete grades given in this class.

Plagiarism is unacceptable. You will be dismissed from the university for plagiarism.

Standard rules of etiquette apply in class.

TOPICS AND SCHEDULE: SUBJECT TO CHANGE
We will discuss specific pages and chapters for assignments as needed.
   Class/Meeting/Date/Topic/Assignment
   1. Jan 24 Intro to class, each other, begin reading Creswell,
   expectations, purposes first five chapters for the next class.
   In-Class Observation Activity 1: Description of the setting
   Field note format demonstration. Students select one area of the classroom to describe in detail. 5 Minutes. Students take turns reading their descriptions working for accuracy and detail. Students critique each other. Activity is repeated following feedback.
   Observation Activity 2: Description of a Person
   Students have 7 minutes to select a person to observe and describe following field note format and with notes to the self. Students read their descriptions and critique each other. Instructor also critiques each writer.
   Reflections: Students describe what they learned about themselves as observers and describers. They give themselves an assessment on a scale of 1–10, 10 being the highest.
   Discussion of all assignments for the term: Details of all assignments, due dates, course requirements, etc.
   2. Feb.7 Questions for research continue, Creswell next five chapters.
   Appropriate methods for particular questions
   In-Class Observation Activity 3: Go to the second floor study area,

the library, or the cafeteria. Find a person to observe and describe. 15 Minutes. In the same spot draw a floor plan of your area. 15 Minutes.

Return to read, critique, and revise descriptions. Reflect on what was learned about yourself as an observer, describer, and writer.

Field Project—Nonparticipant observation assignment updates: Students identify the site for their individual projects and give a rationale for choice of location.

Questions and discussion from today's reading of Creswell.

3. Feb. 21 Nonparticipant observation/Observation/Interview, complete Creswell

Viewing, documents, begin Janesick—four chapters

Library strategies—Observation activity continued

Introduction to Interviewing Activity 1: Find someone in class to interview on the topic: "What is your view of friendship?" Tape the interview. 15 minutes. Reverse roles so that each learner experiences interviewing and being interviewed. Tape the interview. Save the tape for the final class when we begin to pull categories out of the data on tape.

Preliminary discussion of category development from the tapes.

Project updates and discussion.

Questions and discussion from today's readings.

4. Mar 7 Analyzing interview data, continue Janesick

Category development

First assignment due

Interview Activity in Class

Guest Speaker: Steven Bjornstad

Steven Bjornstad will do a presentation on his dissertation study in progress. He will share with the class his proposal and his timeline.

Interview Activity 2: Interviewing a Stranger: Find a stranger in the cafeteria, second floor, the lobby and interview that person on the topic, "What does your work mean to you?"

Take field notes and ask for permission to tape the individual.

Discussion of journal writing as a qualitative technique.

Each individual reports on their project with class discussion of each.

Reflections on the role of the researcher.

Discussion of the readings for today.

5. Mar 28 Document analysis and begin Rubin & Rubin

Archival techniques, complete Janesick

Computer Assisted Data

Analysis, interview

Activity 2: Deconstruction

Small group meetings to discuss the contents of the taped interviews; preliminary category and theme development.

Return to large group and report categories by listing on the board all themes, categories, and subcategories.

Discussion of readings, discussion of ethical issues in fieldwork, model development of what was found in the taped interviews. Questions regarding the major interview project.

6/7. Apr. 25 Qualities of the qualitative, continue Rubin & Rubin

Second assignment due

Marathon class

Multimethod

Descriptive validity, complete all readings

Pair up and report to one another on individual interview projects. Return to full group. Each person then introduces the partner's study to the group at large. Questions and discussion follows. Discussion of pilot study work from this class for your dissertation.

Pulling the class together, final readings, final questions. Preliminary exploration of possible dissertation topics and methodology.

Demonstration in class of various completed qualitative dissertation studies and valuable handouts from same. EG. Sample category development. Models constructed of findings from major studies, etc.

DESCRIPTION OF ASSIGNMENTS:

Assignment 1: Nonparticipant observation assignment: To develop observation skills—Due March 7, 2001

Where:

Restaurant, coffee shop, shopping mall, zoo, place of worship, museum, health club, funeral parlor, skating rink, or any public setting

Why:

To observe a complex public setting. There should be natural public access to the setting and multiple viewing opportunities for you.

How:

Nonparticipant observation. Go to this social setting more than once to get a sense of the complexity and to maximize what you learn. Go at least three times at different times of the day. If you wish to return at any other time, of course, feel free to do so. Take notes. Make a floor plan. See what you are able to hear, see, and learn just by observing.

The Setting: Look around you and describe the entire physical space. Draw a floor plan or take a photo if permitted.

The People: Look around you and describe the people in this setting. Focus on one or two of the people. What are they doing in that social space?

The Action: What are the relationships between people and/or groups? Try to discover something about the people in the setting.

1. Describe the groups and any common characteristics, for example, age, gender, dress code, speech, activity, and so on.
2. Focus on one person in your viewing area to describe in detail. For example, a waitress, a caretaker, a salesperson, and so on, depending on your setting.
3. If you had all the time in the world to do a study here what three things would you look for upon returning to the setting?
4. Be sure to give a title to your report, which captures your observational study.
5. Be sure to use references from our texts this term or any other appropriate texts.

You have 4 weeks plus, to complete this assignment. Be sure to include a self-evaluation and include:

1. Of all the exercises so far, how has this one challenged you?
2. How did you approach this assignment?
3. What difficulties did you encounter in the field setting?
4. What would you do differently if you were to return?
5. What did you learn about yourself as a researcher?

Assignment 2: Interview project assignment
This assignment is due on April 25, 2001
Reminder: This project cannot be handed in any later. No exceptions.

Project: Interview one person, twice, so that you have the experience of going back for an interview. Interviews should be at least one hour in length each. The topic of the interview is:
WHAT DOES YOUR WORK MEAN TO YOU?

Select an educator or other professional to interview about what work means to that person. The first interview should have some basic grand tour questions like:

INTERVIEW PROTOCOL A—FIRST INTERVIEW

1. What does your work mean to you?
2. Talk about a typical day at work. What does it look like?
3. What do you like about your job?
4. What do you dislike about your job?
5. Where do you see yourself in 5–10 years?

You create the questions for INTERVIEW PROTOCOL B

You create the questions based on what you found in the first interview and to get to the goal of the interview.

This should take at least an hour but no longer than 90 minutes, per interview. Aim for each interview to take an hour of time. Be sure to take field notes so you can probe into areas of this first interview, during the second interview. Be sure to tape all this. Be sure to get informed consent. Use either of the sample consent forms which are in the book, Stretching Exercises.

Due on last class night: A paper/report of 10–25 pages, which includes at least the following:

a. Describe in detail why you selected this person

b. Provide a list of all the questions asked in each interview and label them; Interview Protocol A, Interview Protocol B

c. Summarize the responses from both interviews in some meaningful way with precise quotations from the interview

d. Pull out at least THREE THEMES from the interviews

e. Tell the story of what this person's life work means to this person

f. Include the signed consent form

g. Discuss any ethical issues which may have come up

h. A sample of three pages of your best transcript from the tape

i. Finally include a page or more of your own reflections on your skills as an interviewer, as a researcher, and what you learned from this project; be sure to mention any difficulties that came up, what you would change the next time you conducted an interview.

j. Be sure to use references from our texts this term.

k. Be sure to create a title which captures your themes.

Remember that this is a narrative research paradigm, so you should write this in narrative form as if you were telling this person's story. The story is about the person's life work.

Evaluation of your writing rubric: Use this rubric as a tool to understand how your work will be graded. This rubric appears earlier in this text but contains the following categories:

COMPREHENSIVENESS AND ACCURACY

CONVENTIONS OF GRAMMAR AND WRITING

USE OF SOURCES

USE OF APPROPRIATE TOPICAL EXAMPLES

In this section, I will display samples of selected student feedback. Here are samples from various courses of student evaluation from the 1980s and the 1990s.

Examples of Student Feedback

EXHIBIT 1: Course: Multicultural Foundations of Education Summer 1990

1. Describe what you learned and accomplished in this course and how does this relate, if at all, to your program, and future professional life?

    I feel we touched on some of the most important issues facing ed today—AIDS, minority ed., etc.

2. What qualities in yourself were developed in this course?

    Insight, sensitivity, and understanding, particularly as a related to minorities

3. To what extend did the instructor facilitate your work in this course and what qualities in the instructor facilitated your development in this course?

    Dr. Janesick is an excellent mediator of discussions—through her questions and comments she facilitated meaningful class discussions.

4. Would you recommend this course, under what conditions, and to whom?

    Yes! Perhaps as an elective—for the classroom teacher, for counselors—anybody!

5. How would you rate the textbooks, speakers, readings for this class? Which were most helpful? Explain.

    Textbooks—good

    Speakers—some excellent

    Readings—particularly enjoyed Dr. Kubler Ross's book.

EXHIBIT 2: Course: Multicultural Foundations of Education Summer 1990

1. Describe what you learned and accomplished in this course and how does this relate, if at all, to your program, and future professional life?

    I learned about different cultures and that acceptance is very important.

2. What qualities in yourself were developed in this course?

    Openness to discuss topics and to evaluate different points of view.

3. To what extend did the instructor facilitate your work in this course and what qualities in the instructor facilitated your development in this course?

    Enthusiasm, friendliness, and openness.

4. Would you recommend this course, under what conditions, and to whom?

> People who will come in contact with people of different cultures. In short, all people!!

5. How would you rate the textbooks, speakers, readings for this class? Which were most helpful? Explain.

> The textbook was a little dry, but covered a variety of topics. AIDS by Kubler-Ross was excellent, and the speakers were fantastic. I especially enjoyed the videotapes on deaf culture.

EXHIBIT 3: Multicultural Foundations of Education Summer 1990

1. Describe what you learned and accomplished in this course and how does this relate, if at all, to your program, and future professional life?

> I learned many things about multicultural education and how I can implement a multicultural approach to education in my future classroom. I was exposed to many different viewpoints from other people in the class. Very interesting discussion.

2. What qualities in yourself were developed in this course?

> I was forced and challenged to think differently throughout this course.

3. To what extend did the instructor facilitate your work in this course and what qualities in the instructor facilitated your development in this course?

> She always initiated interesting discussions. Dr. Janesick has a great deal of knowledge to share with us. I feel fortunate to have been a part of her last class here at the university.

4. Would you recommend this course, under what conditions, and to whom?

> Yes. Any future educator should take this course—counselors too.

5. How would you rate the textbooks, speakers, readings for this class?

> AIDS book EKR was excellent. Speakers were all very good.

EXHIBIT 4: Foundations of Curriculum Summer 1991

1. Describe what you learned and accomplished in this course and how do you see this relating to your program and life work?

> This course forced me to clarify, through careful reflection, my own orientation to curriculum. Although I have a master's degree in C and I from IMKC, my past training was focused on how to develop curriculum, and I never really was forced to understand why I write the curriculum I do. Now I know that

nearly everything I write is pragmatic, hermeneutic, and expe-
rientialist in focus. This class also forced me to focus on the
way curriculum is used in a district in contrast to the way curriculum could be used in a district. I guess, in the end, the
course revealed and reaffirmed my own philosophical base and
inspired me to continue to pursue more meaningful curriculum
for all students.

2. What qualities in yourself were developed in this course?

This course improved my ability to be a reflective practitioner,
it polished my interpersonal skills through group work opportunities, and it challenged me to keep up with the newspaper
and current events daily.

3. To what extent did the instructor facilitate your work in this course
and what qualities in the instructor facilitated your development?

Dr. Janesick's tolerant, open-minded quest for knowledge and
meaning inspires similar pursuit of knowledge in others. Her
willingness to share her rich and varied experiences breathes
life into the study curriculum.

4. Would you recommend this course, under what conditions, and to
whom?

I would recommend this course to all graduate-level students
who are dealing with education either within the education system or within the community.

5. How would you rate the textbook and did it make sense to you?

Schubert's textbook is a must-read. It is clear, insightful, mentally stimulating, and representative of a broad and varied perspectives.

EXHIBIT 5: Foundations of Curriculum Summer 1991

1. Describe what you learned and accomplished in this course and
how do you see this relating to your program and life work?

This course reaffirmed my teaching philosophy and strategies.
It provided me with a basis and extension ideas for my curriculum design. It encouraged me to continue to pursue and grow
in my approach to teaching.

2. What qualities in yourself were developed in this course?

(1) More self confidence

(2) Ability to be flexible while working with a cooperative group
of varying work experience

(3) Not take things at face value and realizing that the critical
people help keep the balance.

3. To what extent did the instructor facilitate your work in this course and what qualities in the instructor facilitated your development?
> (1) Your openness to accept various applications and "no-put-downs" reinforced cooperation and involvement.
> (2) You tried to keep us on track and make content applicable and practical.
> (3) Your openness about your opinions and willingness to risk sharing them.

4. Would you recommend this course, under what conditions, and to whom?
> I have already recommended the course to other teachers who need one of the choices as a requirement. At least I feel I am leaving a little better for it.

5. How would you rate the textbook and did it make sense to you?
> I appreciated the approach Schubert used (advocacy, criticism, and guest comments). This helped make content meaningful and not abstract.

EXHIBIT 6: Foundations of Curriculum Summer 1991
1. What qualities in yourself were developed in this course?
> I feel this course has enhanced my professionalism . . . . I am somewhat more literate in the processes of curriculum and curriculum development. Reflecting upon paradigms in education made me recognize paradigms in other areas; as a result, I am more aware of my open-mindedness, or lack of it, in other realms of life.

2. To what extent did the instructor facilitate your work in this course and what qualities in the instructor facilitated your development?
> This is the first time I have relied so *completely* on a group for a college course, and I found the cooperative learning experience both *stimulating* and *effective!!* The depth and breadth of the instructor's knowledge base was a tremendous source of inspiration, even (and sometimes especially) when I was in disagreement. I truly appreciated the "values approach." Additionally, the ambiance of the class resulted in my becoming acquainted with many of my classmates. I am certain these relationships can only help me grow professionally.

3. Would you recommend this course, under what conditions, and to whom?
> I would recommend this class to anyone wishing *active* participation, mental stimulation, and/or exposure to alternate para-

digms. This is a *fabulous* instructor. I will certainly try to take
another of her courses.

4. How would you rate the textbook and did it make sense to you?
    Quite honestly, the initial chapters were difficult. After becom-
    ing accustomed to the style and reasoning level of the author,
    however, I found the text fascinating. The author presented dis-
    parate points of view and cited sources for each. It was refresh-
    ing to read a text where the author posed questions rather than
    dictated answers.

EXHIBIT 7: Foundations of Curriculum Summer 1991

1. Describe what you learned and accomplished in this course and
   how do you see this relating to your program and life work?
    Thanks to this course I learned a lot. Now I become fully aware
    of the vital role the curriculum has. The curriculum should pro-
    vide attention to the major concepts, issues, and problems that
    humans face in their lives.

2. What qualities in yourself were developed in this course?
    The positive impact of educators on the society is one of the
    qualities that developed in myself. Society needs a true educa-
    tor capable of making a remarkable contribution by being well-
    versed in knowledge that will reflect on learners.

3. To what extent did the instructor facilitate your work in this course
   and what qualities in the instructor facilitated your development?
    I believe that the instructor did a great job. She gave us enough
    time to voice our ideas, and provided us with constructive feed-
    back. She let us feel that we are persons of worth. In short, she
    is the one I really trust.

4. Would you recommend this course, under what conditions, and to
   whom?
    Absolutely, I recommend this course to every student who is re-
    ally interested in education. This course will help them under-
    stand their expertise whatsoever more fully.

5. How would you rate the textbook and did it make sense to you?
    I love this book; it clarifies many things and gave me awareness
    to the curricular fields.

6. Other comments:
    I believe that God wants me to do good because he helps me
    take this course. This course has widened my understanding
    about Americans; their culture, their sciences, their literature,
    and their lives. This sense has developed especially during

group study and discussion which in turn, created support
among students. All of this was due to our instructor who
helped us appreciate the true meaning of education. Had there
been instructors like her in my country, my people would have
eradicated the darkness in which they live and replaced it with
enlightenment. May Allah bless you.

EXHIBIT 8: Developing Intercultural Awareness Summer 1996
1. What is the most significant idea you have come in contract with in
   this course and explain how it has affected you.
   > I liked knowing the Literacy of stupidification, knowing the
   > meaning of white, and the terrible state of education. No one
   > will leave this class naive, thinking America is equal.
   > I have never looked at whiteness as described in this class. I
   > think it made me more aware of the world and myself.
2. List any insights you have gained from our texts, speakers, field
   trips, and the authors who have influenced you the most. Explain.
   > Too many: Sleeter/McLaren book excellent. This class was a
   > good growing experience (much better than just curriculum
   > building class). Not many classes for you to think.
3. Would you recommend this class to others? Explain why/ why not.
   > Definitely, it should be required for undergraduates. I enjoyed
   > the small intimate class—keep it small.
4. To what extent did the instructor facilitate your learning in this
   class? Explain and rate the instructor.
   > Teacher very engaging with the student, well-rounded. I felt in-
   > ferior to the older, wiser people.
5. Comments:
   > One of my best education classes. Thanks.

EXHIBIT 9: Developing Intercultural Awareness Summer 1996
1. What is the most significant idea you have come in contract with in
   this course and explain how it has affected you.
   > One idea that sticks with me is Macedo's article which describes
   > culture in a multicultural society as a "porous array of intersec-
   > tions where distinct processes criss-cross from within and be-
   > yond it's borders. For me, it expands on Giroux's notion of bor-
   > der cultures as areas of ongoing and active dialogue and
   > situates his complex notion.
2. List any insights you have gained from our texts, speakers, field
   trips, and the authors who have influenced you the most. Explain.

There have been quite a few—too many to enumerate here—hopefully evidence of them will come out in my work. I never thought of the implications of whiteness for example, nor the fact that a certain kind of privilege comes with majority status. I never thought about my own ethnicity either. This class made me think about these things—all the time!

2. Would you recommend this class to others? Explain why/why not.

Certainly, especially because of the professor and the texts/expectations.

3. To what extent did the instructor facilitate your learning in this class? Explain and rate the instructor.

She facilitated my learning by making available critical texts for digesting and providing a forum in which to discuss them. She listened to us too.

EXHIBIT 10: C&I 811 Developing Intercultural Awareness Summer 1996

1. What is the most significant idea you have come in contract with in this course and explain how it has affected you.

Hooks and Peter Mclarin's idea of white representation as "terror." Understanding the perspective from which an African American "sees" the white segmentation allows us, as critical pedagogists, to reposition ourselves to a greater understanding.

2. List any insights you have gained from our texts, speakers, field trips, and the authors who have influenced you the most. Explain.

Both required texts were stimulating intellectually offering many starting points for dialogue, but Phillips & Darder were particularly important to understand the white representation from the other perspective. All 3 speakers were informative and interesting. The trip to Haskell was wonderful, too. Both speakers and field trip informed me a little more about Native American culture and more, something of which I need more.

3. Would you recommend this class to others? Explain why/ why not.

Yes, definitely, because it makes a person think critically about the whole process of education, both as a student and as a teacher.

4. To what extent did the instructor facilitate your learning in this class? Explain and rate the instructor.

This professor is a most valuable resource and is a model of a competent professional and "transformative intellectual" who creates the environment for success and inquiry and dialogue.

5. Comments:

Thanks for another great experience.

EXHIBIT 11: C&I 811 Developing Intercultural Awareness Summer 1996

1. What is the most significant idea you have come in contract with in this course and explain how it has affected you.

> The most significant idea I came in contact with in this course was an understanding of critical pedagogy, the education for social change. Last semester, it was mentioned several times that education was a subversive activity. Through the class readings, my own reading of Freire, the guest speakers, and the discussions, I have come to an understanding of this concept. In my former life as a junior high science teacher, I had unwittingly followed the master narrative. Although I had sensed that something was wrong, I didn't posses the vocabulary and notions to deal with it. As a result of this course, I now posses the vocabulary and notions to deal with it. As a result of this course I now posses the tools to deal critically with the master narrative and to deconstruct it.

2. List any insights you have gained from our texts, speakers, field trips, and the authors who have influenced you the most. Explain.

> Jones's electrifying statement, " I am a Celt," and my own realization that I don't know how to be a Celt.
>
> —Coming to terms with my whiteness via reading McLaren and Haymes.
>
> —The notion of the Big lie in Maccdo and its implications of our official texts (movies, history books, etc.) accounts of our treatment of the native Americans.
>
> —The cultural, linguistic, and selfhood genocide of the Native Americans and the continued onslaught against the other via the American ideology of Protestantism, capitalism, and republicanism (Adams).

3. Would you recommend this class to others? Explain why/ why not.

> I would definitely recommend this class to others (I already have!). The class provides an opportunity to gain a better understanding of critical pedagogy, multiculturalism, and the politics of difference.

4. To what extent did the instructor facilitate your learning in this class? Explain and rate the instructor.

> The instructor provide a framework (readings, speakers, discussion, etc.) that allowed us to construct our one meaning from the texts (all of the class activities) provided. This is my second class with Dr. Janesick, and in this class, as in the previous one (C & I 755), she has been EXCELLENT, for me, she has been very inspiring and encouraging.

5. Comments:
> One of the most thoughtful classes I have had to date.

EXHIBIT 12: Advanced Analytical Methods/Qualitative Research Methods
Fall 1999
1. List three adjectives, which describe yourself and what you learned as a result of the readings and discussions in this class.
> I acquired patience, receptivity, and endurance as a result of the readings and discussion in class. I am a better listener and I have a better understanding of qualitative study. The readings gave me clear reference to do qualitative study. The class discussions allow me to understand and accept opinion of others in a positive way. The required class assignments gave me practical qualitative experience project.

2. List the most significant idea you come away with after completing the readings, writing, and discussions in the course.
> The most significant idea were centered around the class assignment. The miniproject assists my understanding of what is involved in qualitative study.

3. Would you recommend this course to others? Explain.
> Not only would I recommend the class, I think components of it should thread through every course we take. The ultimate good of a doctoral program is to write the dissertation and threading what is learned in this class throughout would enhance the quality of the dissertation.

4. Rate the qualities of the instructor, which enabled you to learn something from the assignments, readings, writing, and discussions.
> Excellent. The instructor's life experiences added greatly to reducing my fears about writing. I am looking forward to getting started on my dissertation. In the past I feared the task. Thanks. I think I can become a good researcher now.

EXHIBIT 13: Seminar in Curriculum and Assessment
Summer 2000
1. List three adjectives, which describe yourself and what you learned as a result of the readings and discussions in this class.
> Inquisitive, empathic, focused. These books and discussions helped me to see things in a different way. I feel ok questioning the norm. My visions towards helping kids are more focused.

2. List the most significant idea you come away with after completing the readings, writing, and discussion in the course.

Educative assessment: This empowers children to develop self-assessment and independence skills. We are teaching kids to help themselves!

3. Would you recommend this course to others? Explain.

Yes, the children of my school will benefit directly as a result of this course. What more could you ask for.

4. Rate the qualities of the instructor, which enabled you to learn something from the assignments, readings, writing, and discussion.

Flexibility. We were allowed to take our assignments in directions that were useful. I appreciate being trusted to find a topic. I was able to do assignments that directly influenced my life outside of school (too often, assignments in school do not reflect my "real life").

EXHIBIT 14: Seminar in Curriculum and Assessment Summer 2000

1. List three adjectives, which describe yourself and what you learned as a result of the readings and discussions in this class.

I learned that I am a postmodern thinker. I am more aware of what authentic assessment is and now (thanks to Wiggins) I am a better administrator. Also, I learned I am a changing individual. I am so happy that I am moving into a better understanding of what it is to be a good teacher, principal, and administrator.

2. List the most significant idea you come away with after completing the readings, writing, and discussion in the course.

To develop a workable schedule for teachers to allow meaningful assessment to happen.

How to market my years of not working. Yahoo!!

Most importantly; I have learned that developing a postmodern school would be very challenging and rewarding.

3. Would you recommend this course to others? Explain.

Yes, firstly the books were excellent (all three of them). Secondly the instructor was stimulating and she made us do an autobiography which was very liberating. Thirdly the class was overall an enjoyable stimulating experience.

4. Rate the qualities of the instructor, which enabled you to learn something from the assignments, readings, writing, and discussion.

She was organized and she was a reasonable person.

Her assignments were useful.

She was thought provoking and she picked excellent books and she gave excellent resources.

I like the fact that she gave us list-serves to go to.

Example B: Sample Doctoral Student Portfolio

In this second example of how a portfolio is developed, kept, and re-vised, we turn our attention to a doctoral student portfolio.

"Writing and fulfilling your own story!"

Personal Professional Portfolio Plan: A model to support your initiation of your Portfolio

Your commitment to beginning your own professional life story will be honored. It will support your advancement professionally, engender a more productive and interesting program for you, and save you time and cost as well. You may add to or alter requests which are provided in this Portfolio model plan.

Since a Portfolio continues with you throughout your doctoral pro-gram and thereafter, please include your planning and your major products. I ask that you prepare and submit your Portfolio on a diskette or on-line by means of Internet or electronic mail. Please turn in your completed task on a 3.5" IBM formatted floppy disk.

The Portfolio is a continuing documentary, but contains two parts:

Sector I Your Professional and Career Planning. This sector incorpo-rates your personal strategic plan to advance yourself in professional competence and career responsibility.

Sector II Your Achievements and Products. This sector incorporates statements of your major achievements as well as your major products during your doctoral program. These products range from seminar pa-pers and conference presentations to internship descriptions and dis-sertation summary.

Sector I: Your Professional Development

Please briefly comment or respond to the following personal, profes-sional, and career inquiries. If you desire to alter these requests or add to them, please do so.

1. Describe you and your interests
    a. What are your professional career interests and even goals?
    b. What are your professional experiences to this time including those which may not be related directly to your career interests and goals?
    c. What are your reasons for pursuing this doctoral program?
    d. Where do you see yourself in 5 years?
    e. Issues you have some passion for.

f. Your personal beliefs about education and your role in education, or your philosophy of education statement.

These issues may and should be priority issues of yours. These may be used in course papers, comprehensive examination and/or the initial thinking related to a dissertation problem. Hopefully you will consider publication with our assistance. Research and publication are critical factors in professional advancement in your area of concentration.

Sector II: Your Academic and Professional Development Process and Products

This sector should be the depository of your finest work. It should contain your writings, a description of your professional achievements, an authentic taxonomy of your professional interests such as issues you are really concerned about, and a litany of the outstanding professionals you have come to know and possibly work with. It should begin with a well-written curriculum vitae which may be improved and made current every year or semiannually.

To begin development of Sector II, please add the following:

A written sequence of your seminar papers, conference presentations, possible publications, description of your internship experience, your comprehensive paper, dissertation, and publications. Include your dissertation proposal as well. Include any critical reflections on the process of studying for your comprehensive exams, etc.

You may have strong papers, examinations, and other documents which you have already completed and which should be incorporated in your Portfolio Sector II. (Source: John Carpenter and Valerie Janesick)

In the following sections, you will find the following: The outline of Saul Stzam's portfolio, his autobiography, and his updated curriculum vitae.

Saul Sztam
Titles and dates of doctoral papers submitted in the program in Higher Education Administration at Florida International University
12/97 Standardized Tests: How effective and culturally sensitive are they?
3/98 Social Change: Are standardized tests effectively predicting intelligence in today's students?
11/98 Group consultancy
12/98 Autobiography: Defining moment
2/99 Book Report: The university, an owner's manual by Henry Rosovski

2/99 Strategic Planning at the School of Journalism and Mass Communication, office of Student Services

4/99 Higher Education Administration: Leadership

4/99 Dialogue with an honor's student

10/99 Comprehensive Research Paper: How can we better understand what high school students and their parents consider the most important factors in deciding on an institution of higher learning?

12/99 America's most wanted: How can college and universities better understand our target student population?

Current Dissertation topic: Selecting a College or University: A study of students and their parents.

Seminar in Curriculum: Autobiography "Defining Moment"
By Saul Sztam

Introduction

My life would forever change one early Saturday morning in New York City back in 1983. The streets were empty as my mom, my sister, and myself rushed to our destination. Of all people to run into, Johnny Carson, the famous late-night talk show host, stood alone on a street corner admiring the rare silence of the city. We had neither the time nor the desire to even address him. Our destination that morning was a hospital. We received a call that morning with the news that my father suffered a heart attack and was in critical condition. Two hours after we arrived we were given the horrible news. I don't remember much about the hospital but I remember many of the faces I saw that morning including the nurse, the doctor, and even the cabdriver on the way home. During this cab ride I remember holding a brown paper bag with my dad's belongings. As a teenager in such need of a father figure, I struggled for months switching from a state of denial to anger. Within six months I also lost my last living grandparent and my favorite uncle. I did a lot of soul searching at a very young age. This was a turning point in my life in which I realized I had a choice to make that could affect me forever. I could continue to castigate myself and blame any future failures on this tragic time period, or I could grow up very quickly for my family and myself on a faster track to becoming a responsible young adult. I chose the latter. At a very young age, I was committed to doing the right thing, to being dependable, to working hard, and to following through. These values are the foundation of my person today. My mother provided a great inspiration, as she remained strong and focussed with the intent of offering the best to her children. Maturity came early for me and I found that this trait would be embraced by many of those around me. Growing up quickly also had its downfalls. I became demanding, somewhat self-centered, and close-minded. I believed life should always be fair, things should work out as planned, and people should be good to one another. Life is just too short. My experience level did not match my perceived maturity level. Many accomplishments and disappointments later, I did eventually achieve a desired balance. My educational experiences have helped me grow. Going to school in a foreign land, Argentina, for four years gave me a totally different perspective. Working in the field of higher education for almost 12 years gave me the opportunity to listen to others, understand them, encourage them, and try to make things right for them. Helping make others stronger and smarter had a similar effect on me. These experiences, my progression through positions, and the chance to work with and learn from other educators as a student, a coworker, and as a willing mentee has contributed to making me the person I am today.

Summary of critical incidents

Two years after this tragic part of my life, my mother bought a house in sunny south Florida where I finished my high school education. The transition from the school system in New York City to the one in Florida was an educational experience I still often refer to. Neither could compare to what I was exposed to in Argentina back in elementary school. Living in this foreign land I developed a respect for education and those committed to it. This level of appreciation I have yet to find in our country. As a student in New York I had the desire to learn and I was encouraged by the competition in the school. My high school in Florida seemed to encourage mediocrity. I got this same feeling from most high schools in the area I later got the opportunity to work with. When I graduated high school my initial plan was to go away to college, but I just did not feel right about following my friends to the University of Florida or Florida State University. I felt a sense of responsibility to stay home with my family. The sensible decision at the time was to attend Broward Community College. The decision would help shape the rest of my life. As a freshman looking for a convenient part-time job, I inquired about an opportunity available in the office of veterans' affairs. Two weeks earlier my previous employer, an electrical distributing company, offered me a full-time job. The right thing to do was to concentrate on school although the offer was tempting. My introduction to education involved not only coordinating veterans' affairs but also working in the department of financial aid. I quickly became an important part of this unit. Upon completing my Associate of Arts degree in 1988, I transferred to Florida Atlantic University for my Bachelor's in Social Sciences. At this time, I was working as an academic advisor. This position was my breaking out. At the very young age of 20, I was making important suggestions and decisions in my very own office. I felt a real sense of accomplishment by helping people. My degree was preparing me for a career in law as it included many political science courses. The closer I got to graduation, the more I thought about a graduate program in education. Working at a college helped me make a more educated decision. I believe I could have made a great lawyer and might still someday. The most attractive aspect of law to me has always been the money. I kept thinking about someday sitting at home on a Sunday afternoon with a wife and kids and getting called in to help a client. The job of an attorney never ends and sometimes forces good people to act immoral. The enjoyment I felt while working with students sounded a lot better than dealing with the daily stress of a job I didn't truly enjoy.

I decided to enroll at Florida International University in 1990, in the Master's program in Adult Education and Human Resource Development. At this point, I was working full-time as an advisor taking every opportunity to get cross-trained. This graduate program would hopefully allow me to network with other professionals and give me some training and experience in management. While the program did serve many purposes, it probably had too much of a concentration in training and human resources and not enough in higher education for my taste. It was clear that my intentions were to continue this career as an educator. I began teaching "college success skills" and was very active in the school's recruitment efforts. My age seemed to be getting in the way of my progress. I was a lot younger than my peers were, many who still remember me as a student. Frustration was starting to set in as I grew out of my position with my experience and education. I turned down a couple of job offers outside of the college because they just didn't feel right and then things started happening for me. I was named the central campus recruitment coordinator in 1994, which made me a strong candidate for the position of admissions and registration coordinator at the central campus. This position meant a lot to me and I finally got my chance in 1996 after coming up second or third so many times for other opportunities. My new official title was Coordinator of Admissions, Registration, and Recruitment at the central campus.

For the first time, I was in a position to implement some of the ideas and concepts I picked up over the years. I served as the acting supervisor on many occasions but never on an official and permanent basis. My boss at the time had so much confidence in me that I had the support necessary to succeed and the autonomy desired to do it my way. I was in charge of a very busy department on a campus of over 13,000 students. Our office had 13 employees, 7 of which were full-time. They all knew me very well and some weren't thrilled with the fact that their new supervisor was, as they thought, a young and cocky know-it-all. On my first day as a supervisor, at 8:15 in the morning, I had to deal with my first conflict. Two full-time employees were yelling at each other over personal problems in the storage room. It was loud enough for everyone in the office that early to hear including students walking by. I've always felt any employee working in this field should always act professionally and this was happening in my office in front of my very eyes. Without hesitation, I let them know that this type of behavior was not acceptable. I spoke to each employee individually and then together and made it clear that conflicts would be discussed privately and properly. Although they reassured me that this occurrence had nothing to do with me, I knew that this would not be the only time I would spend babysitting or acting as a referee. I chalk up every experience, positive or negative, as an opportunity to learn more about myself and about others. My assistant coordinator would also provide me with a challenge. She had served as the acting coordinator for two years but could not apply for the position because she lacked the education. I tried to be as sensitive to this as I could for obvious reasons but I was not always successful in reaching her. We had different philosophies, and her getting demoted to work for her replacement was not an easy pill to swallow. I learned a lot from our relationship and I felt a strong sense of loyalty when she announced her retirement a week after I announced my resignation. Once I was comfortable in my new position, I began my doctorate program at Florida International University in Higher Education Administration. This program seemed to have everything I was looking for. It was structured for college administrators and its curriculum offered me a hands-on approach. Meeting new people in the field including a professional faculty would eventually open up many doors.

After spending over eleven years at Broward Community College, I've always felt a strong sense of loyalty and pride for my employer. Some of the people who made this college the place that it was have retired and the replacements brought in a different perspective. I have seen many things happen over the years. Decisions are not always made with the student's best intention in mind but with close attention to monetary concerns and political positioning. It has never been as blatant as in the last year I was there. It got to the point that I would no longer recommend my institution to people I cared about. These new members of our family all knew how to say the right things but didn't practice what they preached. I served on many search committees and in one particular case the open-door policy of a future supervisor was discussed. During the interviews, she made it a point to announce her willingness to talk to anyone at any time. A week after she was hired, she installed a deadbolt lock in her door, would only talk to staff or students with an appointment, and has since moved her office so far away from the action she hardly sees what happens in the trenches. It was clearly my time to go. If I cannot feel good about the place that I work, there is no longer a reason to stay. I applied for a position at Florida International University in the School of Journalism and Mass Communication as the Director of Student Services. This higher level position seemed like a great move and I was thrilled to have it offered to me. It was still difficult to leave a place I called home for so long but it was the right thing to do at the right time. I have been employed at this position since April of this year and it has been challenging and fulfilling. My department has strong leadership committed to excellence. In the short time I have been there, many strides have been made to improve services to our students. Faculty members, who in the past have been reluctant to discuss student needs, are also becoming more cooperative. We are there for students and it is a great feeling to see their needs met.

Key inspirational people in my professional growth

We are all made up of our experiences and we all have a piece of those who have touched us. I've had the luxury of working with some knowledgeable and influential individuals in this field who have taken the time to teach me. When I first started in financial aid as a nineteen-year-old part-time employee, Judith Berson was the Director of Financial Aid and my coworkers seemed almost intimidated by her. My perception was that she was very demanding but focussed on the goals of the department. Under her supervision, I was encouraged to learn new responsibilities to become more useful in such a busy office. She had a lot of confidence in me from the beginning and always seemed to give me some words of wisdom. Looking back at that time, I was only a part-time employee and she was the Director. I always felt comfortable enough to talk to her and give her my suggestions. As my responsibilities increased while employed in other areas of the college, we had the opportunity to work together on other levels and she trusted my skills time and time again. As the Associate Vice President of Student Affairs, she made me the chair of the college-wide staff development committee. This introduced me to a whole new set of people and I really liked the responsibility of putting together such important workshops for fellow staff members. At my first workshop, my skills were really put to the test. Our keynote speaker was late, very late, and the guest of honor was our President, Dr. Holcombe. I scrambled around and rearranged the program for over 150 employees. I was incredibly surprised with the positive responses we received. I knew our audience very well and I knew how ruthless they could be. Apparently, the content of our program and the advanced planning made up for the small inconvenience. Serving as the chair of such a good committee gave me a strong sense of accomplishment. Dr. Berson later graduated from the same doctorate program I currently attend and continued to serve as one of my mentors over the years.

When I first started my job as an academic advisor, one of the first things I noticed was just how hard my new boss worked on a daily basis. Katherine Tymeson was the Dean of Students and if you didn't know any better you would think she was the hardest working, most caring advisor in the office. She epitomized leading by example. When the office was busy, you really could tell who the hard workers were and who was just killing time. On one particular evening, one other advisor and the two of us saw 100 different students from 4 PM to 8 PM. This must have been some kind of record. Watching her go motivated me to push myself that much harder. She was our boss but was also one of us. I respected her authority and appreciated her constant support. I've been asked on numerous occasions—which previous supervisor have you modeled your leadership style after? Ms. Tymeson always comes to mind first.

Dr. George Young was the Vice President of Student Affairs at Broward Community College for most of the time I spent there. While I was working as an advisor, he offered a one-semester workshop for a selected group interested in becoming a dean or a vice president. There were only five available spots college-wide and many applications. To my surprise, I was chosen. The other four members were deans, directors, and the registrar. They were as surprised as I was to see me at the first meeting. These workshops were networking at its best. Dr. Young clearly sent a message to the rest of the college and myself: I was an up-and-coming student affairs employee recognized by someone at the top. Over the years, many decisions made by Dr. Young were very controversial. I have disagreed with some of them as well. He was never afraid to make a decision but always kept an open mind. He probably was never more appreciated than he is now.

After several attempts to land my first supervisory position, Dr. Stan Mitchell finally gave me my first big break. He made me the Coordinator of Recruitment and later hired me as the Coordinator of Admissions and Registration. He had enough faith in me to tell me to take care of my area the way I wanted to, and told me he would always be in my corner. He confided in me several times and even asked me for my advice in other areas of the department. He recognized the fact that I have seen many things happen over the years and that my number one concern was always the service to the students. He helped me understand some of the realities about the decision making of the college. After serving as the interim Dean of Students for three years, he is now happily retired in Gainesville.

Enrolling in a doctoral program was something I always wanted to do and the time was finally right in the fall of 1997. At an orientation luncheon at the Davie campus of Florida International University, I had the luxury of sitting next to John Carpenter. In a very short time, he not only convinced me to attend the program but was also a tremendous motivator. He seemed like such a genuine and caring person. My first class with him taught me a lot about the man. He arrived hours early to prepare the classroom. His love for his occupation was obvious. He has since also served as an advisor, a mentor, and a friend. On many occasions, I find myself thinking about what could be done and why the system won't allow it. Dr. Carpenter wants to make things happen and finds a way to do it. For someone with so many accomplishments and so much experience, he remains humble and unique. His work ethic is exemplary as he constantly reminds us that change can happen.

The five professionals I have discussed were an integral part of my professional development. Over the years, I've had many negative examples to go by as well. I try to learn from everything, good or bad, but these five special people had qualities in them I will always carry with me in how I do my job. It is an honor to know these types of individuals and hearing them tell me how proud I've made them over the years has served as the most effective positive reinforcement for me.

Influential readings

One of the things I have truly appreciated about this doctorate program has been the opportunity to read. There are so many intelligent professional educators who have expressed their experiences and opinions through writing. We don't always have the opportunity to read and learn more about the field we are in; it unfortunately happens on the job. In this program, we are encouraged to read and we also benefit from discussions with other professionals in the field. I have read many texts and articles and have chosen those which address some issues near and dear to me, many of which I hope to address in some form in my dissertation.

It is my opinion that education is a reflection of our society. It is no secret that our education system at the lower level leaves a lot to be desired. Comparing this to other countries where education is considered sacred even in lower socioeconomic environments, I believe our problem has a lot to do with the way our society thinks. *Seeing Ourselves* by Macionis and Benokraitis, a text assigned by Dr. Carpenter, gave me a compilation of articles written by many well-known authors. This text covered a wide range of topics, many of which crucially help shape our society today. The "family" is an institution that has deteriorated over the years, as effectively pointed out by David Popenoe in his article titled: "The Decline of Marriage and Fatherhood." While Poepenoe concentrated on the decline of fatherhood, I see the real problem in the decline of the family in general. From 1960 to 1990, the percentage of children living apart from their biological fathers more than doubled, from 17 percent to 36 percent (Macionis and Benokraitis, 1997, p. 313). There are many reasons for this increase and most of them are attributed to our financially changing times. Children today are not getting the emotional, financial, or moral support from the family structure they need. This results in many of today's more prevalent issues as described by Popenoe (Macionis and Benokraitis, 1997):

> Father absence is a major force lying behind many of the attention-grabbing issues that dominate the news: crime and delinquency; premature sexuality and out-of-wedlock teen births; deteriorating educational achievement; depression, substance abuse, and alienation among teenagers; and the growing number of women and children in poverty. (p. 313)

The success of the family is not always correlated to which type of family it is. Our lives, in general, have improved, which means we have many more choices than before. A nontraditional family today would seem to have a much better chance to survive than in the past. I agree with Popenoe that there are certain qualities in the male figure and the female figure that together go a long way in developing character in our youth. However, there are many "traditional" families composed of people not fit to be parents. The decline of the family and its influence on our youth is a huge concern of mine, a problem I don't see getting any better.

The quality of our education is again at the center of my concern. *Failing at Fairness: How Our Schools Cheat Our Girls,* written by Myra and David Sadker, addresses some major problems with our school system. This text allowed me to put myself right back into the classroom and relate to some of the problem we have today. Not only are we cheating girls, but we are also cheating boys. From a very young age girls are reminded that not only are they different from boys in a biological sense but in how they will be treated. We have progressed so much, yet many that have benefited from this progress are not helping our youth. This behavior is so accepted, it goes unnoticed.

> The classroom consists of two worlds: one of boys in action, the other of girls' inaction. Male students control classroom conversation. They ask and answer more questions. They receive more praise for the intellectual quality of their

> ideas. They get criticized. They get help when they are confused. They are the heart and center of interaction. (Sadker and Sadker, 1994, p. 42)

This text effectively presented this problem and provided us with sufficient quantitative and qualitative research for support.

The needs we must meet in education change everyday. In higher education the traditional student is now, in some cases, what we used to call the nontraditional student. As our populations change, so does our focus. An article was written, titled "What the Public Wants from Higher Education," which brought some of this to light. We are no longer teaching in traditional classrooms, but in more tailored environments. Lifelong learning is a theme that has become more popular.

> Public support exists for universities to do more than educate 18 to 22 year old undergraduates. A majority of adults think that it's important for universities to provide multiple services, including undergraduate and graduate teaching; teaching older, returning students; providing off-campus technical help; and conducting research. (Dillman et al., 1996)

As college administrators, it would behoove us to pay close attention to the ever-changing needs of our customers. This cycle has begun and will continue as universities battle for the almighty enrollment numbers.

Standardized tests have affected our population and our way of identifying intelligence for many years. I can still remember the stress I felt during my senior year while waiting for my dreaded SAT scores. Was I college material? Was I as smart as the rest of my classmates? Do I have a future? Thousands of high school students face these emotions every year. I strongly believe that we do need some sort of standardized testing. We have to be able to distinguish between the thousands of students applying to our universities. A 4.0 GPA from school A is not the same as a 4.0 from school B. It is virtually impossible to accurately measure performance when dealing with a large number of students.

With roots in intelligence testing that go back generations, the mental measurement establishment continues to define merit largely in terms of test-taking and potential rather than actual performance. The case against standardized testing may be as intellectually and ethically rigorous as any argument made about social policy in the past twenty years, but such testing continues to dominate the education system, carving further inroads in the employment arena as well, having been bolstered in recent years by a conservative backlash advocating advancement by merit (Sacks, 1997, p. 25).

While I believe that testing is necessary, I can understand why there are so many opponents to this method. These tests might be somewhat accurate, but they are also culturally biased. Socioeconomic factors in this process become major considerations. We are constantly trying to find ways to educate more minority students and standardized tests seem to create greater obstacles.

> Frustrated by the small pool of black and Hispanic students, and troubled by the high dropout and failure rates, many in the education establishment have concluded that disparate scores prove not that many minority students are inadequately prepared, but that the tests themselves are biased. Charges of racism and sexism are commonplace, and the College Board has come under increasing pressure to revise the tests so that black and Hispanic students perform better. (D'Souza, 1992, p. 43)

My solution to this problem is to come up with a culturally sensitive test developed by educators with different backgrounds. The development of such a tool would take a long time but much of the research has been done. What is missing is the commitment from one of these nationwide organizations to adjust their tests accordingly.

I've never been much of a historian, but reading *The American College and University* by Frederick Rudolph was very enlightening. It is incredible how our university system has evolved and how many of our principles today come from so long ago. One of Rudolph's chapters was titled "The Collegiate Way." College is a way of life, a family, a fraternity, and a minisociety. These concepts were developed long ago and we have altered them slightly as needed. The college experience is, in my opinion, just as much of a moral and character developer as it is an opportunity to learn. Rudolph describes the collegiate way as: "the notion that a curriculum, a library, a faculty, and students are not enough to make a college. It is an adherence to the residential scheme of thing" (Rudolph, 1990, p.87). This text detailed many of the key factors behind the development of today's college such as: the education of women, the rise of football, and progressivism as it related to the universities.

My philosophy

As defined in Webster's, philosophy is the set of values of an individual or a culture (*Webster's II*, 1978). How we, as individuals, reach this set of values or how we should reach this set of values is what separates our different philosophical concepts. Our perception of how we view the world or education is affected by our experiences, our knowledge, our social position, and an intangible quality within. One's personal philosophy can be expressed in many different ways. Everyone's personal philosophy is correct because it comes from the individual, and not necessarily from a theory or a concept. I strongly believe the world is basically a simple place composed of people with the same simple, basic needs: to be safe, to be loved, to be healthy, and to be happy. What we do to satisfy these needs and the trials and tribulations we go through to accomplish this is what makes us individuals with different views and different levels of satisfaction. What makes us who we are is a combination of our backgrounds, our experiences, our influences, our opportunities, and our inner strength. The world is very real and observable. We are all playing the game of life. While it's not a level playing field, our desire or lack of desire is what ultimately makes the difference. When studying the different philosophies as described by our great philosophers, I liken this experience to the study of psychology or religion. You can find some positives and negatives in each and many of the concepts are relative to the person and the situation. I sometimes have a hard time categorizing my thought process with a particular philosophy because it seems too easy to misinterpret. I have taken several self-study questionnaires and the most common philosophy that I am associated with is progressivism, derived from pragmatism. A text by Gerald Gutek titled: "Philosophical and Ideological Perspectives in Education" describes pragmatism and progressivism clearly. "Pragmatism emphasizes the educational process as a transaction between the person and the environment. Progressivism, a reaction against traditionalism in schooling, stresses the liberation of the child's needs and interests" (Gutek, 1997, p. 6). I once saw a picture in the mall with the following caption: "Happiness is not found at the end of the road, it is found along the way." I've made it a point to always enjoy myself somehow, regardless of my responsibilities. John Dewey, the famous pragmatic philosopher and educator, founded many of his theories on the concept that education is a process of living and not only a preparation for future living. Education changes every day and should continue to do so with the hopes of providing our students with a real life experience.

The future

We never know what the future holds. My original plan was to go to law school, get married by the age of 25 and have 2 kids by the age of thirty. The field of law lost most of its appeal, I was engaged once but not married and I have no immediate rush to have children. My focus at this time is to continue to grow and develop as a person, a process that is ongoing; complete my doctorate program; and advance further within the field of higher education. With my doctorate, I hope to eventually serve as a

Dean of Students or even a Vice President for Student Affairs. I also hope to have the time to conduct further research and publish in the area of student services. Having the experience in so many different aspects of higher education, I would also love to serve as an outside consultant to other universities and colleges. I feel as though I have gained a lot of knowledge in this field and I will strive to increase the scope of my impact. After all, the future of our society depends on education. The future of our education depends on us.

Conclusion

Writing an autobiography forced me to reflect on my life. Looking back on some of the struggles I faced early in my life, I can appreciate them as learning experiences. Life doesn't always seem fair and it's easy to forget that all individuals have a turning point in their lives, some have more than one, and they don't always handle it the right way. When me meet people, present actions displayed can be a result of a plethora of good or bad events. The loss of my father at such an early age presented me with the harsh realities of life. Fifteen years later I still get sad around Father's Day or the anniversary of his death. These times also serve as reminders of many good things such as the memories I have with him, the important people in my life today, and the focus on my part on those things that really do matter. My professional life has exposed me to many challenges and many special people who will always remain a part of me. We never stop learning. Reading, writing, teaching, working, and caring are just some of the ways I hope to keep learning as I have in the past. After 30 years I am very happy with what I have accomplished and what I have learned, acknowledging plenty of room for improvement. They say your life doesn't really start until you turn 30. I hope to be even happier if and when I write my autobiography 30 years from now. If I only had a crystal ball . . .

References

Dillman, D. A., Christensen, J. A., Salant, P., & Warner, P._D. (1996, spring/summer). "What the Public Wants from Higher Education." *The Center for Adult Learning and Educational Credentials, 85,* 1–2,15.

D'Souza, D. (1992). *Illiberal Education: The Politics of Race and Sex on Campus.* New York: The Free Press.

Gutek, G. L. (1997). *Selected Chapter from Philosophical and Ideological Perspectives on Education.* Massachusetts: Allen and Bacon.

Macionis, J. J., and Benokraitis, N. V. (1997). *Seeing Ourselves: Classic, Contemporary, and Cross-Cultural Readings in Sociology* (4th ed.). New Jersey: Prentice Hall.

Rudolph, F. (1990). *The American College and University: A History.* Athens: The University of Georgia Press.

Sacks, P. (1997, March/April). *Change.* 25–31.

Sadker, M., and Sadker, D. (1994). *Failing at Fairness: How Our Schools Cheat Our Girls.* New York: Simon and Schuster.

Webster's II. (1978). Boston, MA: Houghton Mifflin.

Curriculum Vitae

PERSONAL INFORMATION:
NAME: SAUL R. SZTAM
Foreign Language: Spanish
Permanent Address: 80 Wimbledon Lake Drive
Plantation, Florida 33324
Email: *sztams@fiu.edu*

OBJECTIVE:
Administrative position in higher education in which my professional and educational background can be used to benefit students and the institution.

EDUCATIONAL BACKGROUND:
1997–present: Florida International University
Doctorate in Education
Major—Higher Education Administration.
Program is designed to enable selected individuals from the university, community college, and other postsecondary and higher education to develop knowledge and skills to enhance their instructional, administrative, and related research skills. This program is also designed to stimulate student research and development related to the university, community college, and other forms of postsecondary education, particularly in the development on innovative instructional and administrative approaches. All requirements but the dissertation have been completed. Dissertation topic: "Selecting a College or University: an Interview Study of Students and their Parents." Expected completion date is Spring 2001.

1. Florida International University
Master of Science Degree
Major—Adult Education and Human Resource Development. Courses involved the study of all fields in Adult Education and the positive ways to train, manage, and oversee employees. Extensive research was conducted on the field of education including comprehensive studies on Broward Community College. Different management techniques and styles were studied and researched to effectively be implemented in the workforce.

2. Florida Atlantic University
Bachelor of Arts Degree
Major—Social Science. Courses involved the study of Political Science, Social Psychology, and Criminology.

3. Broward Community College
Associate of Arts Degree. Courses covered all of the general education requirements.

PROFESSIONAL WORK EXPERIENCE:
1998–present: Director of Student Services
School of Journalism and Mass Communication
Florida International University, Biscayne Bay Campus
Duties include developing, planning, refining, implementing, and supervising all aspects of student services and training of related staff. Duties also include coordinating graduate and undergraduate recruitment efforts, serving as a liaison for all articulation meetings and conferences, preparing the school's planning and institutional effectiveness reports, maintaining statistical data on enrollment and related trends, monitoring enrollment figures for course planning, serving as the school representative for re-accreditation efforts evaluating faculty advisors, certifying graduation applications, overseeing graduate and undergraduate scholarship programs, developing and implementing an alumni program, managing the student services budget, and serving as the instructor for the school's orientation course.

1998–Present: Instructor, Freshman Experience Course
Florida International University, North Campus
Course covers an orientation to the university, an introduction to college resources, study skills improvement, note-taking, reading, test-taking, stress management, critical thinking, and time management.

1996–1998: Coordinator of Admissions and Registration
Broward Community College, Central Campus
Duties include coordinating campus admissions and registration activities with appropriate departments, supervising admissions and registration staff of thirteen employees, ensuring that federal and state admissions and registration rules are implemented, recommending resolutions to petitions for student fee refunds, coordinating all high school early entry programs, supervising the processing of class rolls and final grade rolls, certifying student enrollment status to appropriate agencies, reviewing and approving student residency affidavits, assisting in the development of the college calendar, managing the departmental budget, reviewing and approving special international

students status requests, representing the college at community programs, and monitoring enrollment at BCC's largest campus (over 13,000 students).

1994–1998: Coordinator of Recruitment
Broward Community College, Central Campus
Duties include coordinating all recruitment efforts with high schools and GED centers, coordinating and conducting visitations and tours for student groups on campus, serving as a liaison to high school brace advisors, participating in career days and similar events at high schools and other locations, distributing materials to prospective students, and coordinating an annual campus open house.

1993–1998: Instructor, College Success Skills Course
Broward Community College, Central Campus
Course covers an orientation to college, an introduction to college resources, study skills improvement, note-taking, reading, test-taking, stress management, critical thinking, and time management.

1. Senior Academic Advisor
Broward Community College, Central Campus
Duties included advising students in planning their educational programs, evaluating students' academic backgrounds in relation to their personal career goals, preparing and explaining graduation evaluations, conducting orientation sessions, conducting group advisement sessions, representing the college at workshops and conferences, and supervising the advisement staff while serving as the lead advisor during evening hours.

2. Financial Aid and Veteran's Affairs Specialist
Broward Community College, Central and North Campuses
My financial aid duties included advising financial aid students, processing short-term loans, and conducting and annual audit of financial aid files. My Veteran's Affairs duties included processing all Veteran's Affairs (VA) paperwork, keeping record of all VA information and changes, attending the state VA conferences, preparing for VA audits, and writing a monthly newsletter.

PUBLISHED MATERIALS REVIEWED:
"Your Choices, Your Life," by William Svoboda. Prentice-Hall Publishing, 1997.
Review completed on 12/6/97:
"I'll Stop Procrastinating," by Richard Malott. Prentice-Hall Publishing, 1997.

Review completed on 11/5/97:

"College-A New Beginning," by Marcia Heiman and Joshua Slomianko.
Prentice-Hall Publishing Company, 1997. Review completed on
9/26/97.

"Keys to Success," by Carol Carter. Prentice-Hall Publishing Company,
1997. End of chapter narrative published in text, completed on
8/25/97.

"Living and Learning," by Gerald, Cindy, and Heidi Jo Corey.
Wadsworth Publishing Company, 1997. Review completed on
9/18/95.

SUMMARY OF PROFESSIONAL PARTICIPATION:

Member of University Student Grievance Committee

Member of University Student Discipline Committee

Member of Phi Kappa Phi Honor Society

Discovered Latin American/Caribbean Scholarship opportunity

Chair of College-Wide Academic Standards Committee

Chair of Student Affairs Staff Development Committee

Attended Noel-Levitz Conference on Student Retention and
Recruitment

Cochair of University Retention Committee

Member of FACRAO (Florida Association of Collegiate Registrars and
Admissions Officers)

Member and selector of college-wide discipline committee

Member of the new system implementation team through the
consortium of Community Colleges

Participated in Dr. George Young's limited access Deaning Seminar

Mentor program counselor and facilitator

Honor's convocation keynote speaker

Graduation Marshall

Member of Dean of Student Affairs search committees

Member of Advisor Search Committees

Academic Standards Committee Member

Campus Advisory Standing Committee Member

Student Affairs Building Reconstruction Committee Member

Classified Staff Standing Committee Member

Writer, producer, and narrator of Community College student
orientation video

Developed and implemented a math awareness program at Ft.
Lauderdale and Piper High Schools

REFERENCES AVAILABLE UPON REQUEST

Example C: Sample Middle School Student Portfolio

We now turn to the example of Michele Galecka, a teacher at the middle school level who incorporates portfolio assessment into her classroom. The setting is Novi, Michigan.

The Novi Experience

Demographic Background: Novi Middle School is a suburban middle school housing over 900 seventh- and eighth-grade students. Novi is located approximately 35 miles northwest of the city of Detroit, Michigan. Currently, the population of Novi is a little more than 40,500 people.

Every student at Novi Middle School maintains a personal portfolio. This portfolio is an evolving collection of each student's work. When the students come to Novi Middle School in the seventh grade, they bring a collection of writing from their elementary school career. These are mostly writing samples and select pieces of writing from various content areas. At the beginning of seventh grade, the students spend time sorting through this work and selecting representative work samples to enter into their middle school portfolio. These portfolios will grow during the seventh and eighth grades, and follow students to the high school.

Novi Middle School has adopted a middle school philosophy in which students are arranged in teams of approximately 112 students. These students have common core academic teachers for math, science, social studies, and language arts. These teachers are responsible for helping students maintain their portfolios. Throughout the school year, teachers provide time for students to set aside work that best demonstrates their strengths and weaknesses and provides a continuum for monitoring growth. This work may include tests, quizzes, essays, group or individual projects, homework assignments, or other written assessments. In addition, students are encouraged to submit work from their exploratory classes, whether that is a piece of artwork, a design from industrial technology, a computer project, or a recipe from foods and sewing. In the past few years, students have begun to use technology to help submit artifacts into their portfolios. A half sheet of paper is attached to all work placed in a student portfolio. This form, completed by the student, identifies the subject and school year the work was completed during and the student's assessment of that piece of work.

At the beginning of each school year, students are asked to reflect on their strengths and weaknesses in order to establish goals to be entered into their portfolio. Toward the end of the school year, students assess these goals. The students, with teacher assistance, must decide whether or not they have achieved each goal, if the goals need revising, or if new goals need to be set. For students, portfolio assessment is a way to monitor growth.

Some teams incorporate portfolio assessment as a tool for student-led conferences. In the spring of each year, teams have the option of parent-teacher conferences or student-led conferences. In student-led conferences, students take responsibility for their learning by showing their parents their academic progress through work samples and goal assessment. Portfolios provide a meaningful sample of work for each subject area. Students are able to select work that represents their goals, their learning, and their growth.

Each team at Novi Middle School uses student portfolios in a slightly different manner. However, there are some overall certainties with portfolio assessment. First, this form of assessment provides flexibility to meet the individual needs of students and teachers. Second, a high value is placed on student work and student growth. Finally, portfolio assessment provides a place to showcase the work that students are proud of and that is meaningful to them.

This half sheet of paper is attached to all work being placed in the student portfolio.

Name: _____   Subject: _____

TEAM 7A ASSIGNMENT REFLECTION

This work is: (pick one)

A. _____ outstanding _____ acceptable _____ needs improvement

B. What does this piece of work tell about you as a learner?
_____
_____

C. What skills or concepts did you learn from this assignment?
_____
_____

A goal sheet like this one is filled out for math, science, social studies, and language arts at the beginning of each school year. The goal statements are formed by combining the area needing improvement with the strategies listed.

Name: _____

MATH GOALS 2000–2001

Listed below are 3-5 of my strengths in math:
1. _____
2. _____
3. _____
4. _____
5. _____

Listed below are 3-5 ways I would   Strategies that I will use to do this:
like to improve in math:
1. _____   1. _____
2. _____   2. _____
3. _____   3. _____
4. _____   4. _____
5. _____   5. _____

My math goals are:
1. _____
2. _____
3. _____
4. _____
5. _____

The goal assessment sheet is filled out toward the end of the school year. The initial goal sheet is used to identify the goals. Each content area teacher monitors this process.

Name: _____   Subject: _____

TEAM 7A GOAL ASSESSMENT

RESTATE GOAL #1
_____

Did you use the strategies you chose for Goal #1? (circle one)   YES   NO
If yes, explain how you used these strategies.
_____
_____

If no, explain why you chose not to use these strategies.
_____
_____

Did this goal help you to become a better student? (circle one) YES NO
Explain why or why not.
_____
_____

RESTATE GOAL #2

_____

Did you use the strategies you chose for Goal #2? (circle one)   YES   NO
If yes, explain how you used these strategies.

_____

_____

If no, explain why you chose not to use these strategies.

_____

_____

Did this goal help you to become a better student? (circle one) YES NO
Explain why or why not.

_____

_____

RESTATE GOAL #3

_____

Did you use the strategies you chose for Goal #3? (circle one)   YES   NO
If yes, explain how you used these strategies.

_____

_____

If no, explain why you chose not to use these strategies.

_____

_____

Did this goal help you to become a better student? (circle one) YES NO
Explain why or why not.

_____

_____

RESTATE GOAL #4

_____

Did you use the strategies you chose for Goal #4? (circle one)   YES   NO
If yes, explain how you used these strategies.

_____

_____

If no, explain why you chose not to use these strategies.

_____

_____

Did this goal help you to become a better student? (circle one) YES NO
Explain why or why not.

_____

_____

RESTATE GOAL #5

_____

Did you use the strategies you chose for Goal #5? (circle one)   YES   NO
If yes, explain how you used these strategies.

_____

_____

If no, explain why you chose not to use these strategies.

_____

_____

Did this goal help you to become a better student? (circle one) YES NO
Explain why or why not.

_____

_____

Which of the goals listed above do you feel you need to continue to
work on? (circle one)

      Goal 1   Goal 2   Goal 3   Goal 4   Goal 5

Explain how you are going to continue working on the goals you
  circled?

_____

_____

_____

If you did not circle any of your goals, please write two new goals for
the remainder of the school year.

Goal A

_____

_____

Goal B

_____

_____

Example D: Sample University Undergraduate Portfolio

EDUC 405–22: Seminar in American Education
Summer Session B: July 5 – August 14, 2000
Monday and Wednesday, 6:30–9:30 PM Christie Ahrens, Instructor
Room 521

Course Description: Development of contemporary American school;
teaching profession, its requirements and expectations; relation of
schools to values and culture of American society; fundamental issues
in American education; philosophical and historical development of
ideas, events, and laws in relation to organization, purpose, and programs of today's school.

Goals: The two primary goals of "Seminar in American Education"
are to focus on historical and philosophical origins of contemporary

educational issues and purposes, within the context of the dynamics of American society, and to trace the evolution of educational thought in dealing with those issues.

Course Objectives: The students will:

1. relate current educational issues to historical precedents.
2. examine the relationship of educational foundations to curriculum and instruction.
3. learn about the political and governmental structure of schools at local, state, and federal levels.
4. become familiar with requirements and expectations of the teaching profession.
5. explore aspects of the preparation process necessary to become professional educators.
6. become acquainted with the working environment of a school and classroom.
7. be introduced to educational policy issues such as school reform, multiculturalism in schools, and improvement of urban education.
8. gain an awareness of educational theories and philosophies.
9. investigate, discuss, and develop their own personal educational philosophies of teaching and learning.
10. realize that learning is a life-long process.

Required Reading:

Ornstein, Allan C., and Levine, Daniel U. (2000). *Foundations of Education.* 7th Ed. Boston: Houghton Mifflin.

Optional Reading:

Adler, Mortimer J. (1982). *The paideia proposal:* An educational manifesto. New York: Macmillan Publishing Company.

Freire, Paolo (1993). *Pedagogy of the oppressed.* New York: Continuum.

Goodlad, John I. & McMannon, Timothy J. (Ed.) (1997). *The public purpose of education and schooling.* San Francisco: Jossey-Bass Inc.

Hansen, David (1995). *The call to teach.* New York: Teachers College Press.

Palmer, Parker (1993). *To know as we are known.* San Francisco: Harper.

Tyler, Ralph W. (1949). *Basic principles of curriculum and instruction.* Chicago: University of Chicago.

Articles assigned by instructor.

Course Methods and Requirements:

1. Instructional methods will include large and small group discussions, problem-solving activities, student presentations, oral readings,

observational data collecting, modeling, demonstrations, lecture (hopefully, very little of this), and interactive idea exchanges. Cooperative learning techniques/strategies will be incorporated into each class session.

2. Class will begin promptly at 6:30 PM. Students are expected to attend all classes, complete all assignments, and actively participate in class activities. Absences may lower final grades, and failure to complete and hand in assignments on time will result in grade reductions. If you are unable to attend a class session, or turn in an assignment on time, notify instructor ASAP.

3. Work will be evaluated for accuracy, creativity, and effort. Quality of work is expected to be at the graduate level.

Assignments and Assessment:
Class attendance and participation (10 pts.). One point will be deducted for unexcused absences and/or tardiness to class.

1. Feedback Folder—class journal activities (10 pts.)
2. * Personal Educational Autobiography (15 pts.)
3. * Group Project (15 pts.)
4. * Book Review and Oral Report (15 pts.)
5. * Significant Voices in Education (15 pts.)
6. * Portfolio (20 pts.)

* A specific rubric for this assignment will be used for assessment. The rubric will be shared with students before the final assignment is due.

GRADES:

100 – 90 = A
89 – 80 = B
79 – 70 = C
< 69 = D

Feedback Folder: This journal activity will be used to provide individual feedback between instructor and students regarding activities, assignments, questions, and information. Specific guidelines will be discussed in first class session.

Personal Educational Autobiography: Each student will write a brief autobiography detailing his/her educational experiences from preschool/kindergarten through the present. The purpose of this assignment is to develop an understanding of one's own personal history and experience in order to become reflective educational practitioners.

Group Project: Students will self-select into groups of four or five, to research educational practices, goals, and purposes related to an issue in American education today. Further information regarding this assignment, and specific issue topics, will be discussed as we cover those areas in the basic text for this course.

Book Reviews/Oral Report:

1. Students will sign up to read one optional book from the list provided. This book review is to be completed on a book that you have not previously read. In a group discussion, students will outline the contents of the book and what features of the book the reviewer found valuable.

2. Students will choose one additional book from the list provided to read and present a brief oral book review to their classmates. This presentation should include a synopsis of the author's pertinent points, specific information you gained which is applicable to the field of education, and a summary of important facts, data, and/or information your classmates might find useful for future reference.

Significant Voices in Education and Portfolio:

1. Students will be asked to research the historical context and ideas that shaped the vision of education of a significant contributor in the history of educational thought. Students will present their findings to the class.

2. The portfolio is a culmination of the particulars we cover in this class. It will provide you with succinct, organized documentation of the learning activities you experience, the authors you will "meet," the instructional strategies you will learn, and the wisdom you will gain in EDUC 405.

All assignments are to be neatly typed, organized, and grammatically appropriate.

Education 405
Final Grade Report

Student _____

Assignment	*Points Awarded*
Attendance	
Autobiography	
Significant Other's Presentation	
Book Review (individual & 5 free pts.)	
Group Project	
Portfolio	
Feedback Folder	

Point Total: _____   *Final Grade:* _____

EDUCATION 405
Personal Educational Autobiography
Student: Heather

CRITERIA	3 POINTS	2 POINTS	1 POINT	0 POINTS
Questions posed in assignment 2.5 Intern years?	All questions considered and related to student's decision to become a teacher.	One of 5 questions not considered or related to decision to become a teacher.	More than one of 5 questions not considered or related to decision to become a teacher.	Most questions not considered or related to student's decision to become a teacher.
Paper organization 3	All points focused, connected, and logically related to topic; appropriately paragraphed.	Plan is clear, most points focused, connected, and logically related to topic; appropriately paragraphed.	Plan is evident, minor digressions, points not clearly focused, connected, and logically related to topic.	Plan is absent, or not evident. Focus is unclear and disconnected.
Conventions: Sentence structure, grammar, usage, and mechanics. 3	No major errors and few minor errors.	Few minor errors, no more than one major error.	Few major errors, some minor errors. Meaning is not impaired by errors in convention.	Many major errors. Meaning is impaired by errors in convention.
Presentation 3	Paper is neatly typed, bound, and organized in a binder. Title page is included.	Paper is neatly typed and bound. Title page is included.	Paper is typed and bound. Title page is included.	Paper is typed.
Overall quality 3	Excellent	Good	Satisfactory	Poor

Total Points: 14.5

Mrs. Childers must have seen your writing potential early on, as did Mr. Burns and Mrs. Matthews. Your paper is very well written. They must have been great teachers—and, I'm sure you were a great learner.

Here is the autobiography of Heather, which was just evaluated.

Heather's Story
Since the age of five I have been immersed in America's public educational system. I began my educational experience in the morning class of

a half-day kindergarten program. I proceeded through elementary school, grade by grade, until I reached the end of my sixth grade year. The following year I was bused to my junior high school, where I spent the next three years going through the terrifying transition of child to teenager. Just as I had reached a certain level of comfort and confidence, I was whisked away to high school, where I was once again, "low man on the totem pole." I graduated from high school with honors and ventured into the world of higher education. I chose to attend a private institution, Drake University, where I learned a great deal about who I was and who I wanted to be. I received a Bachelor of Arts in Art History with a Spanish minor in May of 1995. Hoping to one day teach Art History at the college level, I found it necessary to pursue an advanced degree. I began graduate work at the University of New Mexico, striving for a Master of Arts in Art History with an emphasis on Contemporary Latin American Art. I soon became disillusioned with the field of Art History as a potential profession, but felt it was important to finish what I had started. I continued to work on my Master's thesis while I examined my goals and aspirations. Although I could not explain why, teaching was always of interest to me, so it seemed logical to consider pursuing a degree in education. As I completed the details of my first Master's degree, I began working on the requirements for my second one at Roosevelt University, a Master's in Education. Now, as I face the need to begin developing a personal educational philosophy, I must explore the reasons for what I have considered to be a blind leap of faith into the field of education.

Undoubtedly, my personal educational experiences have had a lot to do with my desire to be a teacher. This includes my exposure to a variety of teachers, both good and bad, and specific lessons I have learned, both in and outside of school. These experiences have molded my beliefs on education and within them lay the answer to, not only why I want to teach, but also what kind of teacher I hope to be.

In looking back over my educational history, I realize I was very lucky to have had far more good teachers than bad. My favorite teachers tended to be those that recognized students as individuals and projected an enthusiasm for learning. I remember my second grade teacher, Mrs. Norton, for knowing (before I told her) that I had a new baby sister. She was genuinely concerned about how I reacted to the addition to our family. Years later, when she had my sister as a student, she still remembered me and was curious about how my life had progressed. Mrs. Childers, my sixth grade English teacher, recognized my ability and would not accept anything less than my best. In eighth grade Spanish class, Señora Freeman's enthusiasm was contagious as she taught us the Spanish language through art, music, food, and dance. In high school, I was exposed to two wonderful English teachers, Mr. Burns and Mrs. Matthews. Mr. Burns challenged us to think critically about the world around us, while Mrs. Matthews created a classroom community in which it was safe to express your ideas. In my undergraduate program there is one professor that stands out in my mind, Dr. Stone; he was not afraid to be human and he genuinely respected his students' thoughts. At Roosevelt University I have been exposed to a number of professors that effectively model behaviors necessary in current educational trends. All of these teachers have served as role models for me, and there are qualities from each that I would want to incorporate into my own teaching style.

While the above teachers have been a positive influence, there are also teachers in my past that have taught me how *not* to behave as an educator. Thankfully, this list is much shorter, but includes teachers that managed the classroom through fear and intimidation, and those that refused to be held accountable for their students' performance. Mr. Bristol, my Algebra teacher in Junior High, terrified his students, shattering chalk as he wrote on the board, crumpling up papers as he graded them, and yelling answers to questions in an exasperated tone. He created a competitive atmosphere in his classroom, posting the best tests on the wall. I truly felt he disliked me because I did well in his class. In High School I faced another teacher that I actually feared. Mrs. Copeland taught Shakespeare, and by the end of the semester we were convinced that she was as evil as Lady Macbeth. Not only was Mrs. Copeland an intimidating person, she refused to be held accountable for her students' less-than-perfect grades. Not a single student received an "A" in her class, however it was absolutely inconceivable to her that this might be a result of her ineffective teaching methods. Mr. Downing, my High School Physics teacher, was forced to face his students' accusations of poor teaching skills after several students complained to the principal. He devoted an entire class session to discussing the problem but he only got defensive and the problems remained unchanged.

The teachers listed above are people who have made a strong impact on my life, either good or bad; they were involved in some of the most defining educational experiences of my life. The lessons they helped me learn have been of great significance in my life and I would like to share a few of them here.

Mrs. Childers taught me to always challenge myself. I was eleven years old when I learned that "just getting by" was not good enough for me. The class was sixth grade English, and Mrs. Childers had assigned a book report. I chose a book that I knew was far beneath my reading level, because I assumed the report would then be easy to write. I read the book and wrote a brief summary, outlining the characters and the basic plot. I got the paper back with the dreaded "See Me" written in red across the top. Mrs. Childers explained to me that if I was going to read such an easy book, she expected even more from the paper. She knew I was capable of much more. In truth, I had found the book so unchallenging that it had been difficult to write the paper. For the next book report she helped me choose a more complicated novel, and I found that having to think about what I was reading made it far more interesting to write about.

Mr. Burns taught me to be critical of the world around me. To be critical meant not only to questions things, but to really examine and evaluate things through your own perspective. This might mean challenging the ideas of highly respected thinkers and writers. This valuable lesson was learned through a critical examination of a work written by Dr. Martin Luther King, Jr. We were required to find an element of the work to disagree with. At first I was completely frustrated because I supported equal rights and agreed with the premise of King's work. In addition, I could not imagine finding fault with the work of a man that was so greatly respected and admired. I eventually found that it was possible to be critical (make judgments, both positive and negative) and disagree with the way something was said, even if I agreed with the overall theme of the paper. It was a difficult exercise, but I learned that even the great thinkers must be challenged so that you come to understand their thoughts in your own terms.

In Dr. Stone's class I learned that some of the best classes are ones where the teacher gives up control. This was a lesson learned both by the students and the professor. The class was an Honors class about Human Rights. We had been reading a novel (*El Infierno* by Carlos Martínez Moreno) and discussing it as a class. One session Dr. Stone was late to class so we began the discussion without him. He walked in and quietly took his seat. He listened to the conversation and soon stepped out to get a cup of coffee. He returned again in silence. Through the entire class he did not speak unless he was asked a question. The discussion amongst the students was thorough and insightful, and followed the course that we directed. At the end of class Dr. Stone stood up and, close to tears, said "Thank you." We had provided him with the best class he had ever had and reminded him that sometimes the best thing for a teacher to say is nothing at all.

These educational experiences have helped me develop into the person that I now am. They have changed the way I look at the world and how I interact with others as well as myself. These lessons are the foundation for my own beliefs in education and help to define what kind of teacher I hope to be. I want to be a teacher that knows my students well enough to know when they are capable of doing more, and well enough to know when they need help. I want my students to know me well enough to understand that I am human too. I want to be a teacher that helps students to understand that their thoughts and ideas are just as valuable as mine. I want to be a teacher that learns from my students. I want to be a teacher that feels responsible for my students' learning; if they are not doing well, I need to rethink how I am teaching.

In general I have had a very positive educational experience, and it has made me who I am today. I look back on the people who have had the most impact on my life and the majority of them are teachers. Teachers wield tremendous power and have the ability to affect the lives of all of our children, both positively and negatively. I do not want to teach because of a desire to be the one in power; rather, I want to teach because I want to provide positive educational experiences for children. In addition, I want to learn from the students what amazing possibilities the future holds. I am thrilled to have opened my eyes and am anxious to see where my leap of faith will land me.

Education 405
Individual Book Review
Student: _____

Book Title/Author: _____

Criteria	*5 Points*	*0 Points*
Written review includes a description of the work, knowledge of book content, and evaluates the quality of the work.		
Oral presentation is thorough and clear, a written review is given to classmates, presenter appears to have complete understanding of the text.		

Point Total: _____

Education 405
Individual Book Review
Student: Heather

Book Title/Author: *Schools That Work*/Wood

Criteria	5 Points	0 Points
Written review includes a description of the work, knowledge of book content, and evaluates the quality of the work.	5—Well-written review.	
Oral presentation is thorough and clear, a written review is given to classmates, presenter appears to have complete understanding of the text.	5—You are a very good speaker. The summary you gave was clear and your enthusiasm was obvious. Great job!	

Point Total: 10

Education 405
Portfolio Assessment
Student: _____

	4	3	2	1
Quotations 4 Points				
Class Activities 4 Points				
Autobiography 3 Points				
Significant Voices 3 Points				
Book Review 3 Points				
Quality & Organization 3 Points				

Total Portfolio Points: _____

Feedback Folder
EDUC 405: Seminar in American Education
Here follows an example of an actual feedback folder from the instructor to the student.

Date:

Wed. July 5

H: Missed class because I misread the schedule. Sorry!

C: Glad you made it through. Better late than never!

Mon. July 10

H: I'm feeling a little overwhelmed and behind. I don't quite understand what we're writing up for our portfolios regarding the in-class activities.

C: Let's discuss portfolio during break or before/after class. I'll explain in more detail.

Remember that things almost always seem overwhelming the first time around. I hope you'll feel better following Wednesday's class.

Wed. July 12

H: *Schools That Work*—Book for individual report. Feeling better today. I'm really enjoying the quotes. It made me remember a class I had in jr. high that we had a quote for the day. I'm trying to remember where the notebook is!

C: Cool—it must have made an impact on you.

Wed. July 17

H: Tonight's activities were a lot of fun. I felt like we really got to know each other a little better. I enjoyed hearing people's experiences, although you scared me a little when you said teachers are born—I'm always questioning what kind of teacher I'll be and rather or not this was the right decision.

C: Don't let me worry you. I've just seen some teachers who weren't really meant to be there I think. You'll know teaching is right for you as you gain more experience. It's already inside.

Wed. July 19

H: I appreciate your sharing real-life examples of activities to do.

C: I've learned that it helps tremendously to learn from doing and from those that have "been there." I owe so much to my colleagues for sharing their own experiences with me. Glad you feel like we're making progress.

Mon. July 24

H: The significant voices presentations are interesting but it's really hard to sit and listen to presentations all class long (or close to the whole class).

C: True and Wed. night is all presentations! We'll need to be sure to take a few short stretch breaks. Can you imagine what is must be like for 5th or 6th graders in regular elementary classrooms who sit for hours and listen to some teachers "talk."

(lecture and/or deliver info?)

Wed. July 26

H: It is interesting to hear how educational theories take so much time to develop and get placed into practice. It is also wonderful to be able to reflect on theories and evaluate my own beliefs and approach.

C: I'm glad you're taking time to reflect. I believe that it's crucial for us to know where we stand, as we will sooner or later have to put those beliefs into action in our own classrooms.

Mon. July 31

H: I have a whole lot of books that I've put on my "to read" list.

C: Really! Too bad we don't have as much time to read as we do lists of books.

Wed. Aug. 2

H: I'm feeling very frustrated with the lack of time. It doesn't seem like there's enough time to do the rest of the significant voices plus the group projects.

C: I am concerned too, but we'll begin right at 6:30 with group projects. Then we'll do significant voices. Carrie is doing her SV on Wed. because she needs to be out of town the 14th. That means we have 6 SV's left. We'll get it all done! Another reason I think we're frustrated is because we're all feeling pretty comfortable with each other now, and we have more to say. Our discussions have become more lively, more lengthy, and more interactive. That's a good thing I think. I wish you the best as you continue your quest to teach. You'll be a fine teacher!

Education 405
Group Project Presentation
Individual Evaluation Form
Student: _____

Criteria	1 Point	0 Points
Group member was individually accountable for their portion of the work.		
Group member served to support and encourage others.		

Criteria	1 Point	0 Points
Group member offered ideas and suggestions.		
Group member met my expectations regarding this project.		
Overall group project evaluation.		

Total Points: _____
Completed by: _____
Comments:

Education 405
Group Project Issue Presentation
Students: _____
Issue: _____

Criteria	*3 Points* Thoroughly answered and clearly explained	*2 Points* Answered and explained	*1 Point* Question not thoroughly explained
What makes this issue an educational issue or an issue for educators?			
How are educators currently addressing the issue? How might they address this issue in the future?			
What appear to be the causes of the issue? Can we stop the problem(s) before it starts?			
How does this issue impact our students?			
Presentation of material: Original, creative, innovative, and held classmates' interest (2); Traditional stand and deliver (1); Boring (0).			

Point Total: _____

EDUCATIONAL AUTOBIOGRAPHY

Education, with all of it academic and social implications, plays a pivotal role in American society as well as America's continuing future role as a world power. We need to develop a lifelong passion in students toward learning and problem solving. The world we live in is constantly changing and the huge advances in technology are having a profound effect on everyone. One must constantly question the current knowledge base and strive to increase one's own understanding of this knowledge. Teaching students to learn by doing, to ask questions, and to assess their own progress will prepare them to deal with these changes in a rational manner. This approach will also fuel their natural inquisitiveness and develop them into lifelong learners. Additionally, it will help to develop and protect their educational self-confidence and self-esteem.

As I pondered my educational experiences, I realized that I have been involved in the formal educational process for forty-two years. The process started when I entered kindergarten and continues through the present day. These experiences have included personal interactions with teachers, trainers, and educators at many levels, exchanges with my children's teachers, and interfacing with various educators as a substitute teacher. The majority of my experiences have been on the receiving end of education, but those times when I functioned in the role of tutor, trainer, and substitute teacher have been personally gratifying and are part of the reason I am pursuing this most noble of professions. Another reason comes directly from my own and my children's educational experiences. While none of these events or experiences seems to have had lasting harmful effects, they have strengthened my opinion that education needs passionate, caring, and enthusiastic individuals to create positive learning environments for America's youth. Finally, a few individual educators and trainers who have demonstrated an absolute passion for education and their subject matters have inspired me. The attached educational autobiography is a summary of my four plus decades of experience with education. It is divided into time frames based on the various stages of my life. As I reflected on these events and experiences, I realized that I have been on a sometimes convoluted and long journey to the educational profession.

Elementary School Years

When I began to reminisce about my experiences in grade school, I was surprised that I was able to remember the names of four of my teachers. They were from grades 1–3 and my 6th grade teacher. As I assessed specific memories from this time, it was the stressful events that I remember the most. Two specific events come to mind that demonstrate how educators can have a negative affect on students, even when they are trying to do what they perceive as the right thing. The third memory from this time is not a specific event as much as the climate of the school as I perceived it.

In the second grade, I developed a reading problem because my teacher was pressuring me to "clean my plate" at lunch so that I would not waste my parents' money. I ended up in the remedial reading group. I was very upset, because I was so anxious to learn to read like my older brother. I remember working very hard at reading and not understanding why I was in the "slow" group. My mother solved the problem by packing a lunch for me with strict instructions to let me eat what I wanted. I was soon reading at acceptable levels. As long as I can remember I have been a voracious reader, thanks to my mother's common sense.

My fourth grade teacher was an aloof person. I remember her as being very "prim and proper" and rarely ever smiling. This was a shock as the other teachers to this point had warm and nurturing personalities. This was the grade where we learned cursive writing. I was so excited. Now I was going to be able to write like adults, not to mention like everyone else in my family. Everyday we learned a new letter. We were not allowed to write our names in cursive until we had learned all the letters. I had been practicing at home with my brother's help and could already write my first name. I was very proud of this accomplishment. However, I was not allowed to use this skill in class until we had learned all the letters in class. I was very frustrated because it took a very long time and I already knew how to write my name.

The third memory I have is not of a specific event. It is my perception of the climate within the school. I have a brother who is two years older than myself. I remember him as being extremely smart. Today he would have been identified as "gifted" in math and science, but we did not have these types of programs in Florida when we were in grade school. He was pretty much a straight "A" student, but received very poor citizenship grades. He spent a lot time in the principal's office for making sarcastic remarks (i.e., sitting in the back of the room and correcting his teachers, especially in science and math). He had quite a reputation. It seemed like every teacher I had knew of him and would eye me suspiciously when they made the connection between us. I always felt like I had to be extra good in order to differentiate myself from him. I tended to be very shy anyway, and I never wanted to have any attention brought upon myself. I began to develop a very bad habit of being extremely silent in class, even when I knew the answers. This attitude would plague me through high school and eventually manifested itself as a fear of class participation, even when I knew the answers. I always received excellent citizenship grades because I never caused any problems. However, I also rarely asked any questions. I was never encouraged to speak up, but then I was a girl so a quiet personality was considered acceptable. When I was a young adult, I made a conscious decision to change and found that I really enjoyed participating in class discussions.

Junior High and Senior High School Years

I have few memories relating specifically to educational experiences, good or bad, in junior high school. This was time of social development and those stressful adolescent years. I remained a B+ student throughout these years. I remember liking my 7th grade science class, taking chorus, and learning to type. I do not remember any real issues with trying to live in my brother's shadow in junior high.

In high school, grades 10–12, I was once again very aware of my brother's presence. He was highly thought of by many of his teachers and seemed to know exactly where he was going. I, on the other hand, did not have the slightest idea of what I wanted to do with the rest of my life. I always felt that I was being compared to him and that I would never be as smart as him.

I remember the following events from this time period. I enjoyed math as a subject, but was not encouraged to develop these skills by anyone at the school. During the second half of my chemistry class, I went from a very low C to an A. Something clicked, and I just understood the subject. The chemistry teacher told my brother how impressed he was with my innate ability in this area, but never once said anything to my parents or myself. As a senior, I took a yearlong review course of algebra and performed so well that by the end of course the teacher indicated that I should have taken a more challenging course.

The last thing I remember about junior high and high school was the practice of grouping students by abilities. I always thought this was counterproductive, because the students who were labeled as remedial always had low self-esteem. They felt like failures and were treated like failures by other students and many school officials. Many were labeled as such in junior high and never were able to break this mold. I remember thinking that these students never got a fair chance at a good education. At the other end were the accelerated students. To be part of this group, students had to excel in all subjects. This practice left out those students who had natural ability in one or two subjects. Unfortunately, these students were never given the opportunity to excel in specific subjects.

College Years

These years were sprinkled with positive educational experiences. I had a few really great professors who took an interest in me as a student and a person, and helped to develop my self-esteem. I changed my major several times and tried out three different schools before I decided on a specific direction. Like so many beginning college students, I had no idea what I wanted to do. I was good in math so I first tried accounting. This did not last long. I had always been enthralled with subjects that were related to any type of science, but I had never dreamt of pursuing science for a career. After all, I had not been on the college track in high school, nor had I ever received any counseling or guidance in that direction. If I had not been sent a copy of my 12th grade Placement Exam scores I may have never found the courage to study biology and chemistry. These exams were given to all beginning high school seniors in the state of Florida. I believe they were aptitude/ability type tests. They covered four areas: science, math, verbal, and one other area related to English. I had scored in the 91st percentile for math, the 89th for science, and in the mid-60th percentile for the other two areas. I immediately knew that I needed to concentrate on math and some type of science. I have often wondered what might have happened differently if my high school had notified by parents of my high scores in math and science.

Throughout the rest of my college career, there were several professors who had positive effects on my education experiences. I will not describe these in great detail. These professors all had certain characteristics in common. They each loved their respective subject area, they loved to impart their knowledge and excitement to others, many continued to do research, and they each took personal interests in their students. They challenged us to do our best, and most of all, they tried to make learning fun. My academic advisor at the university I ultimately graduated from, who remains a personal friend to both my husband and myself, challenged me to have faith in myself. He encouraged us (my husband and me) to enroll in graduate school in biochemistry, which we did.

The other memory I have from my college days was of being a tutor for chemistry and participating in study groups. Within the study groups, I was the one with most of the answers. Therefore, I led many of the discussions. These sessions left me feeling invigorated and with great feelings of accomplishment.

We went to graduate school in the late 1970s for about 2 years. As first year graduate students we were required to teach three different sections of General Chemistry Laboratory. The only requirement was that we complete the required number of laboratories, otherwise we were on our own. We made up our own tests and were responsible for teaching many of the basic concepts like how to name chemical compounds. Looking back, teaching these classes was the most enjoyable part of graduate school. We left without finishing the program mainly because of the professors' inability to get along. I found them to be petty, self-centered, and somewhat immature. In their defense, the biochemistry graduate program was undergoing great change during this time and they were all feeling the effects. I did extremely well academically, but did not have the energy or desire to mediate between the various personalities on my graduate committee. I was tired of going to school. So I left academia for work as a chemist.

Working Years

Anyone who believes that their educational experiences are done when they start work is wrong. While I might not have been in "school," I was continuing to learn many new things. Some were life lessons and some were continuing education. I learned managerial and people skills from my first department manager. She became my mentor in these areas. She provided me with many opportunities for personal and professional development. In the 18+ years that I worked as an industrial chemist and then as a quality director, I have taken numerous continuing education classes and seminars and had several opportunities to train and work with people. The most gratifying experiences have been those where the instructors were enthusiastic, energetic, and demonstrated a strong commitment to their subject matters. I have learned the most from the courses/seminars where I have to put forth a lot of effort and had a lot of hands-on activities. One of the most memorable was the training I received to be an examiner for the Lincoln Foundation's Award for Business Excellence. We had to spend at least 40 hours preparing prior to attending a weeklong training session. During the training, we did many small group activities and presentations to the group. This was the most thorough training I have ever had, and the instructor made the entire process entertaining.

Besides taking training courses, I also had opportunities to teach and train during my working career. I remember these times as being some of the most fulfilling in all my working years. It was always exciting to watch as someone else mastered a new and difficult concept or task and see his or her self-confidence improve. These were times of great satisfaction for myself.

Parent Years

During these years, I entered into another phase of educational experiences: specifically a parent with school-aged children. My children, who will both be in high school next year, have had their share of good teachers, a few exceptional teachers, and one or two less than ideal teachers.

When my son was in first grade, he became very frustrated with math. They were doing timed tests and he was having problems completing the tests. All I knew was that he was in tears at home and saying he hated school. One note to his teacher, and she quickly assessed the problem and turned him around. She allowed him to take one of tests by himself without any other distractions. He realized he could do it, and never looked back. On the other hand, his third grade teacher was giving him grief about his organizational skills (i.e., he had a very messy desk). He made good grades, but he could not keep his desk clean or organized. He was beginning to have self-esteem problems. I solved the problem by giving him a "trapper-keeper," even though they were not supposed to use them in the third grade. He still uses one to this very day.

Ryan's 6th grade teacher taught him to love reading. At the beginning of the year they had to read 20 minutes everyday (7 days a week), and by the end of the year they were reading 40 minutes everyday. His reading skills improved drastically, he found that he loved to read and has continued to read 2–4 books each month for pleasure. As a high school freshman he was reading at a college freshman level (according to his English teacher). His improved reading skills at the end of 6th grade allowed him to be placed in algebra in the 7th grade.

During the 7th grade, Ryan developed problems taking math tests. Ryan's algebra teacher spent every morning for 2–3 weeks helping him develop test-taking strategies. After working with his teacher, his test scores came back up and his grade went back to an A. Ryan is entering his junior year in high school and remains an honor roll student who loves school.

My daughter had two very difficult years in elementary school that were related to her teachers. Her fourth grade teacher had an extremely dry sense of humor and Danielle did not know how to deal with it. She took everything she said very seriously. In fact Danielle admitted to me that her teacher intimidated her and as a result she would not ask for help on anything. Danielle completely lost all of her confidence, especially in math. I spent a lot time working with her at home to maintain her math skills. I requested a conference during the second teacher-parent conference to discuss this issue with her teacher. When I told her teacher that Danielle was very intimidated by her, she kind of sniffed and said that all of the other parents said that their children just loved her. She offered no response and in fact did not seem to care. I was so shocked and angered that I could not respond. I had promised Danielle that I would not make a big issue about it. Danielle was afraid that her teacher would take it out on her. In an effort to provide Danielle with a positive experience, we allowed her to begin playing the flute in April. She took private lessons and progressed very quickly. She was very proud of her accomplishment and by the end of the school year she had adjusted and was once again a happy student.

Danielle's fifth grade teacher was wonderful, especially in math. I explained that Danielle had had a rough prior year and that she had no confidence in her math abilities. Her teacher went out of her way to encourage her and build her self-confidence. She gave the students regular feedback that allowed them to begin to take responsibility for their own progress. Danielle had a good year that year.

Sixth grade was pretty much a disaster, until her teacher had to take a medical leave for the last part of the year. Danielle tended to be extremely social (she talked when she should not have) and her teacher labeled her as a problem. Danielle had also matured physically, even though she was only 11 years old. Her teacher felt she was not behaving enough like a lady. Danielle felt like she was being picked on and did not have a good attitude. She did not participate in class, would not raise her hand, or ask any questions. Her self-esteem once again plummeted. Danielle and I had many discussions concerning her responsibility as a student and that she was partially to blame for her predicament. She worked very hard to change her behavior (i.e., talked at appropriate times, raised her hand to participate, etc.). Unfortunately, her teacher never seemed to notice and continued to make negative remarks to her and on her report card relating to her behavior. Her grades were mostly A's and B's. The all time low point came when Danielle came home and described the following event:

Her teacher was standing at the board with her back to the class. She heard some talking and without looking, told Danielle to be quiet. Danielle had not been talking and was extremely upset by this incident. This incident was confirmed by several of Danielle's classmates. I did not act on this because Danielle was afraid of negative consequences from the teacher. Things were much better for Danielle with the substitute teacher. By this time, Danielle had modified her behavior and the substitute indicated she was a well-behaved class member. The final report card was written by her regular teacher (who had not been class for the last several weeks of class). Danielle received straight A's academically, but her teacher indicated that it was unfortunate that Danielle just did not understand how to behave properly. For the first time in my life, I told one of my children to ignore what a teacher had said. I told Danielle I was very proud of the efforts and improvements she had made.

Junior high school was a very good experience for Danielle. She had many wonderful teachers who encouraged her and brought out the best in her. She did well academically, participated in sports, and made many new friends. She has a great attitude about school and is looking forward to starting high school this fall.

Substitute Teaching

During my first and only year (so far) of working as a substitute, I have been both a teacher and an instructional aide. I'm constantly amazed at the dedication of many of the teachers and upset by the lack of dedication by others. Some teachers seem to have lost whatever passion they may have once had. They do not respect the students as people. Once mutual respect has been lost, there is very little common ground left for building a cooperative learning environment.

Several experiences in the past year convinced me that I capable of teaching. I had the opportunity to teach all levels of 8th grade math twice, each for about one week. It was a lot of hard work but I enjoyed interacting with the students, and they actually learned the material I presented. According to their regular teacher, they enjoyed having me and named me as their substitute of choice. I found that I have a lot to offer students and that I really enjoy working with them. These experiences clenched my decision to enter the education profession.

Return to College

The most positive experience that I had with education came recently when I decide to pursue a Masters in Secondary Education. The very first class I took changed my entire attitude concerning the field of education. All of my past experiences consisted of the traditional approach to teaching (i.e., lectures, taking notes, writing papers, taking tests, and laboratory work, etc.). Since I was very successful in the past with this approach, I felt very comfortable about returning to school. When we received the course syllabus and assignment sheet I quickly looked for the dates of the tests and when papers would be due. Imagine my surprise and dismay when all I saw was project work, both group and individual, class discussions, and reading assignments. Then I saw that we would be assessing our own work according to assignment rubrics and that our instructor would either agree or disagree with our assessment. Disagreements would be discussed. I almost bolted from the classroom, because I had just been pushed into an unknown realm: depending on others for a majority of my grade, assessing my own work, and no tests. I gave this approach a chance and returned for each class. I did my own work as required, participated in great classroom discussions, realized that I could trust others, and learned that I could assess my own work fairly with the help of the rubrics. I not only had fun in this course; I learned a great deal both academically and personally. Our instructor had put each of in charge of our own education. The rubrics were the itineraries for our journey through the class materials. We were solely responsible for how much of the itinerary we completed and therefore, where the journey ended and how enriching the journey was (i.e., grade we received). If this was the future direction of education, then I definitely wanted to be a part of it.

Summary

These situations are the ones I remember because the educators either exceeded my expectations or failed to meet expectations. It is interesting that the incidents I remember negatively concern mainly nonacademic issues. However, these experiences are just as important to the educational process as the academic experiences. If students are turned-off, they tune-out. Once they tune-out, our jobs as educators are much harder. Some will be lost forever. Others may be fortunate enough to be led back by one or more extraordinary teachers who awaken their natural love for learning. I can think of no greater cause in life than to help young people learn how to learn, to revel in their own strengths and weaknesses, and to pursue knowledge as a lifelong endeavor. It is my hope to be one of these teachers. In ten years I see myself as either a middle school or high school teacher involved in teaching science and possibly math. I will strive to find ways to actively involve students in their education, to celebrate their successes, and try to guide them through the difficult times.

AUTHENTIC ASSESSMENT IN TODAY'S WORLD

The politics of schooling most often gets in the way of student progress. Bureaucrats want a score in most cases. They want to measure progress of students with a one-shot score because it's easy. It requires less time. And sad but true, time is indeed money. In the past, educators, researchers, and writers did not question typical tests. But, with the social movements of the 1960s onward, all sectors of society began questioning civil rights, women's rights, gay rights, etc. When people on the macrolevel became concerned with issues of equality, it was not long before this trickled down to the microlevel in the schoolroom. On a global level, people were asking for fairness.

In the schools, asking for fairness was applied to the most basic activity of learning, or how we assess what learners know. It takes much more time, effort, involvement, teacher training, and teacher professional development to put authentic assessment techniques into practice. In the past twenty years, in every state in the country, educators are clamoring to know more about authentic assessment. Why? Put simply, because it makes sense. Ask yourself, do you want your child judged and graded by a typical one-shot test that provides a simple score? Or, would you rather have your child assessed and graded with performance and product tasks that show not only what your child learned, but also what your child can do? I go with the latter. The reasons for preference for authentic assessment are the following:

1. Authentic assessment overall is fair. No one racial or ethnic group is penalized with a one-shot score.
2. Authentic assessment overall tells us a great deal about how a learner connects content knowledge to a given problem under study in the learner's world.
3. Authentic assessment overall provides us with feedback on a learner's progress on a continual basis.
4. Authentic assessment shows us how a learner constructs a product or performance so that we can see the learner's growth.
5. Authentic assessment overall provides for continual feedback, allowing the learner to adjust and improve performance.

These are not the only reasons to select authentic assessment as a solid evaluative technique. Obviously, in today's world, students are bombarded with media images and information technology, and one might say, a sophisticated information explosion. Today's learner we know to be a bit more demanding, a bit more realistic, and a bit more challenging and competitive—all the more reason to give the learner the opportunity to display what he or she has learned through performance-based authentic assessment and actual products that verify a student's progress.

The pace, complexity, and demands of today's world require of us much more when it comes to student learning. Oddly enough, it was years ago, in the early part of the twentieth century, that John Dewey (1859–1952) made similar assertions (1968, 18–19). Dewey is known as America's foremost philosopher of education. He wrote prolifically on the topic of experience and education. He reasoned that students must have an actual experience with learning something or the meaning would be lost. For example, rather than read about how to bake a cake, a student should actually perform the activity of baking a cake. The preparation of material and ingredients, the putting together of the ingredients, baking, frosting, decorating, and so on—all are part of the actual real world experience of the learner. At the time Dewey was writing he encountered mixed reviews. Educators, of course, were intrigued and enthused about his work. Yet he worked in the realm of philosophy applied to the real world of education, earning him the title of pragmatist. He once said there is nothing so practical as a good theory. With an understanding of Dewey's work in experience and education, I see Dewey as the starting point for what we now call authentic assessment. It is important to understand our history, in order to understand where we are now and where we are going. American Pragmatism, the philosophy approach most often represented by America's own educational philosopher, John Dewey, provides us with the first seeds of what we now call authentic assessment. Put simply, experience is one, if not the greatest, teacher. Authentic assessment requires the learner to experience what is being learned, whether it is baking a cake or documenting a semester's work of writing assignments.

CURRENT RESEARCH ON ASSESSMENT

In attempting to define and describe authentic assessment, all of us need to put aside for a moment our previous knowledge of typical, large-scale testing. To put it simply, typical standardized large-scale tests do not prepare learners for the real world. They do not prepare learners for what to "do" with knowledge. Assessment, on the other hand, is about "doing." Learners do make a product or do present a performance. They must connect the knowledge base in action. As writers have pointed out, would we test a lawyer just on her knowledge of torts class? Or, would we judge her on her performance in the courtroom? Would we test the ballet dancer on floor exercises in class or on his performance in the ballet *Apollo* to understand his knowledge of ballet? In other words, we need to assess the learner's knowledge of how the learner prepares for the various roles and opportunities that the learner encounters in the real world of work, study, and play. Knowledge is not all clean cut and easily catalogued. It's messy and uneven out there in the real world. If the learner is to succeed in the real world, the learner must be able to "do" the subject. For example, the medical student who becomes a surgeon will be assessed on a successful surgery, not just on her knowledge of anatomy. Let's examine this a bit further.

The research and writing on assessment clearly shows that there is a tension between authentic assessment and one-shot large-scale testing. On the one hand, authentic assessment tasks are designed to find out what students know and what they can actually do with their knowledge. On the other hand, the generic testing approach requires a learner to memorize facts out of the context of the learning situation and does not require a check on what a student can do. Authentic assessment tasks are designed to focus on understanding and application. Let us look then at some of the key writers and the research on authentic assessment. This will help to clarify the tremendous interest on the part of educators in the assessment movement.

Stop for a moment and think about your own schooling and your own learning experiences. When you learned something in geography class, for example, did you memorize some facts for a specific test? Did you then receive a grade for this? Can you now recall those facts? These are rhetorical questions, but let's face it, most of us went to schools where this behavior was the norm. To further use the geography example, an authentic assessment practitioner would approach this in a different way. He would first decide what was critical to know about the geography unit under study and then design authentic performance tasks to see what the learner could do with the information. For example, let's look at this breakdown:

Typical Geography Test	*Authentic Assessment*
1. Requires memorization of the capitals of all African countries	1. Requires a deep knowledge of trends and changes in politics and society in the major geographic regions of Africa
2. Requires a written test on the capitals	2. Requires a series of projects that might include: interviewing a person from Africa; writing a play about a particular series of events in an African country; scanning the newspaper for reports on Africa as a starting point for the main themes of a geographic unit; using a journal to document thoughts, reflections, and

Straw man

Typical Geography Test	*Authentic Assessment*
	ideas about articles or books about Africa; or selecting a country of Africa, for example, South Africa, and planning a three-week itinerary for a visit to South Africa, naming key sites and documenting their history, developing a budget for such a trip, and integrating all the facts in a way that shows the learner's themes about South Africa in particular and Africa in general.

Thus, the learner uses judgment and strives for competence and mastery of subject matter. With this in mind, let's examine some major themes in the literature in assessment.

Theme One: The Value of Assessment

The development and application of authentic assessment in various disciplines leads us to see the value of assessment. Jacalyn Lund (1997, 25–28), educator and practicing teacher, has written in the area of physical education and authentic assessment. As Lund describes, in the area of physical education, think about the lifeguard at the pool. How did the lifeguard achieve competence? Of course, the lifeguard had some classroom work in terms of reading, writing, and reflection. But beyond that, the lifeguard had further tests. These tests allowed him or her to demonstrate, for example, how to rescue a drowning victim. There were levels of circumstances "surrounding the drowning." Yes, the drowning scenarios were simulations of actual possible drownings, but the prospective lifeguard had to solve these problems with a simulation of the actual event. This simulation of a drowning scenario is an example of authentic assessment. The learner had to show competence against a set of criteria for each of the possible drowning scenarios. The writer points out the fact that authentic assessments are becoming more popular and useful among educators as they seek to make students prepared for the real world tasks facing them. Students must demonstrate a thoughtful understanding of all their book knowledge, so to speak, so that mastery involves more than recall for a test. Using the lifeguard example, a written test could not possibly tell the teacher if the learner were able to rescue a drowning victim. The learner had to demonstrate the ability to do so. Thus Lund reiterates Grant Wiggins's main ideas about authentic assessment. Authentic assessment tasks are set in a meaningful context that allows the learner to make connections between real world experiences and school-based ideas. In the process, authentic assessments focus on higher-level thinking, problem solving, and more complex levels of learning.

In addition to the books Grant Wiggins has written, he also has written numerous articles on authentic assessment. I have selected three of his most powerful articles for consideration here. Wiggins (1989) explains clearly why it is futile to try to teach everything of value to students by the time they leave high school. Rather, he argues, we should instill in students a deep love for learning, a burning desire to keep questioning and asking questions throughout their lives. Wiggins points out that the current rush of books on what every student should know in grades x, y, or z, oddly enough *never* explore *why* students don't know where Mexico is on the map or when the Civil War was fought. He claims that for every student who may not know the exact years of the Civil War, somewhere out there is a well-educated adult who also is unaware of this fact and does not deem it essential. He further points out that quite often teaching is reduced to the written equivalent of TV news sound bites or entertainment. One of the reasons for this is the fact that many groups lobby hard for their ideas to be taught. However, he points out accurately, the problem is, this subject matter may indeed be taught, but it is not *learned*. The problem with student ignorance, he states, is really about *adult ignorance* as to how thoughtful and long-lasting understanding is achieved. He puts it clearly in these terms; the dilemma at the heart of curriculum and instruction is either (1) teaching everything of importance is reduced to trivial forgettable sound bites, or (2) schooling is a necessarily inadequate apprenticeship. The apprenticeship is inadequate because we will have to give up some things in order to learn a few things very well. He advises that students must be enabled to know and learn about their own ignorance, gain control over the resources available for making progress, and then take pleasure in lifelong learning. An authentic education then would be one of developing the "habits" of mind and "high standards of craftsmanship," given the reality of one's own ignorance. Thus, this view stands in contrast to the prevailing view that the more we know, the more we should test in order to show what we recalled for those typical tests.

Another, even more powerful piece by Wiggins develops his fine argument regarding the use of judgment in context. In other words, real learning takes place when a student actually uses judgment to complete an authentic task to show the level of understanding of a given subject. He begins with the question "What is performance?" This is a critical question for Wiggins. He differentiates between drilled skills and performance by use of the famous soccer game example. In soccer, and many other sports, practice drills are the beginning of every practice session. But if a learner practices only these drills can we say that the learner knows how to perform in a game of soccer? The drills in soccer are very much like the test items on the typical test. But all the drills together are never equal to the actual performance test, the actual soccer game. Earlier I used the example from dance and will revisit dance as a metaphor here. The ballet dancer in training begins with numerous drills at the barre, then floor exercises, then combinations of two or three steps put together. But the real test comes in on actual choreographed performance of a ballet. So I ask you, the reader, to ask yourself as you approach various subjects, what is the equivalent of the ballet, or the equivalent of the soccer game for you? He goes further and leaves us with this question. Given the world we live in today, do we really want to put one focus on the precision of test scores? Or, do we want to focus on the intellectual value of the challenge of learning?

The third substantive piece of research and writing by Wiggins (1993) is documented in his work on new schools and new communities. The periodical piece is about "embracing accountability." He basically argues that no teacher can be successful unless the teacher is held accountable. To be held accountable means simply to be responsible for one's work. In fact, he goes so far as to say any hope we have of ever being excellent teachers depends on accountability. He has an involved argument about the importance of feedback for both student *and* teacher. He argues against the view that teaching is merely "teaching to the test." He passionately argues for building a performance appraisal system. He reminds us that the purpose of assessment is to improve performance, not just audit performance. This is a must for those seriously trying to understand the value of assessment.

Theme Two: Examples of Authentic Assessment

The reader may peruse examples of authentic assessment in various disciplines in journals, books, and on the World Wide Web. Because the examples are so numerous, I have selected two examples. The fields that most often use authentic assessment include physical education, the arts, and the humanities. The first example is from the area of literature in the classroom. Walker (1997), an experienced writing teacher, writes of creating a new course to integrate writing, speaking, listening, reading, and literature. She describes a literature class she taught in Native American and colonial literature for high school students in the eleventh grade. For assessment, Walker used a research project as a performance assessment. Students worked in groups to study Native American tribes. They studied migration, ancestors, and the culture. Students used formats such as game shows, panel discussions, interviews, and skits to convey what they learned. Next, the students created a newspaper on the literature of that period. In addition, a thematic mobile, each part of which had a thematic quotation from writers of the period, was constructed. For the final examination, students were required to create a timeline depicting the trends in literature of the colonial period. The overall effect was active, engaged learning. Students had to demonstrate what they learned in written, verbal, and artistic forms—an authentic assessment.

Another example of an authentic assessment of writing is evidenced with the rubric I often use when I ask students to write an autobiographical narrative in how they came into the field of education. Students at the university level write about personal experiences with a teacher in their past. Autobiography is a particular literary genre, yet it can be assessed for form, content, and style. Here is the rubric I created based on experience, trial and error, and common sense.

Rubric for Evaluating Your Writing

Project: Autobiography

1. Chronological accuracy:
   Students must report a chronology of events of their own choosing which describes their own characteristics of race, class, gender, ethnic origins, and schooling.
2. Find supporting literature as needed to indicate their awareness of the categories race, class, gender, ethnicity, and schooling in the literature and connect this to their own situation.
3. Recognition of themes:
   Students are asked to identify at least two recurring themes in their autobiographical account.
4. Summary of themes, indicators, and meaning:
   Students are asked to construct a solid summary of the themes, indicators, and meaning in their essay.

These four categories are assessed in the following scale:
   4 - Element is consistently demonstrated
   3 - Element is frequently demonstrated
   2 - Element is occasionally demonstrated
   1 - Element is not demonstrated

In summary, here are examples of application in the arenas of high school and university literature and research courses. This handbook, and the voluminous resources listed here and on the Internet, are meant to be a starting point for understanding assessment in the new millennium.

SUMMARY

In this chapter authentic assessment was described and explained. A brief review of historical influences that led to authentic assessment was delineated. Examples of the contrast between typical tests and authentic assessment tasks were discussed. The most commonly recognized authentic assessment technique, portfolio development, was described. Examples of rubrics for evaluation were given. Authentic assessment within the political frame of education was discussed. Here is a summary of principles of authentic assessment:

1. The purpose of authentic assessment should be to promote meaningful learning
2. Assessment should be designed to elicit student participation, effort, and commitment to the assessment activity, for example, journals or portfolios.
3. Assessment must occur continually
4. Assessment should be fair
5. Assessment should include exhibits, portfolios, and performances
6. Results of assessments should be clear, definite, and should provide immediate feedback to participants.

REFERENCES

Berliner, David C., and Bruce Biddle. (1995). *The Manufactured Crisis: Myths, Fraud and the Attack on America's Public Schools.* Reading, MA: Addison-Wesley.

Brookhart, Susan M. (1999). *The Art and Science of Classroom Assessment: The Missing Part of Pedagogy.* ASHE-ERIC Higher Education Report, Vol. 27. No. 1. Washington, DC: The George Washington University Graduate School of Education and Human Development.

Dewey, John. (1938/1968). *Experience and Education.* New York: Collier (1968 edition).

Gardner, Howard. (1993). *Multiple Intelligences: The Theory and Practice.* New York: Basic Books.

Gardner, Howard. 1999. *The Disciplined Mind: What all Students Should Understand.* New York: Simon and Schuster.

Lund, Jacalyn. (1997). "Authentic Assessment: Its Development and Applications." *Journal of Physical Education, Recreation, and Dance* 68, no. 7 (September): 25–28.

Resnick, Lauren B. (1990). "Tests as Standards of Achievement in School." In *The Uses of Standardized Tests in American Education.* Proceedings of the 1989 ETS Invitational Conference. Princeton, NJ: Educational Testing Service.

Silver, Harvey F., Richard W. Strong, and Matthew J. Perini. (2000). *So Each May Learn: Integrating Learning Styles and Multiple Intelligences.* Alexandria, VA: Association for Supervision and Curriculum Development.

Tanner, David E. (1997). "The Long (Suit) and the Short (Comings) of Authentic Assessment." Paper presented at the Forty-Ninth Annual Meeting of the American Association of Colleges for Teacher Education in Phoenix, AZ. (Feb. 26–March 1). ERIC Document ED 405 326.

Walker, Michelle. (1997). "Authentic Assessment in the Literature Classroom." *English Journal* 86, no. 1 (January): 69–73.

Wiggins, Grant. (1989). "The Futility of Trying to Teach Everything of Importance." *Educational Leadership* (November): 44–59.

_____. (1993). "Assessment Authenticity, Context and Validity." *Phi Delta Kappan* 75, no. 3: 200–214.

_____. (1998). *Educative Assessment: Designing Assessments to Inform and Improve Student Performance.* San Francisco, CA: Jossey-Bass.

Chapter Two
⌖ Chronology

INTRODUCTION

The assessment movement can trace its origins to the intellectual movement known as postmodernism. However, the testing movement started just after World War I. In order to understand the big picture of assessment, it is necessary to go back even further to the 1880s when Francis Galton, in London, administered tests to hundreds of persons to test sensory reactions and reaction times of volunteers. This was the genesis of intelligence quotient (IQ) testing. In the early 1900s, Alfred Binet and his colleagues in France developed the first intelligence test that actually was designed to find and identify "mentally defective" students, as they were called at the time. It was then that psychologists were writing about the possibility of measuring the mind. It was an era of excitement and possibility. At this time in New York City, Edward L. Thorndike was devising tests, called standard scales, to measure students' performance in reading and mathematics. Later, all school subjects were to be tested. Schools adopted these tests because they were efficient and convenient. American factories and industries were moving toward mass production and efficiency, and the schools reflected society in the rush to adopt standardized testing of students. Then with the advent of World War I, psychologists created tests for the army that sorted out recruits for particular tasks. This was one of the great influences on schools in terms of adopting testing.

POSTMODERNISM

Many sociologists chart the beginning of postmodernism after World War II. They point to the atomic bombing of Hiroshima and Nagasaki as a critical turning point in history. As a result of the atomic bomb, key writers, artists, philosophers, world leaders, educators, and citizens began to raise serious questions regarding Western ways of thinking and doing business. Postmodernism is a theoretical framework and a form of critique that questions the following:

1. The primacy of Western reason, and its social, political, economic, and educational effects
2. Obligatory Western heroes, which supposes a privilege for these heroes
3. Stories of expansionism, progress, and the success of science at the expense of working poor people, who enable that expansionism, progress, and success
4. Western stories that critique other cultures without applying that same level of critical analysis to the Western ideology, mythos, and culture.

POSTMODERNISM AND APPLICATIONS FOR ASSESSMENT

If we take a postmodern view of schooling, one of the main concerns of the educator is to attempt to uncover ways that dominant schooling serves to perpetuate the hopelessness of the oppressed. As a result, those who conduct assessment would assert a framework that:

1. Recognizes the power of race, class, and gender differences and how these shape educational outcomes
2. Exposes the ways that power works to structure inequality
3. Promotes a narrative of hope, complexity, and multiple competing perceptions of social reality
4. Conceptualizes ways that promote a more human and hopeful way to approach school, work, parenting, play, and so on
5. Suggests that all teachers are learners and all learners are teachers
6. Suggests that no one single vision of the world is enough to change the world
7. Suggests that assessment of students be fair.

CHRONOLOGY OF THE ASSESSMENT MOVEMENT

1880s

Francis Galton becomes a pioneer in the testing movement in France and worldwide. His goal is to improve human breeding and, as such, he is often associated with the eugenics movement. The basis of eugenics is the belief that heredity is the major factor in intelligence. Galton attempts to prove that intelligence tests can select the best and brightest for breeding. He is criticized by many worldwide.

1890s

In France scientists like Alfred Binet and his colleagues create intelligence tests. Again, the purpose is to sort out "deficient" children. Binet and Theodore Simon create tests that measure memory, visual traits, imagination, and language skills. Binet always points out that he does not believe one single score is the measure of intelligence. He openly writes of the possibility of error in testing. He strongly rejects his fellow countryman Galton's assertions that intelligence is fixed. Binet prompts the entire field of psychology to research all the relevant issues imbedded in the act of testing. Some writers refer to Binet as the father of intelligence testing.

WORLD WAR I ERA (1914–1918)

Testing is used to sort army recruits for particular jobs.

POST–WORLD WAR I (1919–1939)

Psychologists use the experience with army recruits for continuing their research on testing and develop what they believe are the best intelligence tests. Schools adopt the tests and the notion of testing as important and valid. Teachers still continue to use teacher-made tests. Testing is historically a part of public schooling.

1946–1960

Postmodernism takes root in all disciplines, especially art, dance, drama, language, literature, science, business, philosophy, law, and the humanities in general. Public education enjoys a period of relative calm. After the launch by the Soviet Union of the Sputnik satellite in 1957, politicians in the United States seek to emphasize science and mathematics in school programs. Teachers begin to organize more effectively and unions take a strong hold.

1960s–1970s

The civil rights, feminist, gay liberation, and children's rights movements are launched in earnest. Educational reformers begin to question how schools work. The conflict in Vietnam and the deep division in the country that it engenders, as well as distrust of politicians brought about by the Watergate scandal of Richard Nixon's presidency, work as incentives for teachers to continue their efforts to teach for learning and understanding. Teachers make tests related to their respective curricula. Standardized testing still is used but the emphasis is on testing for a reason.

1970s

Howard Gardner begins a thirty-year period of research on how the mind works and how humans learn. This is the beginning of his theory on multiple intelligences. This research almost single-handedly starts the assessment movement. States begin to see the need to get involved in aspects of education unknown before. For example, school lunch programs in poverty zones, Head Start programs, even breakfast programs are begun with the help of the federal government. States are just beginning to realize the importance of funding education. The National Institute of Education becomes the U.S. Department of Education.

1980s

The Reagan administration attempts to abolish the Department of Education and fails to do so. However, it issues a report entitled

"A Nation at Risk" that begins twenty years of criticism of public schooling and calls for more testing of students. Schools in the United States are compared to the Japanese schools, particularly in regards to test scores. Students in Japan, Korea, and China outshine U.S. students in math. Pundits and politicians call for more testing. Standardized test makers seize the opportunity to make a profit and make more tests. At the same time, the Reagan administration cuts funding for education and for educational research, as money is diverted to the Strategic Missile Defense System (Star Wars) and defense budgeting. Some educators such as David Berliner and Bruce Biddle begin a close examination of the data on student test scores.

1990s

The 1990s bring assessment into prominence. The work of Grant Wiggins in particular is a beacon for educators to keep working on authentic assessment as the best example of tracking students' progress, growth, and development. Teachers unions support assessment. Teachers are given professional development training to learn and incorporate methods of authentic assessment. Berliner and Biddle publish the results of their study, begun in the 1980s, which purports to show that the politicians are outright wrong in accusing U.S. teachers, schools, and students of falling behind the rest of the world in academic achievement. Their work is finally published in the text, *The Manufactured Crisis* (1995). Parents organize and voice opposition to excessive testing and grassroots organizations come alive on the World Wide Web, such as FairTest. Politically, the jargon remains superficial. Absurd claims are made, such as the boast that by the year 2000 U.S. students will be first in mathematics worldwide. Educators develop authentic assessment. State legislatures support these efforts. Districts use resources to support teachers in these efforts. Wiggins and others continue publishing, retraining, and conducting workshops. Many educators document their work on assessment and students show development and growth. Professional organizations such as the National Council of Teachers of English and the National Council for the Social Studies issue strong statements warning against the overuse of high-stakes testing. At the same time, school districts continue to be judged on the results of standardized tests. In many areas of the country—Chicago, for example—each school's test results are published in the newspaper, often without the context of the testing described.

2000–2001

Assessment is clearly part of the educational landscape. It even begins taking root in some southern states, traditionally the states with low scores in all areas. However, the new Bush administration favors standardized testing. But the grassroots movement of parents, educators, administrators, and teachers coming together to support assessment is hard to stop. States, one by one, are incorporating assessment into curricula in many districts (see Appendix B). Universities and colleges even pick up on the use of portfolios in their teacher education programs. Pre-service teachers (student teachers in the process of earning their credentials) are now the generation of those who know about assessment, use these techniques regularly, and as they go into the workforce, will be the generation that puts assessment into effect. The largest professional research association in education, the American Educational Research Association, issues its firm statement against high-stakes testing.

Due to the shift in thinking globally, in terms of postmodernism, one can only expect more questioning of testing to take place, particularly in regard to the profits made by test makers and the implications of race, class, and gender issues in standardized testing. Note that countries that traditionally score very highly on standardized tests like Japan, China, Korea, or even the high-scoring European countries, do not overtest or even regularly test young children. It is not until much later in schooling that those countries even use standardized tests. At the same time, the groundswell of grassroots activism in favor of authentic assessment continues to take shape.

Chapter Three

❧ The Standards Movement and Assessment

Some set great value on method, while others pride themselves on dispensing with method. To be without method is deplorable, but to depend on method entirely is worse. You must first learn to observe the rules faithfully; afterward, modify them according to your intelligence and capacity. The end of all method is to seem to have no method.

—*Lu Ch'ai*
From The Tao of Painting

STANDARDS AND ASSESSMENT

Although these words were meant for students studying painting, they resonate with the current interest in education standards and assessment. I want to begin this discussion with the notion that we are at the point of "depending on method." Let me explain by looking back at the history of the standards movement. It is often linked to the educational reform movement sparked by the report "A Nation at Risk" (1983), the first government document on the state of education. Of course, we can easily claim that educational reform has been a pastime for over a century as many writers have done (see Cuban, 1994). However, more recently individual educators and professional organizations have demanded standards as a remedy for almost every educational problem. Consider the following points regarding school reform movements recently elucidated by Orlich (2000).

Although school reform might be operationally defined as "anything you can get away with," the bulk of reforms in the U.S. seem to exhibit eight general characteristics.

1. The reforms are politically inspired and coerced by state governments.

2. The stress on higher student achievement is based on standards-based reports that were prepared by professional associations, not by local school boards.
3. Content standards tend to be collections of outcomes or student behaviors, assembled in a nonsystematic manner and without content hierarchies clearly shown.
4. Cost-benefit analyses are lacking from the reports on state school reforms.
5. Control of education has shifted to the national and state levels and away from localities.
6. The reform agendas, though fragmentary, are broad in scale and encompass most of the fifty states.
7. Politically inspired as the education reform movement has been, it must still be classified as being theoretical, that is, its basic premises are grounded not in empirically sound studies but rather in political enthusiasms and intuitions.
8. Implied within these reforms is the conclusion that, as a consequence of standards and high-stakes state testing and assessment programs, there should be a dramatic increase in student achievement.

As Orlich has written, "The time has come to challenge the premise that massive funding, written standards, and a firm resolve to create reform will cause students to achieve at higher levels because there are developmental limits to student achievement. Other writers have argued that the notion of setting high standards for all students is hard to resist, For example, it is difficult to argue against high standards. Yet, if we go deeply into the complex issues related to standards, this house of cards may easily crumble."

ETHICAL PROBLEMS WITH
THE STANDARDS MOVEMENT

Keep in mind these eight characteristics—as listed above—of educational reform movements in general and now think about the standards movement framed with the following questions:

1. Who benefits from setting standards?
2. Whose voice is taken into account when the standards are formulated?

3. Are we creating new inequalities by advocating standards?

Obviously, the problems created by setting standards are complex. Let us look at the first problem of who benefits from setting standards. As Gratz (2000) correctly argues, reforms—especially the standards reforms—present us with the problem of overpromising and underdelivering. Likewise, he points out that even if a new idea is tested in one setting, it may never be suitable for widespread implementation. So when we ask, as he puts it, "high standards for whom?" we uncover a host of questions. He reminds us that educational accountability is in its infancy and most often relies on the single measure of test scores. The extremely high monetary cost of the tests themselves, the upkeep of all the preparatory materials, and the like, illustrate the very high cost of testing. Clearly, the testing industry benefits from encouraging testing. In addition, as those of us with a life in education realize, testing is often handled questionably. Some educational leaders suggest that the teacher actually teach for the test alone, thereby casting teaching as test preparation. In fact, the standards movement was initiated with grandiose aims, such as world-class high standards. Yet in actual cases, as in the state of Texas, for example, the standards movement has become distorted by politics and expedience. Let's look at this more closely as we examine this case study of Texas, for it illustrates the political and economic consequences of the push for standards.

The Texas School Reform Case

Spoon feeding in the long run teaches us
nothing but the shape of the spoon.
—E. M. Forster

The well-known researcher Linda McNeil (2000) has done a thorough analysis of school reform movements in her book, *The Contradictions of School Reform*. She particularly examines this reform movement in Texas from the mid-1980s to the present time. She completed the first study to document and track standardized reforms from their beginnings in the state legislature to their effects on the curriculum in schools, teacher reactions, and subsequently, student achievement. The "reform" in Texas was begun by Ross Perot, politician and businessman, and basically took control of schools away from the local public and professional teachers and placed it in the arms of business-controlled external management and accountability systems. This major shift from public to private is a key underlying the barely examined reality. The accountability system in Texas is called Texas Assessment of Academic Skills (TAAS). TAAS is basically promoted for the following reasons:

1. It has shaped up the schools
2. Teachers and principals are held accountable for test scores
3. "Performance contracts" are used for evaluating principals based on test scores
4. Test results are used for decisions about school practice.

Perot was very articulate about how to improve schools through testing and basically argued that "if it's good enough for business, then it's good enough for schools." Thus, the injection of a business orientation, as well as a political one, complicates matters even further. But McNeil (2000) looks closely at this situation and points out the flaws in this simplistic approach to education.

For one thing, she raises the issues of historical inequities in funding schools, staff allocation, investment in materials, and support from the broader community. In fact, many writers point out that what drives the standards movement in general can be distilled into two assumptions, both based on fear:

1. Our nation is losing its competitive edge so we must demand more from all students. We are falling behind other countries and in order to compete in the global marketplace we must push students to learn more and learn faster. We can do this by raising standards.
2. If we raise standards for all students, we automatically address the disparity between high and low achievers. Thus, the argument goes, minority students will benefit because they are generally found in urban schools with low achievement records.

Oddly enough, earlier in our history, John Dewey argued for a child-centered, rather than test-centered, curriculum in the attempt to address some of the key points on inequality. In our present day, test makers argue for more tests as the way to resolve the serious complexities of standards. By raising standards and using an appropriate test to measure achievement, they maintain, we automatically improve education and our place in a competitive global economy. If only it were that simple! Let's look again at the Texas case. McNeil reports on various teachers' reactions and changed behavior when a mandated curriculum driven by testing is in place. Basically, teachers explained that the TAAS preparatory component of their curriculum totally recast their and the principals' roles. Teachers were silenced and marginalized. They had little voice in the matter. Likewise, principals also lost a voice in the matter. But what is the cost of standardization and compliance? Where is the space for the "public" in public schools? As we increase standardization, will we eliminate the voices of parents, teachers, and other community members? Likewise, who benefits most from the noise about raising standards? In the highly politicized milieu of an election year, politicians especially love the opportunity to get tough with standards. In fact, recently in the state of Florida, Governor Jeb Bush announced on numerous occasions that poor-achieving schools would be punished. Not only would the schools that fail to meet standards be announced in public newspapers, they would also be punished by receiving less in terms of resources. Does that make any sense?

Basically, mandatory typical tests will be used as the means for implementing state standards. Gratz (2000) argues that those accountability systems designed to help students and schools almost always downplay cross-school comparisons. Thus, another problem emerges. By aggregating test scores, the reality of disparities within and between schools is masked. For example, a suburban school, he states, may do well in preparing college-bound students. At the same time it may not do well at all in preparing noncollege-bound students. Yet, by aggregating all the scores, someone looking at the test data may see the school as excellent. Thus, the way data is reported is a problem and has political, racial, and economic overtones.

To add to the latest information on the Texas case, Raymond A. Horn Jr. and Joe L. Kincheloe, both noted and well-published authors, have compiled a text, *American Standards: Quality Education in a Complex World, The Texas Case.* This text not only touches on the ethics but also the legal issues involved in Texas. For an example, in 1979 and 1980 the Texas Assessment of Basic Skills (TABS) test was given to students. The results of the tests were used in district planning and specific curriculum content. There was a focus on teaching the state curriculum according to legislative requirements. The teachers also had to pass a basic skills test in reading and writing and another test on specific disciplines. A list of standards was created for teachers and administrators to know and be able to demonstrate to students. Many saw these changes as too rigid and without enough input from educators, parents, and community members.

In 1995 a move toward site-based management began. Some believed that this kind of management would create greater accountability. This plan called for educators, parents, and community members to implement chosen strategies, determine goals, and assess outcomes. Teacher development also became more site based. Campus-level teams were charged with identifying areas in which teachers needed improvement and implementing the programs. TABS evolved into Exit Test TAAS (Texas Assessment of Academic Skills). TAAS is also a test based on state-mandated curriculums, but it is said to involve higher-order thinking skills and problem solving.

However, not everyone agreed with the high-stakes TAAS testing. *GI Forum v. TEA* involved seven minority students who did not receive their high school diplomas. The evidence provided by both sides indicates that TAAS is deeply entrenched in the factory system paradigm of education. It is important for us to remember that the factory system of the past century had a strong racially biased component that was not challenged until the 1960s. Is this the direction that the people of Texas are comfortable with—the direction in which they want to go?

For additional information, please visit the Horn and Kincheloe text.

Teaching for the Test

McNeil (2000) reported that many of the schools she studied in Texas used large amounts of time practicing for tests. Students practiced filling in "bubbles" on stock tests and learned that test makers never have the same letter choice for a correct answer three times in a row. In fact, to help students remember this, a catchy phrase was repeated: "Three in a row, no, no, no." What are we to make of this? Still further, principals who participated in the study reported using the lion's share of the school's budget to purchase expensive study materials. Read McNeil's book for more particular and extensive examples of what can be problematic in terms of standards and testing.

Yet Texas is not the only state preoccupied with standards. Research done in California and Nebraska (Wohlstetter and Smith, 2000) on this issue, shows that some schools can improve but most do not have financial support to do so. They offer networking and partnerships as a solution to offset the heavy cost of school improvement and reform. At the same time, they stress the enormous cost for what needs to be done in schools if we are to authentically improve achievement for all students. Schools must have an infrastructure to accommodate and support the host of reforms, requirements, and ongoing demands of the curriculum. Without this, what chance can any reform hope to have in a climate with few or shrinking resources?

The New Discrimination

What is most distressing about centralized, standardized testing is how it masks ongoing inequality. As McNeil (2000) and others point out, minority students who may be disadvantaged to begin with are now thrown into the pool of the entire school. As the curriculum narrows to a focus on test preparation, a new kind of discrimination emerges. Instead of outright tracking and stratification, the new discrimination uses the *appearance of sameness* to cover up inequalities. Most of the "basics" or a "back to basics" mantra is historically rooted in the mistaken notion that sameness produces equity. Nothing can be further from the truth. Is there any evidence that standardization brings up the bottom-scoring students? One would have to look very far and wide to find evidence for this given McNeil's (2000) text. In fact, she argues persuasively based on the Texas case that the TAAS system is actually harming students, teaching, curriculum development, and faith and trust in public schooling. This makes sense given the almost unquestioned faith in the business model so prominent in states like Texas. McNeil (2000) argues that substituting a rich curriculum in poor and minority population schools with drill and repetition exercises is the new discrimination. Even if standardization and drill and repetition exercises raise scores in the present moment, children's learning is often not enhanced or enriched.

Currently, research is in progress that is designed to examine these issues in Texas and we shall have to wait and see what is found. Walter Haney and others (1993) began questioning the trade-offs in standardized testing and sometime in 2001 will have a published report on the Texas case. In an unpublished paper, Haney (1999) did a study of data from Texas on dropout rates, before and after the TAAS system was implemented. His preliminary results are disturbing. McNeil (2000) summarizes his soon-to-be released data. Haney looked at statistics from 1978 (pre-TAAS) to the present. The data were collected by the Texas Education Agency. In 1978, more than 60 percent of black students and nearly 60 percent of Latino students graduated from high school, 15 percent below the average for white students. Yet by 1990, four years after the Texas reforms, graduation for all three groups dropped. By 1990 fewer than 50 percent of all black and Latino ninth graders made it to graduation. The graduation rate for whites was 70 percent. Thus, the gap between minorities and whites actually grew! Then—even more problematic—Haney found that by 1999 the white student graduation rate had regained ground to about 75 percent, yet the graduation rate for minority students remained at below 50 percent.

Has this enhanced or enriched the curriculum or student learning? This data gives us a great deal to examine more closely. McNeil concludes that we are actually creating new inequalities and we cannot avoid a serious examination of this problem. Again I return to the three questions mentioned earlier:

1. Who benefits from standards?
2. Whose voice is taken into account when standards are formulated?
3. Are we creating new inequalities by advocating standards?

There will always be a debate on these issues. For example in Texas, for every person who complains about problems with the TAAS system, there is someone who thinks it works. In any event, check the data itself.

CONTINUING ETHICAL QUESTIONS REGARDING NORM-REFERENCED TESTS

Related to the ethical concern about standards is the ethical concern about the tests themselves. For example, let's think about the ethics of using norm-referenced tests (NRTs). A norm-referenced test compares a student's score with the scores of others who already took the same exam. Many are now accustomed to seeing scores in the newspaper that disclose a school's percentile rating. This is based most often on a norm-referenced test. NRTs are designed to rank order the test takers to accommodate a bell curve. In other words, test makers want to see that the results of students' scores can be represented by the bell-shaped curve. Test makers, often bureaucrats outside of education, actually construct the tests so that most students will fall in the middle. Only a few are expected to score very high and very low. In addition, most of these tests are multiple-choice tests. Given what we know about the complexity of the mind and how learning and cognition take place, it seems questionable to rely on multiple-choice tests in general. Not only that, the political climate of our times is such that governors and other politicians call for *all* students to score above the national average. However, this is impossible with an NRT. NRTs are deliberately constructed so that half the population falls below the midpoint or average. Thus, we contribute to the "dumbing down" of the educational process. Is it surprising that students feel put upon when they see their own scores or their school's scores below the midpoint? In addition, to compound the problem, NRTs are designed to rank order and compare only *some* of the students' scores. A commercial NRT, such as the California Achievement Test, does not compare *all* the students who take the test in a given year. The test is "normal" on a "sample" that is advertised as representing all in a given group. Why is this done? One reason is that it is easier to do it this way. The problem with doing it this way is that one question right or wrong can cause a student's score to jump up or go down more than ten points. Likewise, if a particularly intelligent student is absent on test day, the school's score might plummet. If a particularly nonintelligent student is absent, the score may skyrocket. In any of the cases, the score is hardly reflective of a given student, class of students, or a school.

Is the Test Score Accurate?

Obviously, the test score cannot be accurate. Since the questions are posed as multiple-choice options, the items on the test reflect only a sample of possible questions. At best, the test score is more like an esti-mate. Anyone who studies testing and measurement knows that no test is completely reliable. To add more confusion, because a school's score goes up or down does not mean that a given school is better or worse. When new tests are used, scores usually go down, for example. Presum-ably this occurs when a test other than the one to which teachers were teaching is administered. Naturally, in such a situation the scores go down. In addition, the claims of politicians that all students will achieve a particular score don't make sense. This is impossible because NRTs are designed so that one half of the test takers score *below* the average. One can only conclude that these test scores are not truly accurate. In fact, test makers actually have gone on record to state that "in elementary or secondary education, a decision or characterization that will have ma-jor impact on a test taker should *not* be made on the basis of a *single score.*" This statement was issued by the American Psychological Associ-ation in its "Standards for Educational and Psychological Measurement" (1990). Furthermore, because NRTs focus on routine, drill, and memo-rization, and because many teachers teach only to the test, one can con-clude that there is more damage done here than is needed. By lowering expectations and by deemphasizing problem solving, critical thinking, and content knowledge, it appears we are not helping children to learn. We are teaching them to conform.

Race, Class, and Gender Bias in Testing

One of the major criticisms of standardized testing is that it is biased. For almost two decades, standardized tests have been criticized for score gaps that indicate race, class, and gender bias. Just to take one example, for the American College Testing (ACT) assessment test ample evidence exists to support claims of test bias. For some background, the ACT is a standardized multiple-choice test. It is intended to predict first-year college grades and success. In 1989 the ACT program actually attempted to respond to its critics and vowed to change the test accordingly. However, there is little evidence twelve years later that this promise has been kept. Many organizations listed in earlier chapters in this text—such as FairTest and The American Educational Research Association—have indicated the glaring biases of the ACT. For example, the data clearly show that whites outscore all other groups. As FairTest, the watchdog organization of the testing industry, points out, if the test were not biased in this category, one would expect Asian Americans to score higher because they take more academic courses than any other group. Likewise, Asian Americans would rank first when scores are not adjusted for family income, course work, and grades. Thus, we see an example of the bias of this test.

Furthermore, there are many other biases of the ACT as disclosed by the FairTest organization. Here are just the main three categories of bias:

1. Biased format. Research shows that a multiple-choice format favors males over females. Guessing, a risk males are more likely to take, is rewarded. Because multiple-choice items do not allow for shades of meaning, they work against females' more complex thinking styles.
2. Biased language. Idiomatic terms such as "thumb its big nose at," and "straight from the horse's mouth," may not be familiar to many test takers, particularly those whose first language is not English, causing them to choose wrong answers.
3. Biased question context. Studies show that test takers do better on questions they find interesting, or that are set in familiar situations. Many more English and Reading ACT passages cover topics that are likely to be more familiar to whites and males than to minorities and females. One reason for this is that people of color and women are seldom featured on the ACT. Of four publicly disclosed tests, one did not include a single reference to a person of color, and two mentioned only one. Similarly, men appeared in items five times more often than women. When people of color and females are mentioned, they rarely have the status of whites and males. For example, one test featured twenty-one white males, including

famous scientists, politicians, and artists. The single minority group member was a nameless Japanese tea master. The five females included a "she" and four characters in a fiction passage as described by FairTest.

Thus, one can only conclude that this test is problematic.

Still further, the ACT does *not* in fact predict freshman grades, as originally claimed. Even the test makers have finally admitted that "high school grades predict college grades better than the ACT scores do." Another problem with this test is its imprecision. The ACT has admitted that individual tests have wide error margins on the 1–36 point scale. For example, 1.5 points in English and Math, 2.21 in Reading, and 2.04 in Scientific Reasoning. So once again, we see the flaws in this test.

Unfortunately, the most glaring problem with the test is that a student's life in school may be seriously cut short because of his or her score on the ACT. The cut-off scores determined by the test makers are used to determine admissions and scholarships. Even one point may be used to deny entrance or scholarship money. Of course, ACT does not condone this, yet at the same time the test maker has done nothing to stop it. In fact, ACT sells study guides, tapes, and other materials to prepare students who can afford them to prepare for the test! Take a look at the following data on 2,000 college-bound seniors' test scores on the ACT and come to your own conclusions:

2,000 COLLEGE BOUND SENIORS' TEST SCORES: ACT
Total Test-Takers: 1,065,138 of whom 57.0 percent are female
All Test-Takers 21.0
Gender
  All Males 21.2
  All Females 20.9
Ethnicity
  African American/Black 17.0
  American Indian/Alaskan Native 19.0
  Caucasian American/White 21.8
  Mexican American/Chicano 18.6
  Asian American/Pacific Islander 21.7
  Puerto Rican/Hispanic 19.5
  Other 19.5
  Multiracial 21.2
Household Income
  Less than $18,000/year 18.3
  $18,000–$24,000/year 19.1

$24,000–$30,000/year 19.8
$30,000–$36,000/year 20.4
$36,000–$42,000/year 20.7
$42,000–$50,000/year 21.1
$50,000–$60,000/year 21.6
$60,000–$80,000/year 22.1
$80,000–$100,000/year 22.6
More than $100,000/year 23.4

Source: ACT High School Profile Report: H.S. Graduating Class of 2000 National Report.

Again, one can only conclude that this test is flawed. I use this one example of the ACT to point out these problems and to emphasize that each of these flaws raises serious ethical questions. We have not even begun to address these ethical questions. I call on all educators to raise some of these questions in their respective local settings. On a hopeful note, there is one group already challenging gender bias in testing, and that is the group of female athletes in those universities that are members of the National Collegiate Athletic Association (NCAA). Student athletes have filed suit against the NCAA, not the test makers themselves. They decided that it would be more effective to challenge the NCAA, since the NCAA relies on test scores of standardized tests to systematically eliminate female athletes from select athletic programs. This suit is in process and may take years to resolve. However, the public statement has been made.

ETHICAL QUESTIONS ARISING FROM WORK ON MULTIPLE INTELLIGENCES

The theory of multiple intelligences was developed by Dr. Howard Gardner and his colleagues at Harvard University and became known through the text *Frames of Mind.* Also, the text *Multiple Intelligences: The Theory and Practice: A Reader* helped to fully explain this work. Gardner has worked for over twenty-five years on this research and was guided by the questions of how we learn what we learn and how the mind works. Basically, Gardner found that we have at least eight intelligences. These include bodily kinesthetic intelligence, visual-spatial intelligence, mathematical-logical intelligence, musical intelligence, linguistic intelligence, interpersonal intelligence, and intrapersonal intelligence. An eighth category, naturalist intelligence, was added after 1996. Unfortunately, our school system functions with attention to only two of these intelligence categories: mathematical-logical and linguistic. Thus, so much of what could be possible in schools is left out. First let us examine the basic categories and the definitions of each intelligence.

1. Bodily kinesthetic intelligence refers to knowledge gained through bodily movement, which is seen as a type of problem solving. For example, to express emotion through the body as in dance, or to invent something physically, or to play a game such as football involves bodily kinesthetic intelligence.
2. Visual-spatial intelligence refers to problem solving through visualizing an object such as in map reading, navigation, drawing, etc.
3. Mathematical-logical intelligence refers to the ability of individuals to solve problems mathematically and nonverbally. Many scientists show evidence of this, especially in solving a problem nonverbally before putting the solution down on paper. Thus a solution is found before it is articulated.
4. Musical intelligence refers to the ability to compose music and/or play a musical instrument by virtue of the problem solving involved and the creation of a product, in this case music.
5. Interpersonal intelligence refers to the ability to get along with others and all that that entails.
6. Intrapersonal intelligence refers to the ability to understand oneself and work with oneself, as well as to be intuitive and creative.
7. Linguistic intelligence refers to the production of words and language.
8. Naturalist intelligence refers to observing, collecting, categorizing, and understanding patterns in the natural environment much as a researcher or naturalist would do.

Thus, the work of Gardner expands our understanding of how the mind works. Just because schools pay attention to only two of these categories by and large does not mean we should forget about the others. Furthermore, our standardized tests cater to only two of these intelligences. Does that make any sense, given what we know about the complexity of the brain?

In addition, Gardner is striving for a clear vision of what education ought to be. Rather than a mere use of testing to illustrate what a student knows, Gardner and his colleagues remind us that deep understanding of content should be our goal. Furthermore, students should work toward understanding whether something is considered true or false and why it is thus, and should be able to recognize what is beautiful and even unexplainable. We need to expand our understanding of human knowledge, and human differences in respect to culture, context, and the social world. The theory of multiple intelligences can help teachers and students to enhance understanding in at least three ways:

1. By providing powerful points of entry. Knowing when to introduce subject matter and how to introduce it and which students learn in which primary mode of the multiple intelligences can be beneficial.
2. By offering apt analogies. Teachers may use analogy to convey the complexity of a subject.
3. By providing multiple representations of an idea or topic. In other words, rather than rely on only one or two of the multiple intelligences, teachers should try to use as many ways as one can to introduce content.

In his book *The Disciplined Mind,* Gardner uses extensive examples to illustrate these major ideas, especially in respect to his vision for schooling and learning. All rest on the notion that students are best served when we strive for deep understanding of any given content. But this is along with the notion that students must have ways to grapple with what is true and false, what is beautiful and what is not, and what is good and what is reprehensible. It seems to me that this alone calls into question many of our practices regarding the testing of children.

EASY ANSWERS TO COMPLEX QUESTIONS: THE MANUFACTURED CRISIS

*Facts are stubborn things; and whatever may
be our wishes, our inclinations, or the dictates
of our passions, they cannot alter the state of
facts and evidence.*
—*John Adams*

When faced with criticism of the public schools, many look for easy answers and quick fixes to make the situation better. Often arguments are weak, such as "American students don't work hard enough." Individual cases aside, there is very little compelling evidence to support such a claim. Will students work harder for drill and repetition-type work or harder on cognitively developmentally appropriate work? You be the judge. Berliner and Biddle (1995) have warned against the rush to easy answers. In fact, they conducted research over time trying to understand the public distrust in education and reveal some myths behind the attacks on education. Their text is the most powerful repository of evidence arguing against the politicization of issues like standards, testing, and school reform in general. They debunk the phony claims and false statistics used by newspapers, politicians, and others that are simply wrong. With mounds of evidence, Berliner and Biddle (1995) show the reader that, in fact, schools are performing amazingly well, given that in just a short span of thirty years or so schools have widened the pool of students by including the disenfranchised in every single so-called measure of accountability. For example, the authors counter with evidence the politicians' claims that SAT scores are lower, private schools are better than public, and that privatization of schools somehow will fix all problems. The data show that these kinds of claims are almost impossible to support. They refer to the myths as the *Manufactured Crisis,* the title of their book, and one myth after another uncover some of the threads that relate directly to the standards movement and its endless problems. Let's look at some of the misconceptions the authors purport to have exposed:

1. Student achievement in American primary schools has declined
2. The performance of American college students has declined
3. The intellectual abilities and abstract problem-solving skills of American students have declined
4. America's schools always come up short when compared with other nations' schools
5. America spends more money on schools than other nations
6. Investing in schools has not brought success or money is not related to school performance
7. The productivity of the American worker is down
8. American teachers are not prepared to teach
9. Private schools are better than public schools.

This is just a part of what Berliner and Biddle address in their text and show that these claims are utterly phony. They are manufactured not to help students or teachers succeed, but they are designed to deter us from the facts. Berliner and Biddle carefully follow the attack on American schools since the 1980s and explain how a change in the political climate at that time might have contributed to it. In their view, the business and industry model for all aspects of life took the place of the social services and learning model. The authors believe that not only are the myths perpetuated about American education foolish, but they can be harmful. The harm comes in preventing students of all groups from learning, and additional harm is found in the simplistic notion that all can be fixed with simple solutions. I invite the reader to carefully read this text, as it provides a context for understanding how the standards movement and testing as the easy answer, can be framed. In addition, I agree with the authors that if we are to have effective school reforms of any type, adequate funding and the structure for reform should be the first goal. Thus the notion of simple answers can never address the complexity of the issues before us. In particular, the idea that setting standards for students and testing them will in some way automatically insure high achievement simply does not make sense. Remarkably, there are many writers who echo these same thoughts and in particular, the work of Grant Wiggins (1998), stands out.

THE IMPORTANCE OF EDUCATIONAL ASSESSMENT

People write the history of experiments on those born blind, on wolf-children, or those under hypnosis. But who will write the more general, more fluid, but also more determinant history of the examination—its rituals, its methods, its characters and their roles, its play of questions, and answers, its systems of marking and classification? For in this slender technique are to be found a whole domain of knowledge, a whole type of power.

—Michel Foucault

Standards make sense when the assessment system in place makes sense. Wiggins (1993) argues that there are equitable, fair, and authentic means of assessment. He offers us a new way to look at standards and testing. Here are some of his major guidelines:

1. Assess the student's accomplishments and progress, not merely the total score that results from points subtracted from a collection of items. In other words, score longitudinally toward exemplary performance at exemplary tasks, not by subtraction from "perfection" on simplistic and isolated tests.

2. Devise a scheme that assigns degree of difficulty points to assignments and test questions, thus distinguishing the quality of the performance from the degree of difficulty of the task.
3. Give all students the "same" demanding work but differently scaffolded assessments based on equitable expectations.
4. Devise a sliding grading system wherein the proportions of what is counted over time varies. Move toward increased emphasis on achievement with a weight for effort and progress.

In other words, Wiggins (1993, 1998) has suggested that there are ways to test students, to still maintain standards, and to be fair and equitable in the process. His system of authentic assessment (1998) is based on the following premises:

1. Authentic tasks must be realistic. The task or tasks must match the real knowledge and abilities based in the real world of experience with that task.
2. Authentic assessment requires students to use their judgment and their imagination. The learner has to use knowledge, theory, and skills wisely and inventively in order to solve problems or pose problems.
3. Ask students to "do" rather than recite, memorize, replicate, or restate information. In other words, let students demonstrate what they have learned.
4. Authentic assessments are related to the real world context in which adults are tested in the workplace. Typical tests are contextless (p. 24). He argues that students need to experience what it is like to do tasks in real life situations.
5. Assess the learner's ability to efficiently and effectively use a repertoire of skills and knowledge to negotiate complex tasks.
6. Allow appropriate opportunities to rehearse, practice, consult resources, and get feedback on and refine performance and products.

Thus, Wiggins asks us to imagine a new way to look at testing and assessment and a new way to help students learn and grow. If we follow his tenets, there is room to use information from authentic assessments in a way that is healthy, respectful, fair, and demanding for students, without reducing their work to one and only one indicator.

WHY "STANDARDS" AND "TESTING" ARE IMPORTANT WORDS

Words are loaded pistols.
            —Jean-Paul Sartre

After considering the complexities of all those issues that relate to standards and testing, there still remains an important consideration about standards and testing that relates to language. If words are loaded pistols as Sartre suggests, then the words "standards" and "testing" are surely like bullets. One must be careful with language, not just because of the political consequences of these words as shown in the Texas case and others mentioned in this piece, but also because of the emotional consequences of these words. If we are to take seriously proposals about setting standards and how to measure the standards, we need to be aware of the social and political effects of language. Recently, Patton (2000) argued on the importance of sensitivity to and skillful use of language while in the process of evaluating, assessing, setting standards, and measuring.

PROBLEMS WITH HIGH-STAKES TESTING

To fully understand the importance of the assessment movement, one needs to put into perspective the problem with high-stakes testing. *High-stakes testing* is the term used to label tests for which the consequences of a student's score are extremely serious. For example, a test that by itself would determine whether a student advanced to the next grade level would be a very "high-stakes" test for that student. Recently, the high stakes involved for entire school districts have included:

1. The state of Florida's governor mandating testing and adding the proviso that low-scoring schools' scores would be published in the newspaper. Moreover, these poor-scoring schools would have their money taken away. Quite often, these schools are the schools that need the money most.
2. In the Chicago public schools, test scores of each school are published as either passing or failing. Most often the lower-scoring schools are those with a high enrollment of minority children. This is high stakes because by listing schools as failing, the students of that school internalize that they, too, are failing.

Historically, this kind of testing went on in the American south. Southern states have never funded their schools to the extent that other states have. Many writers and critics believe that this lack of commitment to education has roots in racism. Indeed, President George W. Bush wants to impose national testing on all school children, grades three through eight. This would be a case of "federally mandated test abuse, designed to hurt poor children" as described by Dr. Monty Neill, executive director of the National Center for Fair and Open Testing, also known as FairTest. He has also called this "an unnecessary and harmful intrusion in the process of school reform." FairTest maintains its own Web site (www.fairtest.org), and urges all citizens to get active about this serious problem. Neill and others listed in the resources section of this book have long argued that there is no need to require all states and all children to fit into a "one size fits all" model. The Bush plan also would take away federal funding from those schools that surely need it most. The belief that we can test our way to better schools makes no sense. If one looks at the results from states that employ high-stakes testing, the approach clearly has not succeeded. Why would the entire country want to adopt a model that has failed? Likewise, if the government did employ such a model, it would harm low-income, minority students the most.

WHAT FAIRTEST IS TEACHING US

FairTest has numerous publications and calls to action on its Web site. In addition, it keeps track of what is happening in terms of testing in each state. It also has rated the states as to what extent assessment is used to help children. FairTest has established "A Report Card on Assessment," choosing to focus on the positive aspects of assessment, rather that the negative aspects of testing.

A brief history of standardized testing is in order here to frame the assessment debate. Basically, since the 1920s, we have used standardized tests. At that time, only a few students went to school compared to today's student population. In our society at that time the factory model of education was in full swing. Students were sorted hierarchically by virtue of their test scores. Indeed, the hope and promise of the school reform movement of the 1990s and into this decade is the hope to break with the factory model. Assessment of students offers a strong alternative to support high standards without standardization. In the study conducted by FairTest on how well states are seriously using assessment practices, standards were used to judge the merits of each state's progress. In 1995 a publication called "Principles and Indicators for Student Assessment Systems" was disseminated. This statement was written by a coalition of education and civil rights groups from the National Forum on Assessment.The "principles" document calls for assessments that are:

1. Grounded in solid knowledge of how students learn
2. Connected to clear statements of what is important for students to learn
3. Flexible enough to meet the needs of a diverse student body
4. Able to provide students with the opportunity to actively do work, to produce work, and *demonstrate* learning.

Surprisingly, investigators found that two-thirds of the states fundamentally have not used assessment, but rather, continue using standardized tests. Even worse, some states have relabelled testing as assessment! Most programs rely on traditional, multiple-choice tests, and often use them inappropriately as a high-stakes indicator. Overall, the detailed survey and data sources revealed that:

1. One-third of the state systems need a *complete* overhaul
2. Another third need major improvements
3. The remaining third have positive components, but still need improvement.

Thus, we have a long way to go. FairTest reminds us that two-thirds of the states need serious work. In those states testing systems *impede* rather than help students. Here is the summary of their findings on how this two-thirds uses testing systems. They are not advancing reform because

1. Rather than holding schools accountable for providing a rich, deep education and reporting on such achievement to the public, most state testing programs provide information on a too-limited range of student learning in each important subject area
2. Rather than supporting and assessing complex and critical thinking and the ability to use knowledge in real-world situations, most state tests continue to focus too much on measuring rote learning
3. Rather than making decisions about students based on multiple sources of evidence, too many states use a single test as a mandatory hurdle.

THE MAJOR PROBLEMS

As we review the major problems with standardized high-stakes testing, it is a good idea to categorize the problems into the following areas:

1. Problems with the construction of the tests
2. Problems with scoring and interpretation of tests
3. Problems with penalties of the tests if test takers are below par
4. Problems with issues of fairness
5. Problems with teachers teaching to the test.

Throughout this text, the reader has seen each of these issues addressed and many resources were listed for getting more information on these issues. With any luck at all, the text will give the reader a tool for finding the type of information needed. In a sense this text is like a fishing pole. The reader is being taught to fish rather than just given a fish dinner.

HOPE FOR THE FUTURE

Educative assessment offers hope to teachers, students, parents, administrators, and all community members. Assessment allows for developing a sense of community. For example, because parents are involved in portfolio development, they obviously have more contact with the teacher and feel welcome in the school. Thus, by virtue of coming into the school building, the first steps toward a stronger community spirit are taken. When interested parents, teachers, students, and administrators get together and work on assessment in its many forms, good things happen for all. But this is only one sign of the hope offered by educative assessment. As the chapters in this text unfold, other characteristics of assessment offer hope for the future. For example, look at this list to see the possibility of stronger schools and communities.

Educative assessments do the following:

1. Ask that students be actively involved in learning by having them create, perform, produce a product, or *do* something
2. Ask of students that they use problem-solving skills regularly
3. Require actual people to score, grade, and evaluate a student's work, rather than have a machine do so
4. Demand new roles of teachers and administrators.

Based on this evidence, I hope you will agree with me that there is hope for the future in our schools. For those who are dissatisfied with the standardized testing movement, authentic, educative assessment is a good and powerful alternative. Assessment must be part of a learning environment. Students' ability to perform learning tasks with the ability to think, to solve problems, to articulate what and why they are doing something are all those parts of a learning environment.

REFERENCES

Anyon, Jean. (1997). *Ghetto Schooling: A Political Economy of Urban School Reform*. New York: Teacher's College Press.

Berliner, David C., and Bruce J. Biddle. (1995). *The Manufactured Crisis: Myths, Frauds, and the Attack on America's Public Schools*. Reading, MA: Addison-Wesley.

Brady, Marion. (2000). "The Standards Juggernaut." *Phi Delta Kappan* (May): 649–651.

Cuban, Larry. (1994). "The Great School Scam." *Education Week* (15 June): 44.

Gallagher, Chris. (2000). "A Seat at the Table: Teachers Reclaiming Assessment through Rethinking Accountability." *Phi Delta Kappan* (May): 681–687.

Gardner, Howard. (1993). *Multiple Intelligences: The Theory and Practice: A Reader*. New York: Basic Books.

_____. (1999). *The Disciplined Mind: What all Students Should Understand*. New York: Simon and Schuster.

Gratz, Donald. (2000). "High Standards for Whom?" *Phi Delta Kappan* (May): 681–687.

Haney, Walter. (1999). "Study of Texas Education Agency Statistics on Cohorts of Texas High School Students, 1997–98." Unpublished paper. Center for the Study of Testing, Evaluation, and Educational Policy, Boston College.

Haney, Walter, George Madaus, and Robert Lyons. (1993). *The Fractured Marketplace of Standardized Testing*. Boston: Kluwer.

Heubert, Jay, and Robert Hauser, eds. (1998). *High Stakes: Testing for Tracking, Promotion and Graduation*. Washington, DC: National Research Council.

House, Ernest R. (1966). "A Framework for Appraising Educational Reforms." *Educational Researcher*.

Kelly, Thomas F. (1999). "Why State Mandates Don't Work." *Phi Delta Kappan*: 541–546.

McNeil, Linda. (2000). *The Contradictions of School Reform: Educational Costs of Standardized Testing*. New York: Routledge.

———. (2000). "Creating New Inequalities: Contradictions of Reform." *Phi Delta Kappan:* 729–734.

Ohanian, Susan. (1999). *One Size Fits Few: The Folly of Educational Standards.* Portsmouth, NH: Heinemann.

———. (2000). "Goals 2000: What's in a Name?" *Phi Delta Kappan:* 345–355.

Patton, Michael Quinn. (2000). "Overview: Language Matters." In *New Directions in Evaluation, No. 86.* San Francisco: Jossey-Bass.

Slattery, Patrick. (1995). *Curriculum Development in the Postmodern Era.* New York: Garland.

Wiggins, Grant. (1993). *Assessing Student Performance: Exploring the Purpose and Limits of Testing.* San Francisco: Jossey-Bass.

Wiggins, Grant. (1998). *Educative Assessment.* San Francisco: Jossey-Bass.

Chapter Four
✸ Pulling This All Together

SUMMARY

For educators, politicians, parents, and the public in general, assessment is a hot topic. Newspapers and the popular press are quick to jump on any news that shows a school is falling behind. Even happier are the writers who claim that our students are failing, test scores are going down, and the public schools are failing. If people took the time to get the facts however, we would find that this is simply not the case. In the nineties, when people were crying about falling Scholastic Aptitude Test (SAT) scores, it turns out that in fact the scores stayed steady or rose. Not only that, they rose for more students of all races, cultures, and backgrounds. To some, this could look like success, not failure. So the issue is how do we find out what students know and how the schools really are doing? One way is to use assessment techniques to find out what students learn and how they progress through their studies. Thus, assessment of students at all grade levels, stages, and ages is important. But in our day and age, assessment is clouded with many issues aside from the basic questions of what do students know and how do they progress through their studies. Our schools are multicultural, multilingual centers. Many writers wonder, based on evidence, whether typical tests are biased against minorities and those who are from nonmainstream groups. Thus, the issues surrounding testing and assessment are complex, politically charged, and multilayered.

In addition, in the last thirty years, researchers are finding out more and more about how we learn and how the mind works. For example, data shows that all of us learn in multiple modes. We possess many intelligences such as musical intelligence, spatial intelligence, and kinesthetic intelligence. All of this is in addition to the verbal and mathematical intelligences. In this text, we looked at definitions of assessment and how the assessment movement evolved. We examined the historical influences that shaped the current interest and pursuit of assessment for students that is authentic, fair, and that allows students to progress in their schoolwork. We gave many resource lists on assessment in print and nonprint media. This book is a reference book for anyone interested in learning about assessment in this, our new millennium.

In a book of this nature, there is a certain unwieldy character. Many of the chapters are lists of references and suggestions for further research on the part of the reader. Know that the field of assessment is alive and growing. Perhaps, by the time you read this text another slew of references that are not listed here, are in publication. In any event, please take advantage of the print and nonprint media listed here. Get involved in your local schools. If you have children in school, take time to meet your child's teacher and even share this text with the teacher. Assessment is here to stay.

REMEMBERING KEY ASPECTS OF ASSESSMENT

In attempting to summarize the key and memorable points on assessment, I would like to use an example from everyday activity to illustrate. Recently, I was fortunate enough to attend two sessions of professional development on assessment conducted by Grant Wiggins. He asked participants, by way of introduction, to think about the best assessment they had experienced in recent day-to-day life. I am currently studying and developing my yoga practice. It was easy to pull out an example from yoga class. The yoga *asana,* or posture, is called in Sanskrit *Adho Mukha Svanasana* or "Downward Facing Dog." Many yoga teachers will tell you that Downward Dog is a critical pose. This particular *asana* strengthens the arms, the legs, opens your hips and shoulders, and stretches the entire back. Since the head is below the heart, it also offers a mild inversion. Picture in your mind an upside-down "V." Imagine your body in that position and think of your waist as the center of the upside-down "V." As you can see it is a demanding and strenuous pose. Imagine further, a class of thirty people of all ages and stages of yoga practice attempting to do this correctly. Even now, I recall the energy required to get into the pose let alone hold it. But as I took the stance, my teacher came up and said, "now elongate the spine, breathe steadily and just let go . . . let it happen." "Don't try so hard and relax into it." With this specific feedback and these words of assessment, I had my example for the workshop. In addition during that class, the yoga teacher returned many times to check in with me on this posture.

Now let's back up a bit. I was not able to do this in a vacuum. I began studying yoga in Ann Arbor in the 1970s. Off and on since then I have studied and practiced yoga. I also have many years of studying ballet, modern dance, and folk dance, which certainly contributes to preparing the body for yoga. Likewise, I have many books on yoga so I naturally have read about this posture, Downward Dog, and have seen many pictures of it in print in books and on my yoga teacher's Web site. The detailed descriptions I have read about this probably at some level, helped me undertake this. For example, take a look at this description of Downward Facing Dog. This is taken from a number of texts that focus on the Iyengar restorative series of yoga, the Ashtanga flow series, and basic Hatha yoga. In addition, another yoga tradition, John Friend's Anusara Yoga Principles of Alignment series, was part of the summary composed below.

"Directions for the Pose Downward Facing Dog"

Come to your hands and knees. Bring your wrists under your shoulders, with the creases of your wrists parallel. Spread your fingers wide and root your hands, finger tips, and heel of the hands. Hug the muscles of the feet and hands to your bones. Draw your energy into the heart and the base of the sternum. Shoot the energy to your hands and ground them. Keep a tiny bend in the elbows. Lift the ribs and hips and straighten your legs completely as you take the pose. Do not let the lower back sag. Stretch the spine evenly and expand the collarbone. Stretch the sole of the feet back from the ball of the feet and keep your feet parallel. You shall find your center and your comfort zone. The hands remain firmly pressed down, with all fingers stretched out like a star. Be sure your arms are straight. All four limbs should be strong. Relax your head and back and breathe. Hold the pose and keep breathing in a steady succession of breaths. To release, bend the knees to meet the mat. Rest your forehead on crossed hands. Relax and rest.

My point in detailing the description of the posture is that even with all this knowledge, it is not that easy to do. I was not able to fully learn its meaning without the direct feedback from my teacher. But feedback is one part of the activity. Now in reflecting on that feedback, and returning to the workshop, we were asked to list the characteristics and qualities of the assessment we all received, whatever our personal examples. All responded and had remarkably similar qualities in the assessment. We came to agreement that all assessments that were authentic and meaningful exhibited the following:

• Observation and demonstration
• Some type of coaching

- Awareness of limits
- Genuineness
- Feedback was continuous
- Was enjoyable and challenging
- Feedback was immediate
- New learning was based on prior knowledge
- There was a "can do" attitude

In effect then we are promoting what Wiggins aptly named his organization, "relearning by design." In other words, learning does not take place by sheer dumb chance or luck. It takes place by design. For me in the yoga class, I had the benefit of book knowledge, observing fellow classmates, and my own previous training by design. This, together with the challenge of the current yoga class and the immediate feedback from the teacher, enabled me to learn by design. The result was understanding the meaning and purpose of the pose. I learned the pose, Downward Facing Dog, because of the intellectual and physical components to learning. The presence of a good teacher constantly giving feedback made this a learning experience. Wiggins pointed out in the workshop that the goal is not instant reform or instant knowing but rather a continuous process that results in understanding.

As I look back over all this written in this text, as far as assessment resources, two things stand out about assessment:

1. The role of the teacher
2. Stages of backward design

Recall your own experience with a recent assessment and the role of the assessor/teacher. That person most likely wore many hats. For example, instructor, coach, evaluator, critical friend, and disciplinarian come to mind. Likewise, going back to the Wiggins workshop, he mentioned three parts to "backward design."

1. Identify the results you want
2. Determine acceptable evidence
3. Plan your learning experience

To return to the example of my yoga class, the teacher had over thirty years of training, study, and teaching. The teacher's planning was evident and the result was demonstrated. The teacher assumed all the roles listed above as constant feedback was forthcoming. The evidence was there in the doing of the posture.

If the reader remembers anything from the text about assess-ment, these are the main elements to recall. For those pining for the good old days of testing and standardization, I close with the poetry of W. H. Auden, from his poem "At Last the Secret Is Out."

At last the secret is out, as it always must come in the end,
The delicious story is ripe to tell to the intimate friend,
Over the tea cups and in the square
The tongue has its desire,
Still waters run deep my dear,
There's never smoke without fire.
Behind the corpse in the reservoir,
Behind the ghost on the links,
Behind the lady who dances,
And the man who drinks,
Under the look of fatigue,
The attack of the migraine, the sigh
There is always another story
There is more than meets the eye.

—W. H. Auden
From *The Collected Poems*

Chapter Five

◦← Selected Resources

In this chapter, the reader has the benefit of viewing a portion of the extensive resources available in print and nonprint forms and on the World Wide Web. This chapter is intended as an introductory guide as the amount and types of literature available are extensive and too numerous to catalogue. In short, assessment is one of the major foci in education today.

PRINT RESOURCES

Here are some of the most powerful books on the topic of assessment.

Books

Bellanca, James, Carolyn Chapman, and Elizabeth Swartz. *Multiple Assessments for Multiple Intelligences.* Arlington Heights, IL: Skylight Training & Publishing, 1994.

A most useful handbook for educators, this text goes beyond the basics of authentic assessment. While following the tenets of assessment, the authors add the important elements of Howard Gardner's work on multiple intelligences. They clearly explicate how and under what circumstances to use exhibits, performances, journals, logs, demonstrations, products, problem-solving processes, graphic organizers, and major projects. The chapter that explains the guidelines for rubrics is truly helpful. The emphasis of the text is on the use of multiple methods of assessment for multiple intelligences.

Berliner, David C., and Bruce J. Biddle. *The Manufactured Crisis: Myths, Fraud, and the Attack on America's Public Schools.* New York: Addison-Wesley, 1995.

This book sets the stage for understanding the political context of school reform and testing. The authors trace from 1983 the politically motivated attacks on public education and systematically debunk one false claim after another. This book lays the historical context for understanding the ethical issues surrounding testing and assessment.

Bernhardt, Victoria. *The School Portfolio: A Comprehensive Framework for School Improvement.* Larchmont, NY: Eye on Education, 1999.

A school portfolio is a nonthreatening self-assessment tool that exhibits a school's goals, progress, achievements, and vision for improvement. This book shows you how to develop a school portfolio specifically tailored to your school, reflecting its unique challenges and opportunities.
    The features in this book include:

1. Easy-to-use workbook format
2. A framework for school improvement
3. Sample questionnaires and analysis forms.

Contents:
1. Introduction: The Need for a Framework for School Improvement
2. Assessing School Improvement
3. Information and Analysis
4. Student Achievement
5. Quality Planning
6. Professional Development
7. Leadership
8. Partnership Development
9. Continuous Improvement and Evaluation
10. Putting It All Together
11. Appendices

Bernhardt, Victoria L., Leni Von Blanckensee, Marcy Lauck, Frances Rebello, George Bonilla, and Mary Tribbey. *The Example School Portfolio: A Companion to the School Portfolio.* Larchmont, NY: Eye on Education, 2000.

This book presents a prototype school portfolio, along with annotated explanations and suggestions. Although this book describes a hypothetical elementary school, the data and examples come from real schools at which the authors worked, and the recommendations can be applied to any level school engaged in systemic reform.

Contents:
Part I: Introduction and Overview
Part II: The River Road School Portfolio
 1. Information and Analysis
 2. Student Achievement
 3. Quality Planning
 4. Professional Development
 5. Leadership
 6. Partnership Development
 7. Continuous Improvement and Evaluation
Part III: Summary and Conclusions

Brookhart, Susan M. *The Art and Science of Classroom Assessment: The Missing Part of Pedagogy.* Washington, DC: ASHE-ERIC Higher Education Report (Vol. 27, No. 1). The George Washington University, Graduate School of Education and Human Development, 1999.

In this text, Brookhart uses an informal, understandable approach to describe the art and science of classroom assessment. Teachers, parents, and other educators will appreciate the numerous examples of how to assess student's work authentically. She also offers many scoring rubrics that help to guide teacher and student though the nuts and bolts of assessment. She gives clear directions and examples of some practices and techniques for evaluating writing, essay exams, and peer evaluation strategies. She also includes a lengthy section on portfolio assessment as an example of authentic assessment. The final section in the text explains grade distribution and grading policies by reviewing related literature on grading. Her summary of how to design authentic performance assessments and how to write good tests is a useful tool for any educator.

Burke, Kay. *How to Assess Authentic Learning.* 3d ed. Columbus, OH: Merrill, 1999.

This text presents a wide range of alternative forms of assessment. They are presented in a meaningful and practical format that makes their use easily applicable to those in schools and classrooms searching for more authentic forms of assessment. They will prove valuable to teaching teams wishing to collect data to evaluate their curriculum and instructional decision making. They will assist in communicating more thoughtfully to parents. Most importantly, they will signal to students that self-assessment is the ultimate goal of the mindful school. Its non-threatening approach offers explanations of learning standards, performance tasks, portfolio development, and scoring rubrics. This book was written to help educators expand their repertoire of strategies to provide a more balanced assessment of student learning and to help students increase achievement and meet both knowledge and performance standards.

Eby, Judy W. *Reflective Planning, Teaching, and Evaluation, K–12.* 2d ed. Columbus, OH: Merrill, 1996.

This text used in teacher preparation programs is valuable on many levels. The author walks the reader through all aspects of designing authentic tasks and authentic assessments. She describes the importance of the knowledge level, the comprehension level, the application level, the analysis level, the synthesis level, and evaluation level of all authentic performance assessments.

Fischer, Cheryl Fulton, and Rita M. King. *Authentic Assessment: A Guide to Implementation.* Thousand Oaks, CA: Corwin, 1995.

This book assists in understanding the methods of implementing authentic assessment. The authors discuss the problems associated with traditional student testing practices and stress the advantages of moving to authentic assessment. The authors elaborate on the teacher's role in authentic assessment approaches and they divulge the means for developing and implementing an authentic assessment program at the district, school, or individual classroom level. They also discuss the administrator's role in developing and maintaining an authentic assessment program. Finally, they offer a series of helpful hints on how to involve students, parents, and community members in the learning process.

Gardner, Howard. *Multiple Intelligences: The Theory in Practice.* New York: Basic Books, 1993.

Here Gardner describes more fully his groundbreaking research on multiple intelligences to stress an unknown number of separate human capacities for learning. He describes his nearly three decades of research on the human mind and explains the educational implications of his theory of multiple intelligences. Of course, this has further repercussions for testing, and Gardner makes the case for moving from the typical one-shot test to a more naturalistic, contextual assessment. He defines linguistic, logical-mathematical, spatial, musical, bodily kinesthetic, interpersonal, and intrapersonal intelligences. He argues for a plurality of intellect. Through this approach, we all may come to a more lucid understanding of human thinking and learning. Ultimately, Gardner argues that if we can mobilize the full range of human intelligences and use them ethically, we can increase the likelihood of survival on this planet.

_____. *The Disciplined Mind: What All Students Should Understand.* New York: Simon and Schuster, 1999.

In this, his latest book, Gardner synthesizes his thirty years of research in cognitive and biological sciences, as well as fifteen years in education. His dedication to understanding how the mind works has led him to look at the big picture in education. He writes in a user-friendly, informal style to explain difficulties in learning and obstacles to understanding how children and adults think. He then offers frameworks for understanding. Although not directly on authentic assessment, the book helps readers understand the complexity of the mind. By knowing more about how the mind works, the way we assess what students know, how they know, and what they do with knowledge, we come to see the value of authentic tasks for evaluating students' learning. In addition, Gardner asks that we include in the entire process of education not just the content but the understanding of the difference between good and evil, and that which is beautiful and true and that which is not. He emphasizes that we will never agree on one single best method of education and he offers various ways to approach education, given what we know about the theory of multiple intelligences. This text recognizes and places Gardner's work in context as groundbreaking—perhaps more so than even Jean Piaget, Jerome Bruner, or John Dewey.

Goodwin, A. Lin. *Assessment for Equity and Inclusion Embracing All Our Children.* New York: Routledge, 1997.

This book contains several essays that confront the debate between standardized testing and alternative assessment methods, suggesting strategies of assessment that include rather than exclude students to create a diverse community of learners. The collection of essays serves as a substantive discussion of assessment and alternative assessment, and expands the notion of alternatives by presenting multiple possibilities of innovative practice. The collection gives a thoughtful analysis from theoretical, historical, practical, and critical perspectives and shows how assessment, equity, and inclusion are inextricably intertwined.

Hammond, Linda Darling. *The Right To Learn: A Blueprint for Creating Schools that Work.* San Francisco: Jossey-Bass, 1997.

Although this text is not per se on assessment, it does clearly describe learner-centered schools. The author used in-depth interviews, observations, and documents from highly successful schools. She shows that good schools best serve learners by allowing good teachers to flourish and by favoring competence over procedures. The sophisticated descriptions of the schools reveal how authentic assessment is critical to learners, teachers, and administrators.

Hammond, Linda Darling, Jacqueline Ancess, and Beverly Falk. *Authentic Assessment in Action.* New York: Teachers College Press, 1995.

This book examines how five schools have developed authentic, performance-based assessments of students' learning, and how this work has interacted with and influenced the teaching and learning experiences students encounter in school. Case studies of two elementary and three secondary schools describe how they are using a number of different strategies for personalizing instruction, deepening students' engagement with subject matter, and assessing learning in rigorous and holistic ways. The case studies examine how authentic assessment supports changes in curriculum, teaching, and school organization and how it is, in turn, embedded in and supported by these aspects of school life. The cases document the changes in student work and learning that can accompany new approaches to assessment when these are embedded in a schoolwide effort to create learner-centered education.

Herman, Joan L., Pamela R. Aschbacher, and Lynn Winters. *A Practical Guide to Alternative Assessment.* Alexandria, VA: Association for Supervision and Curriculum Development, 1992.

The authors offer guidance on the creation and use of alternative measures of student achievement. They present a systematic, integrative, and iterative process model that links assessment with curriculum and instruction, based on contemporary theories of learning and cognition. The authors review the progress of assessment and provide a substantive rationale for alternative structures. They work to clarify the critical conceptual and technical aspects of using alternative assessments, which is to provide authentic and meaningful feedback for improving student learning, instructional practice, and educational options.

Kohn, Alfie. *The Case Against Standardized Testing, Raising the Scores, Ruining the Schools.* Boston: Houghton Mifflin, 2000.

Our students are tested to an extent that is unprecedented in American history and unparalleled anywhere in the world. Politicians and business people, determined to get tough with students and teachers, have increased the pressure to raise standardized test scores. Unfortunately, the effort to do so typically comes at the expense of more meaningful forms of learning. That disturbing conclusion emerges form Alfie Kohn's devastating new indictment of standardized testing. Drawing from the latest research, he concisely explains just how little test results really tell us and just how harmful a test-driven curriculum can be. Kohn's central message is that standardized tests are "not like the weather, something to which we must resign ourselves. . . . They are not a force of nature but a force of politics—and political decisions can be questioned, challenged, and ultimately reversed." The final section demonstrates how teachers, parents, and students can turn their frustration into action and successfully turn back the testing juggernaut in order to create classrooms that focus on learning.

Lidz, Carol S. *Dynamic Assessment: An Interactional Approach to Evaluating Learning Potential.* New York: Guilford, 1991.

The text contains numerous essays on various aspects of "dynamic assessment." The inadequacy of static assessment—that is, typical tests—is explored. Dynamic assessment allows for a way to access and encourage the potential of each child for the purpose of learning. The book focuses on cognitive learning. This classic text exposes the folly of so-called intelligence tests, which are static measures of ability and do not predict the ability to learn.

_____. *Practioner's Guide to Dynamic Assessment.* New York: Guilford Press, 1991.

This follow-up text to Lidz's earlier text reiterates that dynamic assessment goes beyond procedures. It is an approach to assessment that represents an attitude as well. Dynamic assessors usually believe that all children can learn if sufficient time and effort is used to discover what intervention is best for them. Dynamic assessment depends on testing, feedback, instruction or intervention, retesting, etc. In this respect, it is very much like Grant Wiggins's model of authentic assessment. The assessor in both models strives to provide the appropriate intervention or instruction with detailed constructive feedback.

Linn, Robert L., and Norman E. Gronlund. *Measurement and Assessment in Teaching.* 8th ed. Columbus, OH: Merrill, 2000.

The market leader, this popular text introduces future teachers to those elements of measurement and assessment essential to good teaching. Its straightforward treatment is predicated on the authors' belief that evaluation of learning plays a pivotal role in the instructional process and that its effectiveness depends on a teacher's ability to construct and select valid evaluation instruments. Written with the introductory student in mind, it assumes no prior knowledge of statistics, and uses illustrative examples generously to explain and expand upon topics.

Marzano, Robert F. *Designing a New Taxonomy of Educational Objectives.* Thousand Oaks, CA: Corwin, 2001.

Robert Marzano brings Bloom's educational model known as Taxonomy into the twenty-first century with a new model that incorporates the latest in cognitive science and research on how we learn. Students and educators reap the benefits of new ways to design instruction, curriculum, and assessment. From student-led conferences to policy assessment implications, this definitive work brings assessment concepts up to date and offers practical solutions for today's classrooms.

Mather, Nancy, and Rhia Roberts. *Informal Assessment and Instruction in Written Language: A Practitioner's Guide for Students with Learning Disabilities.* Barndon, VT: Clinical Psychology Publishing, 1995.

This text contains over 350 pages of examples of how to assess student writing. Although the text was written by specialists in the field of learning disabilities, the examples are useful for all levels of learners. Guidelines and examples of actual student work offer practitioners practical assessment techniques and rubrics.

McMillan, James H. *Essential Assessment Concepts for Teachers and Administrators.* Thousand Oaks, CA: Corwin, 2001.

Assessment is at the forefront of reform in education. Now, a renowned expert in the field of assessment shows how to effectively integrate assessment with teaching and learning to attain today's educational goals—a concise and practical book that can be understood and applied by teachers, administrators, and other school personnel.

Nitko, Anthony J. *Educational Assessment of Students.* 3d ed. Columbus, OH: Merrill, 2001.

This highly respected core text provides complete and detailed practical coverage of teacher-constructed classroom assessments, including paper-and-pencil assessments, informal assessments, performance and product assessments, standardized assessments used in schools, and measurement issues that determine assessment quality. This text teaches concepts that are critical for good teaching. Easy to read, it is written for the introductory student. It uses a large number of real-life examples to serve as models for assessment practice. Organization, presentation, and use of rubrics are explained clearly and for the neophyte.

Oosterhof, Albert. *Classroom Applications of Educational Measurement.* 3d ed. Columbus, OH: Merrill, 2001.

This is a core text for educational tests and measurement courses. It presents comprehensive and balanced coverage of all aspects of assessment relevant to classroom teachers, including the construction and use of paper-and-pencil tests, performance assessments, and portfolios, as well as coverage of performance objectives, validity, reliability, grading, standardized testing, and judging assessment quality.

Paris, Scott G., and Linda R. Ayres. *Becoming Reflective Students and Teachers with Portfolios and Authentic Assessment.* Washington, DC: American Psychological Association, 1994.

This text explains clearly how students must be actively involved participants in assessment of their own learning rather than passive respondents to a series of tests. Using examples from Ann Arbor and Walled Lake, Michigan, schools, the authors explain how third-grade students developed portfolios that chronicle their achievement for a year. They explain how authentic assessment must support classroom instruction, collect evidence from multiple activities, promote learning and teaching among participants, and reflect local values, standards, and controls. The authors offer examples of portfolio development specifically with reflection documented in multiple formats. A chapter on strengthening home and school connections is valuable for explaining how parents can also be part of the reflective process of learning. The appendix of the book is a short, clear description of the nature of the learning process, the construction of knowledge, and higher-order thinking. Themes of diversity and multiculturalism are also addressed in the final sections.

Perrone, Vito. *Expanding Student Assessment.* Alexandria, VA: Association and Curriculum Development, 1991.

This book contains several essays, including "Authentic Assessment,

Evaluation, and Documentation," "Authentic Assessment: Beyond the Buzzword," "We Must Take Care: Fitting Assessments to Functions," and "Moving Toward More Powerful Assessment." This book is directed toward finding better ways to assess student learning and to challenge test makers, teachers, curriculum developers, and principals to question themselves about their educational goals and to then develop assessment methods that support these goals.

Rogers, Sheri Everts, and Kathy Everts Danielson. *Teacher Portfolios: Literacy Artifacts and Themes.* Portsmouth, NH: Heinemann, 1996.

This book shows the range of achievement that portfolios can illustrate for individuals. The message should be that a portfolio and its artifacts are uniquely individual. The authors include ideas that have made sense for them and that best illustrate what reflective, talented learners teachers are. The examples are given in the hope of encouraging readers to make the same decisions for their own portfolios.

Routman, Regie. *Invitations: Changing as Teachers and Learners K–12.* Portsmouth, NH: Heinemann, 1994.

Primarily a text that examines teaching strategies and successful techniques, the book includes many excellent examples of authentic assessment tasks. Especially in the area of writing and language arts, lengthy chapters describe authentic activities. An entire chapter is devoted to journal writing. Assessment strategies are described and forums on multiculturalism and students with disabilities are included. This book helps to describe and illuminate perspectives on evaluating students with disabilities.

Salvia, John, and James E. Ysseldyke. *Assessment.* 7th ed. Boston: Houghton Mifflin, 1998.

This is a comprehensive text on assessment. It offers evenhanded, documented evaluations of standardized tests in each domain, straightforward and clear coverage of basic assessment concepts, and illustrations of applications to the decision-making process. Each chapter also provides a list of sites on the World Wide Web where students can find additional information related to the topics within the chapter. The selected Web sites are relevant to the materials presented in the chapter and are likely to endure—that is, sites maintained by publishers, professional or scientific organizations, or university research centers with a record of longevity. Each chapter also contains additional readings and projects to expand student understanding.

Schurr, Sandra. *How to Evaluate Your Middle School: A Practitioner's Guide for an Informal Program Evaluation.* Columbus, OH: National Middle School Association, 1997.

This hands-on text is a must for teachers who wish to see some models of evaluating school programs. It is designed for practitioners at the middle grades; however, the premises hold for all levels. The text discusses how to find exemplary parts of the programs, alternative tools and techniques for evaluation, and what can be learned from case studies.

Silver, Harvey F., Richard W. Strong, and Matthew J. Perini. *So Each May Learn: Integrating Learning Styles and Multiple Intelligences.* Alexandria, VA: Association for Supervision and Curriculum Development, 2000.

This text shows that using an integration of multiple intelligences and learning styles models creates a holistic model that allows educators to engage the full range of human diversity and meet rigorous academic standards at the same time. The book includes:

1. Rationales and research-based principles of learning that support integrated learning.
2. Many classroom examples, activities, and organizers to help educators process ideas and analyze their current practices.
3. Instruments for readers to identify their own style and intelligence profiles.
4. Planning templates for designing integrated lessons, assessments, and curriculum. The authors show educators at all grade levels and in all content areas how to implement a holistic learning program that integrates learning styles and multiple intelligences into instruction, curriculum, and assessment.

Smith, Jeffrey K., Lisa F. Smith, and Richard De Lisi. *Natural Classroom Assessment.* Thousand Oaks, CA: Corwin, 2001.

Here is a fresh perspective on assessment that starts from one's strengths in the classroom and results in improved instruction and learning. Teachers can learn how to analyze results in their classrooms (using their own particular teaching styles) and how to evaluate the assessments of others. Even the beginning teacher can learn how to use assessment to help students focus on strengths and overcome weaknesses.

Wiggins, Grant P. *Assessing Student Performance: Exploring the Limits of Testing.* San Francisco: Jossey-Bass, 1993.

In this book, the author describes the differences between assessment and testing. He argues that testing alone can never provide accountability. He explores and critiques the old and problematic practices of testing such as excessive secrecy, unethical distracters, scoring on a curve, and restricted formats that allow students no explanation of their answers. Wiggins further points out that test design standards serve technical test makers rather than serving students' needs. In contrast, Wiggins argues that authentic tests give useful and timely feedback that enables student growth. The strength of the text is its persuasiveness about assessing student performance, accomplishments, and progress rather than merely totaling a score. In other words, why not have a system that scores "toward" exemplary performance on exemplary tasks, instead of "subtracting" from perfect scores on isolated tests?

_____. *Educative Assessment: Designing Assessment to Inform and Improve Student Performance.* San Francisco: Jossey-Bass, 1998.

This book is the most comprehensive, up-to-date, and descriptive text on authentic assessment. Wiggins gives numerous examples of the tools, techniques, and issues that educators might consider as they develop assessments. He provides a strong argument in favor of authentic assessment over typical tests. He believes that assessment should be used to improve and educate student performance, not merely to audit it on a one-shot basis as most school tests currently do. Authentic tasks, feedback, and understanding are clearly described. The author asks educators to think like assessors. The seventh chapter explores scoring rubrics and criteria. Good and bad rubrics are used to indicate how educators may do the best job possible in assessing student performance. The final sections of the text describe and explain the practical results of using the new assessment. Obviously this affects forms of grading and reporting. The author closes with a plea to educators to embrace accountability for the good of the students.

Articles

The number of articles on assessment is so numerous that I hope the reader will be contented with the examples listed below. They were selected for currency and content. Likewise, this emphasizes how prominent assessment is in the educational literature today.

Barksdale-Ladd, Mary Alice, and Karen F. Thomas. "What's at Stake in High-Stakes Testing—Teachers and Parents Speak Out." *Journal of Teacher Education* 51, no. 5 (November–December 2000): 384–397.

If one can read only one article on assessment, this is the one! It is probably the only current example of actual data from interviews with parents and teachers, reporting from interviews with fifty-nine teachers and twenty parents in two large states. Most impressive is the actual verbatim written record of teachers' and parents' reactions to high-stakes testing, policies, and standards related to their children's work. Equally critical is that teachers finally spoke out about the harmful effect of testing and the erosion of the learning environment. Both have standards, attendant benchmarks, and standardized tests to assess students on the standards. Interview protocols from teachers and parents rendered data informing us about (a) teacher and parent knowledge of state standards and testing; (b) teacher test administration and student preparation practices; (c) effects of tests on teachers, parents, and students; (d) how teachers make instructional decisions based on these tests; and (e) the value of such tests. Teachers and parents were unanimous about (a) the intense stress on all involved, (b) the undermining of meaningful instruction and learning, and (c) the high stakes involved. Differences existed between teachers and parents in the two states. Implications address the need for stakeholders in children's education to make known the deleterious effects of state testing to those in charge of state-mandated testing. The researchers interviewed a total of fifty-nine teachers. Thirty-five of these teachers were from a large southern state. Twenty-four of the teachers were from a northern central state. The majority of the teachers interviewed were students in either a masters degree program or doctoral program, thus indicating their commitment to further education. In addition twenty parents, ten from each state, were also interviewed.

What is most impressive about this study is the actual verbatim written record of teacher and parents reactions to high-stakes testing, policies, and standards related to their children's work. What is equally critical, is that teachers finally spoke out about the harmful effect of testing and the erosion of the learning environment. For example,

Regarding the pressure put on teachers to teach to the test, one participant stated:

> It's awful. I just cringe every time I walk in the Teacher's room because testing is the only topic of conversation there and it raises your anxiety just to hear how scared everybody is. A few years ago, I really loved teaching, but this pressure is just so intense . . . I am not sure how long I can take it.

Likewise, many teachers felt uneasy about job security. Here for example one participant offered:

> They (the tests) really impact me as a teacher because it's getting to
> where if our kids don't pass, we don't get paid for it, and we could get
> booted out of teaching that grade level if our children don't pass the
> test.

To offer an example from a parental viewpoint, when asked how the tests and preparing for the tests affected the children one stated;

> If I thought that getting ready for the test was going to make them (chil-
> dren) a whole lot smarter, I might be able to support it, but it just
> doesn't. They get all worried and nervous and upset about the test.
> They get beat up for nothing . . .They don't learn anything that's going
> to help them for life. They are just children. It's crazy.

Thus, the article carries some powerful personal testimonial from two parts of the country. The views of teachers and parents are recorded to get the personal side of high-stakes testing and its impact on people.

Campbell, David. "Authentic Assessment and Authentic Standards." *Phi Delta Kappan* 81, no. 5 (May 2000): 405–407.

What our school systems are creating may not be education. For many people, getting an education is the act of passing tests and classes. David Campbell of the Department of Educational Studies at California University of Pennsylvania shows how this is not real learning and documents the unfortunate spread of this mentality and what to do about it.

Students are given a standard curriculum to fit everyone. They memorize the facts provided in the classroom long enough to take a standardized exam that will test how well they can memorize. Society then has made the assumption that the student will take this answer from the test that they have chosen out of five possible answers, and integrate that into their lives for future use. Learning and integration cannot happen immediately. For integration to take place, the individual must be able to create connections between the different ideas and facts. These connections are created and grow with the individual's experiences, not by pushing more random facts into their memory. Unfortunately, this type of knowledge is not convenient to evaluate. Standardized tests with only one possible correct answer are much easier to evaluate and be given a grade by the teacher.

However, David Campbell has found this type of "learning" to happen even with people who are currently preparing to teach in the schools. He came up with several questions to ask people who were interviewing for student teaching. The questions did not have short answers that the student could easily pull from their textbooks. The answers that would be given would require reflection about the world and their role in it. The questions were not limited to one right answer, so each person could develop their answer around their own knowledge, experiences, and connections. The unfortunate facts that David Campbell found with his questions were that many of the students and their professors didn't know any answers to the questions and complained that questions requiring this in-depth understanding shouldn't be asked of them. He argues that, teachers who have the mindset of giving their students facts to memorize, testing them, and moving on to the next subject are going to have to adjust their program. Teachers who are working toward success realize they must work with their students. They coach them and give them time to build their own connections. They need to give them opportunities to experience their world. Students who can't use the information anywhere but on the test they are given, have not learned. Once the person has moved beyond tests, knowledge and education will be examined simply through the real life performance.

Clark, Donald C., and Sally N. Clark. "Appropriate Assessment Strategies for Young Adolescents in an Era of Standards-Based Reform." *Heldref Publications* 73, no 4 (September 2000): 201–204.

The authors argue that standards should guide assessment practices. They are especially concerned with middle school children's performance. They delineate why standards are important and further describe the purpose of goals.

1. They delineate what nearly all students should learn, not just what they should be taught.
2. They establish more challenging norms for acceptable levels of student performance.
3. They ensure that in all classrooms across all schools in a local school system, teachers consistently apply common expectations for what students should learn and how well they should learn it.
4. They hold school systems, schools, administrators, and teachers accountable for students' performing at standard.

They further describe the importance of goals:

Goals and Purposes of Assessment

In designing appropriate assessment strategies for young adolescents, middle-level educators must have a clear understanding of assessment and its goals and purposes. Assessment should (a) complement the curriculum and encourage expansion, (b) encourage teachers to assume professional responsibility for evaluation, and (c) make schools accountable on their own terms. Finally, the author's review the importance of authentic assessment and recall from critical conditions for authentic assessment in classrooms:

1. The nurturing of complex understandings
2. The development of reflective habits of the mind
3. The documentation of students' evolving understanding
4. The use of assessment as a moment of learning.

Henderson, Pamela, and P. J. Karr-Kidwell. (1998) "Authentic Assessment: An Extensive Literary Review and Recommendations for Administrators." ERIC Document 418 410, pp. 1–53.

This paper provides an extensive literature review and recommendations for authentic assessment, and then provides recommendations for administrators to implement authentic assessment in elementary schools. It contains forty-seven references and an additional bibliography of ten sources. A lack of comfort with the way in which standardized tests seem to dictate what teachers teach as part of the curriculum, was a contributing factor to interest in authentic assessment that requires and enhances problem-solving skills. To promote a more complex picture of students, schools need to advocate authentic assessment by becoming familiar with the principles of sound assessment. Parent and community support are essential for the implementation of authentic assessment. Some discussions with educators who are using authentic assessment emphasize these points. The key to the development of changes toward authentic assessment is collaborative decision making.

Kohn, Alfie. "Fighting the Tests: A Practical Guide to Rescuing Our Schools." *Phi Delta Kappan* 82, no. 5 (May 2001): 349–357.

Kohn urges readers to make the fight against standardized tests their top priority because, until they have chased this monster from the schools, it will be difficult, perhaps even impossible, to pursue the kinds of reforms that can truly improve teaching and learning.

LaBoskey, Vicki Kubler. "Portfolios Here, Portfolios There . . . Searching for the Essence of 'Educational Portfolios.'" *Phi Delta Kappan* 81, no. 8 (August 2000): 590–595.

According to LaBoskey, educational portfolios can happen, even within organizational structures that seem extremely incompatible—and, if they are consistent with the four characteristics that LaBoskey identifies in the article, they can make a profound difference in the lives of teachers and learners.

Publication from the Educational Researcher. (2000) Position Statement of the American Educational Research Association Concerning High-Stakes Testing in PreK–12 Education, Washington, D.C.

This is the American Educational Research Association's formal statement on high-stakes testing.

The American Educational Research Association (AERA) is the nation's largest professional organization devoted to the scientific study of education. The AERA seeks to promote educational policies and practices that credible scientific research has shown to be beneficial, and to discourage those found to have negative effects. From time to time, the AERA issues statements setting forth its research-based position on educational issues of public concern. One such current issue is the increasing use of high-stakes tests as instruments of educational policy.

This position statement on high-stakes testing is based on the 1999 *Standards for Educational and Psychological Testing.* The *Standards* represent a professional consensus concerning sound and appropriate test use in education and psychology. They are sponsored and endorsed by the AERA together with the American Psychological Association (APA) and the National Council on Measurement in Education (NCME). This statement is intended as a guide and a caution to policymakers, testing professionals, and test users involved in high-stakes testing programs. However, the *Standards* remain the most comprehensive and authoritative statement by the AERA concerning appropriate test use and interpretation.

Many states and school districts mandate testing programs to gather data about student achievement over time and to hold schools and students accountable. Certain uses of achievement test results are termed "high stakes" if they carry serious consequences for students or for educators. Schools may be judged according to the school-wide average scores of their students. High school-wide scores may bring public praise or financial rewards; low scores may bring public embarrassment or heavy sanctions. For individual students, high scores may bring a special diploma attesting to exceptional academic accomplishment; low scores may result in students being held back in grade or denied a high school diploma.

These various high-stakes testing applications are enacted by policymakers with the intention of improving education. For example, it is hoped that setting high standards of achievement will inspire greater effort on the part of students, teachers, and educational administrators. Reporting of test results may also be beneficial in directing public attention to gross achievement disparities among schools or among student groups. However, if high-stakes testing programs are implemented in circumstances where educational resources are inadequate or where tests lack sufficient reliability and validity for their intended purposes, there is potential for serious harm. Policymakers and the public may be misled by spurious test score increases unrelated to any fundamental educational improvement; students may be placed at increased risk of educational failure and dropping out; teachers may be blamed or punished for inequitable resources over which they have no control; and curriculum and instruction may be severely distorted if high test scores per se, rather than learning, become the overriding goal of classroom instruction.

This statement sets forth a set of conditions essential to sound implementation of high-stakes educational testing programs. It is the position of the AERA that every high-stakes achievement testing program in education should meet all of the following conditions:

Protection against High-Stakes Decisions Based on a Single Test

Decisions that affect individual students' life chances or education opportunities should not be made on the basis of test scores alone. As a minimum assurance of fairness, when tests are used as part of making high-stakes decisions for individual students such as promotion to the next grade or high school graduation, students must be afforded multiple opportunities to pass the test. More importantly, when there is credible evidence that a test score may not adequately reflect the student's true proficiency, alternative acceptable means should be provided by which to demonstrate attainment of the tested standards.

Adequate Resources and Opportunity to Learn

When content standards and associated tests are introduced as a reform to change and thereby improve current practice, opportunities to access appropriate materials and retraining consistent with the intended changes should be provided before schools, teachers, or students are sanctioned for failing to meet the new standards. In particular, when testing is used for individual student accountability or certification, students must have had a meaningful opportunity to learn the tested content and cognitive processes. Thus, it must be shown that the tested content has been incorporated into the curriculum, materials, and instruction students are provided before high-stakes consequences are imposed for failing examination.

Validation for Each Separate Intended Use

Tests valid for one use may be invalid for another. Each separate use of a high-stakes test, for individual certification, for school evaluation, for curricular improvement, for increasing student motivation, or for other uses requires a separate evaluation of the strengths and limitations of both the testing program and the test itself.

Full Disclosure of Likely Negative Consequences of High-Stakes Testing Programs

Where credible scientific evidence suggests that a given type of testing program is likely to have negative side effects, test developers and users should make a serious effort to explain these possible effects to policymakers.

Alignment between the Test and the Curriculum

Both the content of the test and the cognitive processes engaged in taking the test should adequately represent the curriculum. High-stakes tests should not be limited to that portion of the relevant curriculum that is easiest to measure. When testing is for school accountability or to influence the curriculum, the test should be aligned with the curriculum as set forth in standards documents representing intended goals of instruction. Because high-stakes testing inevitably creates incentives for inappropriate methods of test preparation, multiple test forms should be used or new test forms should be introduced on a regular bases, to avoid a narrowing of the curriculum toward just the content sampled on a particular form.

Validity of Passing Scores and Achievement Levels

When testing programs use specific scores to determine "passing" or to define reporting categories like "proficient," the validity of these specific scores must be established in addition to demonstrating the representativeness of the test content. To begin with, the purpose and meaning of passing scores or achievement levels must be clearly stated. There is often confusion, for example, among minimum competency levels (traditionally required for grade-to-grade promotion), grade level (traditionally defined as a range of scores around the national average on standardized tests), and "world-class" standards (set at the top of the distribution, anywhere from the 70th to the 99th percentile). Once the purpose is clearly established, sound and appropriate procedures must be followed in setting passing scores or proficiency levels. Finally, validity evidence must be gathered and reported, consistent with the stated purpose.

Opportunities for Meaningful Remediation for Examinees Who Fail High-Stakes Tests

Examinees who fail a high-stakes test should be provided meaningful opportunities for remediation. Remediation should focus on the knowledge and skills the test is intended to address, not just the test performance itself. There should be sufficient time before retaking the test to assure that students have time to remedy any weaknesses discovered.

Appropriate Attention to Language Differences Among Examinees

If a student lacks mastery of the language in which a test is given, then that test becomes, in part, a test of language proficiency. Unless a primary purpose of a test is to evaluate language proficiency, it should not be used with students who cannot understand the instructions or the language of the test itself. If English-language learners are tested in English, their performance should be interpreted in the light of their language proficiency. Special accommodations for English-language learners may be necessary to obtain valid scores.

Appropriate Attention to Students with Disabilities

In testing individuals with disabilities, steps should be taken to ensure that the test score inferences accurately reflect the intended construct rather than any disabilities and their associated characteristics extraneous to the intent of the measurement.

Careful Adherence to Explicit Rules for Determining Which Students Are to Be Tested

When schools, districts, or other administrative units are compared to one another or when changes in scores are tracked over time, there must be explicit policies specifying which students are to be tested and under what circumstances students may be exempted from testing. Such policies must be uniformly enforced to assure the validity of score comparisons. In addition, reporting of test score results should accurately portray the percentage of students exempted.

Sufficient Reliability for Each Intended Use

Reliability refers to the accuracy or precision of test scores. It must be shown that scores reported for individuals or for schools are sufficiently accurate to support each intended interpretation. Accuracy should be examined for the scores actually used. For example, information about the reliability of raw scores may not adequately describe the accuracy of percentiles; information about the reliability of school means may be insufficient if scores for subgroups are also used in reaching decisions about schools.

Ongoing Evaluation of Intended and Unintended Effects of High-Stakes Testing

With any high-stakes testing program, ongoing evaluation of both intended and unintended consequences is essential. In most cases, the governmental body that mandates the test should also provide resources for a continuing program of research and for dissemination of research findings concerning both the positive and the negative effects of the testing program.

Publication from the International Reading Association. (1999) "High Stakes Testing."

The International Reading Association believes that important conceptual, practical, and ethical issues must be considered by those who are responsible for designing and implementing testing programs. This article explores them.

The International Reading Association strongly opposes high-stakes testing. Alarmingly, U.S. policy makers and educators are increasingly relying on single test scores to make important decisions about students. For example, if a student receives a high score on one high-stakes test, it could place him in an honors class or a gifted program. On the other hand, if a student receives a low score on one test, she could be rejected by a particular college. These tests can also be used to influence teachers' salaries, or rate a school district in comparison with others.

Assessment should be used to improve instruction and benefit students rather than compare and pigeonhole them.

Shepard, Lorrie A. "The Role of Assessment in a Learning Culture." *Educational Researcher* 29, no. 7 (August 2000): 4–14.

This article is about classroom assessment, including historical perspectives on curriculums, psychology, and measurement. It also provides samples of a conceptual framework with new theories of curriculum, learning, and assessment, while improving the content and form of assessments. It also looks at protecting the classroom assessment from the negative effects of high-stakes accountability testing and using assessment in the process of learning.

VIDEOTAPES ON PERFORMANCE ASSESSMENT

ASCD 1998 Assessment Conference on Teaching and Learning Set

Type:　Audio cassette
Length:　not available
Cost:　ASCD member price: $64.00;
　　　　Nonmember price: $80.00
Date:　1998
Source:　Association for Supervision and Curriculum Development (ASCD)
　　　　1703 N Beauregard Street
　Alexandria, VA 22311-1714
　800-933 ASCD or 703-578-9600
　Fax: 703-575-5400
　http://www.ascd.org

This is a complete set of audiotaped live recordings from the 1998 Assessment Conference on Teaching and Learning.

Assessment in Math & Science—What's the Point?

Type:　VHS format
Length:　22 minutes
Cost:　$15.00
Date:　1998
Source:　www.learner.org
　Annenberg/CPB Fall 2000 Video Catalogue
　Individual programs:

1. Will this be on the Test? Knowing vs. Understanding
2. What'd I get? Scoring Tools
3.* Is this Going to Count? Embedded Assessment
4. didn't know this was an English Class! Connections Across the Discipline
5. You WILL be tested on this: Standardized Testing
6.* That Would Never Work Here! Seeing Assessment Reform in Action I
7.* That Would Never Work Here Either! Seeing Assessment Reform in Action II
8.* When I was in School . . . Implementing Assessment Reform

* pertains to assessment directly

Assessment Interactive Training Multimedia Package

Type: VHS format
Length: Four 60-minute videotapes
Cost: $799.00 for all four
Date: 1997
Source: Phi Delta Kappa International
         408 N Union Street
         PO Box 789
         Bloomington, IN 47402-0789
         800-766-1156
Fax: 812-399-0018
Email: WEBMASTER@pdkintl.org
http://www.pdkintl.org

This package, created by Richard J. Stiggins of the Assessment Training Institute, is designed to introduce educators to sound classroom assessment. The four 60-minute videos cover all the bases on practical exercises for authentic performance assessment. The videos are:

1. Creating Sound Classroom Assessments
2. Assessing Reasoning in Classrooms
3. Student Involved Classrooms
4. Common Sense Paper and Pencil Assessments

Performance Assessment in the Classroom: A Video Journal of Education

Type: VHS format

> *Length:* Includes two videotapes: Program 1 is 29 minutes,
>   Program 2 is 31 minutes
> *Cost:* $315.00 for both
> *Date:*   1993
> *Source:* Teach Stream, Inc.
>   8686 S 1300
>   E Sandy, UT 84094
>   800-572-1153
>   Fax: 888-566-6888
>   http://www.videojournal.com

These tapes by Jay McTighe, director of the Maryland Assessment Consortium, include a performance-based assessment, an instruction video, and a "Creating Performance Tasks" video.

Performance-Based Assessment in Quality Elementary and Middle Schools

> *Type:*   VHS format
> *Length:* 30 minutes
> *Cost:* $189.00 for members
> *Date:*   1996
> *Source:* The National Association of Elementary School
>   Principals (NAESP)
>   1615 Duke Street
>   Alexandria, VA 22314-3483
>   800-386-2377 or 703-684-3345
>   Email: naesp@naesp.org
>   http://www.naesp.org

This video provides information on performance-based assessment, sample rubrics, and teacher testimonials.

Redesigning Assessment

> *Type:*   VHS format
> *Length:* 98 minutes
> *Cost:*   ASCD member price: $680.00;
>   Nonmember price: $780.00
> *Date:*   1991
> *Source:* Association for Supervision and Curriculum
>   Development (ASCD)
>   1703 N Beauregard Street

Alexandria, VA 22311-1714
703-578-9600 or 800-933-ASCD
Fax: 703-575-5400
http://www.ascd.org

This "classic" three-part series includes an introduction video, a more in-depth treatment of performance assessment and its impact on classrooms and learning, and a video on portfolios. Featured educators include Grant Wiggins, Richard Stiggins, Monte Moses, and Paul LeMahieu.

What's New in Schools: A Parent's Guide to Performance Assessment

Type: VHS format
Length: 14 minutes
Cost: Member price: $65.00; Non-member price: $95.00
Date: 1996
Source: Association for Supervision and Curriculum
Development (ASCD)
1703 N Beauregard Street
Alexandria, VA 22311-1714
703-578-9600 or 800-933-ASCD
Fax: 703-575-5400
http://www.ascd.org

This video includes examples of tasks, projects, and portfolios with comments by students, teachers, and parents. It also comes with a leader's guide.

WEB SITES WITH PERFORMANCE ASSESSMENTS

Assessment and Accountability
Internet address: http://www.nwrel.org/eval/index.html

This is a site by the NW Regional Lab (NWREL) and includes bibliographies of assessment information, a model writing assessment, and information about NWREL's "Alternative Assessment Toolkit" that is focused on the National Council of Teachers of Math (NCTM) standards implementation.

Authentic Assessment Samples
Internet address: http://www.miamisci.org/ph/default.html

Miami Museum of Science provides rubrics, lessons, and materials. Includes other assessment help and a "constructivist" approach to helping students learn.

The National Center for Evaluation, Standards, and Student Testing (CRESST)
Internet address: http://cresst96.cse.ucla.edu/index.htm

This federally funded resource center provides material for educators. This site has helpful reports and a database of assessment descriptions with information on how to contact people with these assessments.

WEB SITES ABOUT PERFORMANCE ASSESSMENT

About Alternative Assessments
Internet address: http://www.aurbach.com/alt_assess.html

Materials presented on this site provide definitions and characteristics of various samples of alternative assessment modes. It also has an excellent listing of resources through hyperlinks to provide additional information.

Alternative Assessment for Adult Learners
Internet address: http://www2.nu.edu/nuri/llconf/conf1995/reif.html

Note: Must be a student to access this site.

This article contains materials aimed at adult learners and illustrates the importance of making goals clear for effective instruction and assessment.

American Association for Higher Education
Internet address: hppt://www.aahe.org

The Assessment Forum has the "Nine Principles of Good Practice for Assessing Student Learning." The AAHE has selected four campus assessment sites as being particularly useful. They are listed below with AAHE's annotations.

Eastern New Mexico University Assessment Resource Office. This site includes 10 surveys used at Eastern New Mexico University, links to the New Mexico Higher Education Assessment Directors Association, and includes a section about the use of CYBER CATS: Classroom Assessment Techniques administered and reported via the Internet. Maintained by the Assessment Resource Office.

Student Outcomes Assessment at Montana State University. This site includes a list of suggested assessment techniques, and assessment information for general education and capstone courses. Maintained by Cel Johnson.

Undergraduate Assessment & Program Review at Southern Illinois University Edwardsville. This site offers extensive assessment information, including an essay entitled "Why do assessment," an annotated bibliography of assessment resources, and thorough descriptions of Primary Trait Analysis and of Classroom Assessment Techniques that can be used via the WWW. Maintained by Doug Eder.

University of Colorado at Boulder, Undergraduate Outcomes Assessment. This well-known site contains an extraordinary comprehensive list of on-line resources. Browse down the page and click on "High Education Outcomes Assessments On The Web." This site was designed by Ephraim Schecter, of Student Affairs Research Services.

Student Outcomes Assessment Page and Internet Resources for Higher Education Outcomes Assessment are two additional comprehensive sites.

Assessment
Internet address: http://www.interactiveclassroom.com

This site provides information on outcomes, assessment, and materials for practicing in-service teachers.

Assessment, Accountability, and Standards
Internet address: http://www.serve.org/assessment/

This site provides information on accountability of teachers related to state standards.

Assessment-Related Sites, Index
Internet address: http://tiger.coe.missouri.edu

This university maintains a site to provide links to information on state standards, accountability, and rubrics used by teachers.

Authentic Portfolio Assessment
Internet address: http://www.teachersworkshop.com/twshop

This site provides many models of portflio assessment in all forms for pre-kindergarten through high school levels.

Automating Authentic Assessment with Rubrics
Internet address: http://stone.web.brevard.k12.fl.us/html/comprubric.html

This site is maintained by educators for the pre-kindergarten through twelfth-grade levels and supplies multiple models of assessments.

ERIC Clearinghouse on Assessment and Evaluation
Internet address: http://ericae.net/ftlib.htm

The ERIC Clearinghouse on Assessment and Evaluation has opened the Text Internet Library at this site. Here you will find links for full-text books, reports, journal articles, newsletter articles, and papers on the topics of educational measurement, evaluation, and learning theory. They include documents based upon criteria that are widely accepted in the library and in the community and they have provided a framework so that you can easily browse.

IMMEX Home Page
Internet address: http://night.immex.ucla.edu/

This site provides educators with multiple examples of how to assess problem-solving skills and critical-thinking skills.

Influence of Performance-Based and Authentic Assessment
Internet address: http://www.eduplace.com/rdg/res/literacy/assess2.html

This site provides educators and parents with clear information on performance-based assessment. Many fine examples are used from the arts and physical education.

An Introduction to Science Portfolios
Internet address: http://www.accessexcellence.org

This is mostly a biology Web site that explains the why and how of portfolios as well as guidelines from the California State Department of Education for portfolio use. It also has some Web links and a chat room in which parents, students, and educators communicate.

The National Center for Evaluation, Standards, and Student Testing (CRESST)
Internet address: http://cresst96.cse.ucla.edu/index.htm

This site has helpful reports and a database of assessment samples. The site emphasizes rubrics and assessment techniques.

SUMMARY

In this chapter, major books, key articles, videotapes, and websites were noted to allow the reader some understanding of the growing literature on assessment. In the next chapter, we will visit the list of organizations devoted to assessment. In addition, major organizations that are committed in general to educational research and evaluation will be described.

Chapter Six

◆ Organizations Supporting Performance Assessment

ORGANIZATIONS THAT PROVIDE INFORMATION ON ASSESSMENT

American Association of Colleges for Teacher Education (AACTE)
1307 New York Avenue, NW
Suite 300
Washington, DC 20005-4701
202-293-2450 ext. 561
Fax: 202-457-8095
Email: kmccabe@aacte.org
http://www.aacte.org

The American Association of Colleges for Teacher Education (AACTE) provides leadership for the continuing transformation of professional preparation programs to ensure competent and caring educators for all America's children and youth. It is the principal professional association for college and university leaders with responsibility for education preparations. It is the major voice, nationally and internationally, for American colleges, schools, and departments of education, and is a focus of discussion and decision making on professional issues of institutional, state, national, and international significance.

American Federation of Teachers (AFT)
555 New Jersey Avenue, NW
Washington, DC 20001
202-879-4400
www.aft.org

The AFT represents 900,000 teachers, paraprofessionals, school-related personnel, public and municipal employees, higher education faculty and staff, and nurses and other health professionals. It advocates national standards for education, the professionalization of teaching, and disciplined and safe environments for learning.

The AFT has actively promoted safe schools practices over the years. One recent initiative is its "Zero Tolerance" policy for drugs, weapons, violence, and disruptive behavior in and around schools. The AFT is currently waging a national campaign called "Responsibility, Respect, Results: Lessons for Life." It has a strong antiviolence component and promotes higher academic and disciplinary standards.

Bilingual Education Clearinghouse
George Washington University
Center for the Study of Language and Education
2011 Eye Street, NW
Suite 2001
Washington, DC 20006
202-467-0867
Fax: 202-467-0867
Email: askncbe@ncbe.gwu.edu
http://www.ncbe.gwu.edu

The Bilingual Education Clearinghouse provides information to practitioners in the field on curriculum materials, program models, methodologies, and research findings on the education of limited English proficient (LEP) individuals. It also offers a free electronic information system to access a database of curriculum materials and literature related to the education of LEP persons. An electronic bulletin board contains news from federal, state, and local education agencies, conference announcements, and other current information. A newsletter and other publications are available, many of which are free of charge. They can answer such questions as:

1. How do you mainstream language minority students?
2. What computer programs exist to assist in teaching limited English proficient students?
3. What are some of the issues and practices involved in meeting the needs of gifted and talented minority language students?
4. How can parents become involved in the education of limited English students?
5. How can teachers integrate multicultural materials in instructional programs?

Chicago Principal Assessment Center
http://www.pencul.org

The Center is self-described as the "Partnership to Engage the Next Century's Urban Leaders" (PENCUL) by providing additional support to aspiring principals and to the local school councils. It identifies, recruits, and helps in the principal selection process based on the Chicago Principal Association standards of school leadership, parental involvement, student-centered learning climate, professional development, school management, instructional leadership, and interpersonal effectiveness.

Education Commission of the States (ECS)
707 17th Street
No. 2700
Denver, CO 80202-3427
303-299-3600
Fax: 303-296-8332
http://www.ecs.org

The Education Commission of the States (ECS) is a nonprofit organization that assists governors, legislators, and state education officials in the identification, development, and implementation of policies that help improve student learning. The ECS functions in conjunction with corporate leaders and Fox River Learning, Advantage Learning Systems, and Voyager Expanded Learning. The ECS provides an information clearinghouse; convenes leadership development conferences; holds state, regional, and national policy seminars (National Forum and Annual Meeting); and offers a variety of publications, and video and audio materials including their *State Education Leader,* published three times a year.

Education Publications Center
United States Department of Education
PO Box 1398
Jessup, MD 20794-1398
301-470-1244
Fax: 301-470-1244
http://www.ed.gov

The Nation's Report Card, the National Assessment of Educational Progress (NAEP), is the only nationally representative and continuing assessment of what America's students know and can do in various subject areas. Since 1969, assessments have been conducted periodically in reading, mathematics, science, writing, history, geography, the arts, and other fields. By making information on student performance—and instructional factors related to that performance—available to policymakers at the national, state, and local levels, NAEP is an integral part of our nation's evaluation of the condition and progress of education.

Educational Research
Office of Educational Research and Improvement's Information Service
U.S. Department of Education
Education Information Branch
555 New Jersey Avenue, NW
Capitol Plaza Building, Suite 300
Washington, DC 20208-5641
800-424-1616
http://www.ed.gov/offices/OERI

The Education Information Branch staff specialists can provide information on topics such as early childhood education, elementary and secondary education, higher education, adult and vocational education, education finance, longitudinal statistical studies, and special education. They have publications and reports, many of which are free. They can answer such questions as:

1. What statistics are there on the number of students who receive loans, grants, and work-study assistance from state sources?
2. What are the statistics on private postsecondary education, such as enrollment, earned degrees conferred, full- and part-time faculty members and their salaries, and more?
3. What information is available on how to choose a school for a child and what makes a school good?
4. How can parents help their children become better readers?
5. What are the enrollment outcomes for recent master's and bachelor's degree recipients?

Educational Resources Information Center (ERIC)
Aspen Systems Corporation
2277 Research Boulevard
Rockville, MD 20850
800-LET-ERIC
Fax: 301-309-2084
Email: accesseric@access.ericorg
http://www.accesseric.org

The Educational Resources Information Center (ERIC) is a nationwide information service set up to collect materials about current developments in education and make them available to the public. The system includes sixteen clearinghouses, each of which is responsible for acquiring, processing, and disseminating information about a particular aspect of education. The ERIC database contains bibliographic information, including key descriptors and abstracts, on over 950,000 research documents, journal articles, curricular materials, and resource guides. The clearinghouses offer a wide variety of services and products and can answer questions about subject fields; run computer searches; develop short bibliographies, newsletters, and other free or inexpensive materials; publish monographs; publish handbooks; and develop materials to help you use ERIC.

ACCESS ERIC is the main center for the ERIC clearinghouses. It answers all questions on how to use ERIC and helps anyone stay up-to-date on the latest developments in the education field. They can answer such questions as:

1. How can I use ERIC to answer my education question?
2. What is required to have a database search run on a topic?
3. How can I have something that I have written entered into the ERIC system?
4. Where can I find the latest statistics on an education topic?
5. How can school administrators develop new management tools and practices?

Educators for Social Responsibility (ESR)
23 Garden Street
Cambridge, MA 02138
617-492-1764 or 800-370-2515
Fax: 617-864-5164
http://www.benjerry.com

The ESR provides resources and services for educators and parents, including publishing books; developing curricula; and sponsoring workshops and training on violence prevention, conflict resolution, intergroup relations, and character education. Query the Web site for information on the highly regarded Resolving Conflict Creatively Program and other materials.

ERIC Clearinghouse on Educational Assessment and Evaluation
College of Library and Information Services

1129 Shriver Laboratory
University of Maryland
College Park, MD 20742
301-405-7449 or 800-464-3742
Fax: 202-319-6692
Email: feedback@ericae.net
http://ericae.net

The Clearinghouse on Assessment and Evaluation provides information on the assessment and evaluation of education projects or programs, tests, and other measurement devices, methodology of measurement and evaluation, and more. A publications list and price sheet are available. They can answer such questions as:

1. Do statistics show that tests discriminate against certain minority groups?
2. What tests are given to handicapped children and what is the research behind these tests?
3. Is the Scholastic Aptitude Test (SAT) an effective tool of measurement?
4. What is computer-assisted testing?
5. How often are SAT tests updated and who designs the questions? ERIC Clearinghouse on Assessment and Evaluation, a link to a good site with information and resources. The site includes ways to locate and evaluate tests and search ERIC databases for information and news on assessment and the text of ERIC essays and digests on assessment. The index is at http://tiger.coe.missouri.edu.

ERIC Clearinghouse on Information and Technology
Syracuse University School of Education
621 Skytop Road
Suite 160
Syracuse, NY 13244-5290
315-443-3640 or 800-464-9107
Fax: 315-443-5448
Email: eric@ericir.syr.edu
http://www.ericit.org/index.shtml

The Clearinghouse on Information and Technology provides information covering educational technology and library and information science at all levels. Materials are available on instructional design, development, and evaluation with emphasis on educational technology including computers, audio and video recordings, and more. They can answer such questions as:

1. What is the latest research on the value of using computers and applying video technology to enhance learning?
2. What are the various studies comparing the different types of computer-based media?
3. Is there an overview of instructional television and its effectiveness for teaching children?
4. At what grade level are computers introduced in the classroom, on average?
5. Are audio recordings an effective tool for teaching foreign languages?

ERIC Clearinghouse on Teaching and Teacher Education
American Association of Colleges for Teacher Education
1307 New York Avenue, NW
Suite 300
Washington, DC 20005
202-293-2450 or 800-822-9229
Fax: 202-457-8095
Email: query@aacte.edu
http://www.ericsp.org

The ERIC Clearinghouse on Teacher Education acquires, publishes, and disseminates documents conveying research, theory, and practice in teacher education and in all aspects of health education, physical education, recreation education, nutrition education, and more. They can answer such questions as:

1. What are the teacher certification requirements?
2. How effective are student teachers in the classroom?
3. What computer games are there to help kids learn math?
4. What techniques can a teacher use to improve classroom productivity?
5. What are "at risk" students and how can they best be served?

ERIC Clearinghouse on Urban Education
Teachers College
Columbia University Institute for Urban and Minority Education
Main Hall, Room 303, Box 40
New York, NY 10027

212-678-3433 or 800-601-4868
Fax: 212-678-4012
Email: eric-cue@columbia.edu
http://www.columbia.edu

The Clearinghouse on Urban Education provides information on the programs and practices in schools in urban areas. In addition, the education of racial and ethnic minority children and youth in various settings is studied. A publications list and price sheet are available. They can answer such questions as:

1. What is the current research on effective programs for reducing the dropout rates among inner-city high school students?
2. What research is available on the number of pregnant, minority teenagers who obtain their high school diplomas in inner-city schools?
3. What information is there on mentoring programs?
4. What issues are involved in linking schools with human service agencies?
5. Are urban schools financed equitably?

The Galef Institute
6053 West Century Boulevard
3d Floor
Los Angeles, CA 90045
310-645-1960 or 800-473-8883
Fax: 310-645-1915
Email: gallettis@galef.org

Founded in 1989, the Galef Institute is a nonprofit educational organization whose primary goal is to work with educators in public schools, schools of education, and other reform agencies to improve student achievement by strengthening the teaching profession. To achieve this goal, the institute assembled a leading team of educators and researchers to develop the comprehensive school reform initiative known as "Different Way of Knowing Research & Development for Middle Grades." This initiative trains teachers in multiple methods of assessment and developing students' critical thinking.

Maryland Assessment Consortium
Linthicum, MD 21090
401-691-5133

Fax: 410-691-5135
Email: mdac1381@erols.com
http://www.cep.cl.k12.md.us

The Consortium of twenty-four school systems provides high quality staff development training in assessment. The focus is on authentic assessment models. The Consortium offers year-round and summer workshops for teachers.

National Alliance of Black School Educators (NABSE)
2816 Georgia Avenue, NW
Washington, DC 20001
202-483-1549
Fax: 202-483-8323
http://www.nabse.org

The Alliance consists of black educators and community leaders whose focus is the equitable education of black youth. NABSE advocates through legislative practice, public awareness, network building, and professional preparation of educators.

National Association of Secondary School Principals (NASSP)
1904 Association Drive
Reston, VA 22091-1537
703-860-0200
Fax: 703-476-5432
http://www.nassp.org

Established in 1916, the NASSP has more than 41,000 members and is the nation's largest school leadership organization for middle and high school administrators. It provides a wide range of programs, services, and publications; promotes the interests of school administrators in Congress; provides consulting services on such topics as instructional improvement, student government, and urban education; and sponsors student-oriented programs such as the National Association of Student Councils, the National Honor Society, and Partnerships International.

National Association of State Boards of Education (NASBE)
1012 Cameron Street
Alexandria, VA 22314
703-684-4000
Fax: 703-836-2313
Email: boards@nasbe.org

The NASBE is a nonprofit, private association that represents state and territorial boards of education. Its mission is to strengthen state boards of education by serving and representing them in their effort to ensure quality education. In 1994 the NASBE conducted a study group on violence and its impact on schools and learning. Countering policy trends that rely solely on the blanket expulsion of students caught with weapons, the NASBE's resulting report, *Schools without Fear,* has called for addressing the U.S. youth violence epidemic on multiple fronts, "using a creative balance of preventive as well as punitive strategies that target the individual, the home, the school, and the community."

National Board for Professional Teaching Standards
26555 Evergreen Road
Suite 400
Southfield, MI 48076
810-351-4444
Fax: 810-351-4170
http://www.nbpts.org/

The National Board for Professional Teaching Standards is an independent, nonprofit, nonpartisan organization governed by a sixty-three-member board of directors. Most of the directors are classroom teachers. The others are school administrators, school board leaders, governors and state legislators, higher education officials, teachers union leaders, and business and community leaders. Their mission is to establish high and rigorous standards for what accomplished teachers should know and be able to do, to develop and operate a national, voluntary system to assess and certify teachers who meet these standards, and to advance related education reforms for the purpose of improving student learning in American schools.

National Center for Education Statistics (NCES)
1990 K Street, NW
Washington, DC 20006
202-502-7300
http://www.governmentguide.com

The NCES is self-described as the primary federal body that collects and analyzes education data, disseminating it through quick links to K–12 practitioners. It also supplies postsecondary education data, the "Nation's Report Card," information on conferences and training, and college opportunities on-line.

National Center for Fair & Open Testing (FairTest)
342 Broadway
Cambridge, MA 02139
617-864-4810
Fax: 617-497-2224
http://www.fairtest.org

FairTest is an advocacy organization dedicated to ensuring fairness, equity, and high quality in assessment instruments, practices, systems, and policies. FairTest believes that reliance on standardized testing undermines the quality of education. At the same time, standardized testing often creates and reinforces barriers to equal opportunity by perpetuating social and structural inequities based on race, class, income, gender, language, culture, and disability. To accomplish its mission, FairTest promotes assessment of students, workers, and others that is fair, open, accurate, relevant, accountable, and educationally sound, and works to end the abuses, misuses, and flaws of standardized testing. To that end, FairTest organizes testing reform campaigns, educates the public, provides technical assistance, and serves a national clearinghouse for assessment information.

National Center on Educational Outcomes
University of Minnesota
350 Elliot Hall
75 East River Road
Minneapolis, MN 55455
612-626-1530
Fax: 612-624-0879
http://www.coled.umn.edu/NCEO

This organization describes itself as providing national leadership in the participation and continuance of students with disabilities and limited English proficiency in public schools by helping to identify outcomes, indicators, and assessments that help monitor the development of students with disabilities. The Center provides training, resource materials, consulting services, and technical assistance to organizations across the country. It offers a broad list of publications, technical reports, self-study guides, directory of assessment projects, and a national network regarding assessment issues.

National Council for Accreditation of Teacher Education (NCATE)
2010 Massachusetts Avenue, NW

Washington, DC 20036-1023
202-466-7496
Fax: 202-296-6620
http://www.ncate.org

The NCATE is the teaching profession's mechanism to help establish high-quality teacher preparation. Through the process of professional accreditation of schools, colleges, and departments of education, NCATE works to make a difference in the quality of teaching and teacher preparation today, tomorrow, and for the next century.

NCATE is a coalition of thirty-three specialty professional associations of teachers, teacher educators, content specialists, and local and state policymakers. All are committed to quality teaching, and together, the coalition represents over 3 million individuals. It is the performance-based accrediting body for teacher education programs in higher education. NCATE offers on-line publications, policy briefs, and research studies.

National Middle School Association (NMSA)
4151 Executive Parkway
Suite 300
Westerville, OH 43081
800-528-6672
http://www.nmsa.org

The NMSA is a 20,000-member professional organization of teachers, administrators, parents, educational consultants, and community leaders expressly focused on the needs of the young adolescent. In addition to an annual national conference, state conferences and workshops, and several networks such as the National Forum for Middle Grades Reform, the NMSA provides professional development, consultant services, and a wealth of resources from books and periodicals to web links and newsletters. The Association sets national standards for higher education teacher preparation programs and is the leading international voice for middle grades education.

National School Boards Association (NSBA)
1680 Duke Street
Alexandria, VA 22314
703-838-6722
Fax: 703-838-7590
http://www.nsba.org

The NSBA offers information on policies, regulations, and laws, particularly those involving gun-related issues, drug-related issues, antiviolence initiatives, school-related initiatives, issues of child victimization, public relations and media strategies, and publications and clearinghouse services and dissemination.

National Staff Development Council (NSDC)
PO Box 240
Oxford, OH 45056
513-523-6029
http://www.nsdc.org

This is the major professional organization to focus exclusively on the professional development of educators and the organizational development of educational institutions. The NSDC holds a conference early each December, publishes the quarterly *Journal of Staff Development,* and the monthly *Results* and *School Improvement Team Innovator.* The NSDC maintains an active connection with educational research and theory but keeps its approach very practical and practitioner oriented. The NSDC's specialty is bridging the gap between research, theory, and practice. Members are balanced between school personnel, private consultants, regional educational service center and laboratory staff, and university faculty. The NSDC has thirty-six state and provincial affiliates that provide local support to staff developers. (See the section titled "Events" on this site for more information.)

Relearning by Design
65 South Main Street
Building B
PO Box 210
Pennington, NJ 08534
609-730-1199
Fax: 609-730-1488
Email: info@relearning.org
http://www.relearning.org

Relearning by Design helps educators build schools around the student's needs as a learner. Relearning by Design provides consultations, in-service workshops, professional development seminars, and national conferences to improve the ways that educational goals and means are organized and assessed. They also provide a variety of printed materials, publications, videotapes, audiotapes, and software on student assessment and curriculum design. Relearning by Design is headed by Grant Wiggins.

Most importantly, the organization helps educators keep alive the difficult questions at the heart of education:

1. How do we set high standards while also setting fair and reasonable expectations?
2. How do we know that what gets an "A" in our schools is judged to be quality work in the best schools?
3. If "you are what you assess," why do we so often test only what is easy to test, not what goes to the heart of our aims?
4. Is student boredom inevitable or is it a sign that our curriculum is not authentic and ineffective?
5. If feedback is central to learning, why do schools so rarely survey students, parents, alumni, and our institutional clients as to what does and does not work?

A vision statement is one thing; policies that make it real and lead to the changes in bureaucratic traditions are quite another. Relearning by Design asks educators to judge the gap between their intent and their effect and helps them design systems that make it likely that the gap is examined and closed.

RELATED KEY ORGANIZATIONS

The following notable educational organizations are major professional groups. Although not solely devoted to assessment, that topic would certainly be of interest to some members in both organizations.

American Educational Research Association (AERA)
1230 17th Street, NW
Washington, DC 20036-3078
202-223-9485
http://www.aera.net

The American Educational Research Association (AERA) is concerned with improving the educational process by encouraging scholarly inquiry related to education and by promoting the dissemination and practical application of research results.

The AERA is the most prominent international professional organization with the primary goal of advancing educational research and its practical application. Its more than 23,000 members are educators; administrators; directors of research, testing, or evaluation in federal, state, and local agencies; counselors; evaluators; graduate students; and behavioral scientists.

The broad range of disciplines represented by the membership includes education, psychology, statistics, sociology, history, economics, philosophy, anthropology, and political science. AERA was founded in 1916.

American Evaluation Association
505 Hazel Circle
Magnolia, AZ 71753
888-232-2275 or 870-234-7433
Email: AEA@kistcon.com
http://www.eval.org

This is an international, professional organization devoted to the application of program evaluation, personnel evaluation, and technology. All forms of evaluation are of interest. The organization seeks to improve evaluation practices and methods. Assessment would surely be one of the categories of interest.

International Reading Association
Public Information Office
800 Barksdale Road
PO Box 8139
Newark, DE 19714-8139
302-731-1600
Fax: 302-731-1057
Email: pubinfo@reading.org
http://www.ira.org

The International Reading Association is a dynamic and diverse organization that includes classroom teachers, reading specialists, consultants, administrators, supervisors, college teachers, researchers, psychologists, librarians, media specialists, students, and parents. The Association has more than 90,000 members in 99 countries and represents over 350,000 individuals and institutions through its affiliated councils worldwide.

The organization seeks to promote high levels of literacy for all by improving the quality of reading instruction through studying the reading process and teaching techniques. It serves as a clearinghouse for the dissemination of reading research through conferences, journals, and other publications and actively encourages the lifetime reading habit.

Phi Delta Kappa International (PDK)
408 N Union Street
PO Box 789
Bloomington, IN 47402
800-766-1156
Fax: 812-339-0018
http://www.pdkintl.org

Phi Delta Kappa is an international association of educators. The mission of PDK is to promote high-quality education. Its emphasis is on publicly supported education as essential to a democracy. It sponsors professional development workshops regularly in all areas of interest to educators, including assessment. It offers a newsletter; a journal, *The Phi Delta Kappan;* a series of books; and travel seminars.

RELATED EDUCATIONAL GROUPS

Association for Supervision and Curriculum Development (ASCD)
1703 N Beauregard Street
Alexandria, VA 22311-1714
703-578-9600 or 800-933-ASCD
Fax: 703-575-5400
http://www.ascd.org

The Association for Supervision and Curriculum Development (ASCD) is a unique international, nonprofit, nonpartisan association of professional educators whose jobs cross all grade levels and subject areas. Diverse members share a profound commitment to excellence in education. Founded in 1943, ASCD's mission is to forge covenants in teaching and learning for the success of all learners. ASCD sponsors workshops, conferences, and professional development sessions. In addition, books, journals, and videos on topics of interest to educators are available.

Current ASCD Networks on Assessment

ASCD sponsors numerous networks that help members exchange ideas, share common interests, identify and solve problems, grow professionally, and establish collegial relationships. The following networks may by of particular interest to readers of this book:

Authentic Assessment
Contact: Kathleen Busick, Pacific Region Educational Laboratory, Suite 1409m 1164 Bishop Street, Honolulu, Hawaii 96813. Telephone: (808) 532-1900. FAX: (808) 532-1922.

Designing District Evaluation Instruments for Math and Science Process Skills
Contact: Shelley Lipowich, Math/Science Consultant, 6321 North Canon del Pajaro, Tucson, Arizona 85715. Telephone: (602) 299-9583. FAX: (602) 886-2370.

Thinking Assessment
Contact: Sally Duff, Maryland Center for Thinking Studies, Coppin State College, 2500 West North Avenue, Baltimore, Maryland 21216. Telephone: (410) 396-9362.

National Center for Research on Evaluation, Standards, and Student Testing (CRESST)
GSE&IS, Mailbox 951522
300 Charles E. Young Drive North
Los Angeles, CA 90095-1522
310-206-1532
Fax: 310-825-3883
http://www.cse.ucla.edu

Funded by the U.S. Department of Education's Office of Educational Research and Improvement, the National Center for Research on Evaluation, Standards, and Student Testing (CRESST) is a unique partnership of UCLA's Graduate School of Education & Information Studies and its Center for the Study of Evaluation. The CRESST mission focuses on the assessment of educational quality, addressing persistent problems in the design and use of assessment systems to serve multiple purposes. Other distinguished CRESST research partners include the University of Colorado, Stanford University, the RAND Corporation, the University of Pittsburgh, the University of California (Santa Barbara), and the Educational Testing Service. During its current funding period, CRESST research is organized into three programs of sustained R&D and one program for dissemination integrated into the following research model.

CRESST Conceptual Model

The four CRESST programs are briefly described below.

- Program One, Assessment in Action: Teaching and Learning,

addresses fundamental problems in improving the utility of assessment at the school and classroom levels. Researchers are developing new assessments and conducting inquiries into the ways teachers and others respond to and use various types of assessments.

- Program Two, Accountability, Equity, and Public Engagement, focuses on critical issues of validity, equity, and utility of results from large-scale assessment systems. The program combines active, scholarly reflection on the purposes, implementation, and effects of large-scale assessment systems with action-oriented, practical responses to pressing problems in current system design and interpretation.
- Program Three, Validity, Equity, and Utility, brings together leading experts to advance theory in construct validity, measurement accuracy, assessment of progress, and reporting, with special emphasis on the equity issues involved in each. Regular symposia in this program will synthesize findings and methodological advances across CRESST programs to address specific problems of the field.
- Program Four, Outreach and Dissemination, communicates CRESST research findings and policy recommendations to key audiences through a diverse array of publication, videos, workshops, conferences, advanced interactive technologies, and the Internet.

CRESST research products, now moving to practical applications in classrooms, districts, and state assessments, include the design of computer-supported measures and the development of integrated, project-based simulations. The initial version of a CRESST-developed electronic school portfolio uses true 3-D technology and integrated video to provide a tool for school-based planning and continuous improvement.

For further information, please contact Ronal Dietel, CRESST Director of Communications, at (310) 206-1532 or ron@cse.ucla.edu.

National Council for the Social Studies (NCSS)
NCSS Information Services
3501 Newark Street, NW
Washington, DC 20016
800-296-7840 ext. 106
Email: information@ncss.org
http://www.ncss.org/about/background.html

Founded in 1921, the National Council for the Social Studies has grown to be the largest association in the country devoted solely to social studies education. The NCSS engages and supports educators in strengthening and advocating social studies. With members in all fifty states, the District of Columbia, and sixty-nine foreign countries, the NCSS serves as an umbrella organization for elementary, secondary, and college teachers of history, geography, economics, political science, sociology, psychology, anthropology, and law-related education. Organized into a network of more than 110 affiliated state, local, and regional councils and associated groups, the NCSS membership represents K–12 classroom teachers, college and university faculty members, curriculum designers and specialists, social studies supervisors, and leaders in the various disciplines that constitute the social studies.

College and University Faculty Association of the National Council for the Social Studies Oppose High Stakes Standardized Tests!
Whereas high stakes standardized tests represent a powerful intrusion into America's classrooms, often taking up as much as 30 percent of teacher time,

And whereas the tests pretend that one standard fits all, when one standard does not fit all,

And whereas these tests measure, for the most part, parental income and race, and are therefore instruments that build racism and anti-working class sentiment—against the interest of most teachers and their students,

And whereas these tests deepen the segregation of children within and between school systems, a move that is not in the interests of most people in the US,

And whereas, the tests set up a false employer-employees relationship between teacher and students that damages honest exchanges in the classroom,

And whereas we have seen repeatedly that the exams are unprofessionally scored, for example in New York where thousands of students were unnecessarily ordered to summer school on the grounds of incorrect test results,

And whereas the tests create an atmosphere that pits students against students and teachers against teachers and school systems against school systems in a mad scramble for financial rewards, and to avoid financial retribution,

And whereas the tests have been used to unjustly fire and discipline teachers throughout the country,

And whereas the exams represent an assault on academic freedom by forcing their way into the classroom in an attempt to regulate knowledge, what is know and how people come to know it,

And whereas the tests foment an atmosphere of greed, fear, and hysteria, none of which contributes to learning, And whereas the high-stakes test pretend to neutrality but are deeply partisan in content.

And whereas the tests become commodities for opportunities whose interests are profits, not the best interests of children,

Be it therefore resolved that the National Council for the Social Studies join with the National Council of Teachers of English, the International Reading Association, and the American Educational Research Association in supporting long-term authentic assessment, opposing all high-stakes standardized examinations such as but not limited to the SAT9 in California, the Michigan MEAP, the Texas TAAS, Florida's FCAT, and the New York Regents Exam. Moreover we support student and educator boycotts of the exams.

National Council of Teachers of English (NCTE)
1111 W Kenyon Road
Urbana, IL 61801-1096
800-369-6283
Fax: 217-328-9645
Email: public_info@ncte.org
http://www.ncte.org

The National Council of Teachers of English, with 77,000 individual and institutional members worldwide, is dedicated to improving the teaching and learning of English and the language arts at all levels of education. Its membership is composed of elementary, middle, and high school teachers, supervisors of English programs, college and university faculty, teacher educators, local and state agency English specialists, and professionals in related fields.

English Teachers Pass Resolutions on High Stakes Testing and the Rights of Test Takers. November 22, 2000

Members of the National Council of Teachers of English (NCTE), recently passed resolutions urging reconsideration of high stakes testing and asking for the development of a test taker's bill of rights.

The resolutions were adopted by members attending the Council's Annual Business Meeting on Friday, November 17, 2000, in Milwaukee Wisconsin.

The new resolutions appear below. See the NCTE web site (*http://www.ncte.org/resolutions*) for past resolutions.

Resolution on Urging Reconsideration of High Stakes Testing
Background: The National Council of Teachers of English passed a resolution in 1999 expressing concern over the prevalence of high stakes
tests in the United States. The use of such tests has continued to esca-
late and to cause evident measurable damage to teaching and learning
in U.S. schools. Other professional organizations have likewise voiced
strong objections to the use of a single test for making significant decisions. Be it therefore

Resolution

RESOLVED, that the National Council of Teachers of English affirm
the following statement:

The efforts to improve the quality of education, especially in under-
achieving schools, are laudable, and the desire for accountability is understandable. However, high stakes tests often fail to assess accurately
students' knowledge, understanding, and capability. Raising test scores
does not improve education. Therefore, the use of any single test in
making important decisions—such as graduation, promotion, funding
of schools, or employment and compensations of administrators and
teachers—is educationally unsound and unethical.

High stakes testing often harms students' daily experience of learning, displaces more thoughtful and creative curriculum, diminishes the
emotional well-being of educators and children, and unfairly damages
the life-chances of members of vulnerable groups. We call on legislators
and policymakers to repeal laws and policies that tie significant consequences to scores on single assessments. We further call on legislators
and policymakers to join with professional organizations to develop
better means of improving public education.

BE IT FURTHER RESOLVED, the NCTE invite other organizations to
support, publicize, and promote a reconsideration of high stakes testing.

Background: Since the 1970s language and literacy professionals
consistently and increasingly have been concerned about the nature,
uses, and abuses of standardized testing. In fact, NCTE has passed numerous resolutions addressing these concerns. Although NCTE continues to be concerned about standardized testing, particularly high
stakes testing at all levels, we recognize that testing is a pervasive fea-
ture of American education. However, the practices surrounding high
stakes testing vary dramatically from state to state. Some states, for example, have passed on secrecy and deny access to the test at the potential expense of students and teachers. It seems especially important,
then, that standards of open practice that allow for public scrutiny sur-

rounding testing be developed and disseminated. A test taker's bill or rights would include items such as:

- the right to insist that standardized tests be adopted through an open, public process that considers the design and appropriateness of the test;
- the right to know before the test date the form of any given test;
- the right to experience a challenging curriculum that is not constrained by any given test;
- the right to know how the results of the test will be used;
- the right to arrange accommodations for documented learning differences and/or unforeseeable circumstances;
- the right to display competencies through various means;
- the right to an open process of review of test items and results;
- the right to challenge test scores and have them changed if they are incorrect; and
- the right to a process that corrects tests and/or individual items found to be invalid or unreliable.

Be it therefore

RESOLVED, that the National Council of Teachers of English, in conjunction with other professional and public policy organizations and learned societies, develop a Test Taker's Bill of Rights.

BE IT FURTHER RESOLVED, the NCTE encourage decision-making groups at the district, state, and federal levels to adopt a Test Taker's Bill of Rights in order to protect students, parents, teachers, and the general public.

National Education Association (NEA)
1201 16th Street, NW
Washington, DC 20036
202-833-4000
http://www.nea.org

The NEA is one of the most influential teacher unions and lobbies in the United States. NEA members are doing things that improve conditions for children and public schools. The NEA influences educational legislation, practice in classrooms, and professional development for teachers. The NEA offers synopses of the latest in educational research as well as various materials for in-service, practicing teachers.

National Science Teachers Association (NSTA)
1840 Wilson Boulevard

Arlington, VA 22201-3000
703-243-7100
http://www.nsta.org

The National Science Teachers Association (NSTA), founded in 1944 and headquartered in Arlington, Virginia, is the largest organization in the world committed to promoting excellence and innovation in science teaching and learning for all. The NSTA's current membership of more than 53,000 includes science teachers, science supervisors, administrators, scientists, business and industry representatives, and others involved in science education.

To address subjects of critical interest to science educators, the Association publishes five journals, a newspaper, many books, and many other publications. The NSTA conducts national and regional conventions that attract more than 30,000 attendees annually.

✎❖ A List of State Coordinators for Testing Reform

Note: This was the most recent list as of February 2001.

State	*Contact*	*Email*	*Phone*
Alaska	Ken Jones	afkwj@uaa.alaska.edu	not available
Arizona	Gabie Gedlaman	ggedlaman@bigfoot.com	480/539-1337
North California	Lysa Tabachnick	lysat@cruzio.com	831/469-4280
South California	Rich Gibson	rgibson@pipeline.com	619/583-6886
Colorado	John McCluskey	McFort3@cs.com	970/484-5914
Connecticut	Pedro Mendia-Landa	pedro.mendia@yale.edu	203/439-8121
Delaware	Denise Davis	denisedavis@eclipsetel.com	410/755-6891
Florida	Gloria Pipkin	gpipkin@i-1.net	not available
Georgia	Lisa Amspaugh	amspaugh@excelonline.com	770/963-2431
Hawaii	Verlie Malina-Wright	vmalinawri@aol.com	808/261-3714
Idaho	Dan Kmitta	kmitta@uidaho.edu	208/885-7637
Illinois	Harvey Daniels	smokeylit@aol.com	312/441-6635
Iowa	Dick Hanzelka	dhanzelka@aea9.k12.ia.us	319/344-6301
Louisiana	C.C. Campbell-Rock	parentjustice@hotmail.com	504/948-6250
Maine	Bo Hewey	khewey@maine.rr.com	207/774-0419
Maryland	Bess Altwerger	altwerg@saber.towson.edu	410/830-3188
Massachusetts	Karen Hartke	khartke@fairtest.org	617/864-4810
Michigan	Rich Gibson	rgibson@pipeline.com	313/577-0918
Minnesota	Wade Nelson	wnelson@vax2.winona.msus.edu	507/285-7589
Mississippi	Libbie Love	llove@watervalley.net	662/473-9268
Missouri	Debra Smith	d_smith@vax1.rockhurst.edu	816/501-4148
Nevada	Chuck MacLeod	castausa@hotmail.com	775/826-7848
New Hampshire	Arthur Pelletier	ajpell@email.com	not available
New Jersey	Dee Bucciarelli	deenb@worldnet.att.net	609/924-3416
New York	Jan Hammond	jdh77777@aol.com	914/257-2812
North Carolina	Irv Besecker	besecker@sprynet.com	336/766-6160
Ohio	Mary O'Brien	sobrien@columbus.rr.com	614/487-0477
Oklahoma	Will Muir	wmuir@norman.k12.ok.us	405/364-4465
Oregon	Bill Bigelow	bbpdx@aol.com	503/916-5140
Pennsylvania	Melissa Butler	mab@icubed.com	412/421-1724
South Carolina	Andrew HaLevi	AHTeacher@aol.com	843/723-3734
South Dakota	Kim Hanes	khanes@sd.value.net	605/734-4052

Tennessee	Gilda Lyon	gdlyon@yahoo.com	423/825-0844
Texas	Eileen Weinstein	lilefty@aol.com	713/629-8233
Utah	Michelle Bachman	michelle.bachman@slc.k12.ut.us	801/485-5608
Vermont	Susan Ohanian	SOhan70241@aol.com	802/425-4201
Virginia	Mickey VanDerwerker	wmzemka@aol.com	540/586-6149
Washington	Juanita Doyon	Jedoyon@aol.com	253/846-0823
Washington D.C.	Aleta Margolis	aleta@artistryinteaching.org	202/822-8081
Wisconsin	Bob Peterson	REPMilw@aol.com	414/265-6217

Note: If a state is not listed, it most likely is in need of a coordinator. If you would like to volunteer to act as coordinator of your state, please contact www.fairtest.org

Source: The Assessment Reform Network, 2001.

Appendix B

◑ State-by-State Report on Assessment among States that Replied to the Survey

The National Forum on Assessment listed *Principles and Indicators for Student Assessment Systems* in order to help guide assessment reform. FairTest used surveys to gather data along with follow-up interviews and selected document review. Listed below are the state findings.

FairTest adapted the *Principles and Indicators* to create appropriate standards for large-scale assessment. The standards are:

Standard 1: Assessment supports important student learning.
Standard 2: Assessments are fair.
Standard 3: Professional development.
Standard 4: Public education, reporting, and parents' rights.
Standard 5: System review and improvement.

Scoring Guide

The **Fairtest** organization evaluated and assigned the following scores to the states.

Level 1. State assessment system needs a complete overhaul. Such a state system exhibits *three or more* of the following negative characteristics: Uses all or almost all multiple-choice testing; Tests all students in one or more grades with a norm-referenced test; Has a single exam as a high school exit or grade-promotion requirement; or Exhibits generally poor performance on the other standards.

Level 2. State assessment system needs many major improvements. Such a state system has *two* of the following negative characteristics: Uses all or almost all multiple-choice testing; Tests all students in one or more grades with a norm-referenced test; Has a single exam as a high school exit or grade-promotion requirement; or Exhibits generally poor performance on the other standards.

Level 3. State assessment system needs some significant improvements. Such a state system has some positive attributes but still has *one* of the following negative characteristics: Uses all or almost all multiple-choice testing;

Tests all students in one or more grades with a norm-referenced test; Has a single exam as a high school exit or grade-promotion requirement; or Exhibits generally poor performance on the other standards.

Level 4. State assessment system needs modest improvement. Such a state system generally performs well across the standards, has none of the major problems described at previous levels, but does not show all the characteristics of a model system, including use of sampling and classroom-based assessments for accountability and public reporting.

Level 5. A model system. Such a state system performs well across all the standards, including use of sampling and classroom-based assessments as significant portions of accountability and public reporting. It may need minor improvements in some areas.

Not scorable. The state does not have an assessment system and does not mandate any assessments for districts to use, or is otherwise not scorable.

Discussion. This scoring guide gives the most weight to Standard 1. If an assessment system does not support high quality teaching and learning, it should be completely overhauled.

State Date Table, 1996–1997

State	Level	State	Level
AK	1	MT	2
AL	1	NC	1
AR	2	ND	2
AZ	1	NE	2
CA	2	NH	4
CO	4	NJ	2
CT	4	NM	1
DE	0	NV	2
FL	1	NY	2
GA	1	OH	2
HI	1	OK	2/1
IA	0	OR	3
ID	2	PA	3
IL	3	RI	3
IN	2/1	SC	1
KS	?	SD	2
KY	4/3	TN	1
LA	1	TX	2
MA	2	UT	1
MD	3	VA	1
ME	4	VT	5
MI	3	WA	2
MN	2	WI	2
MO	4/3	WV	1
MS	1	WY	0

Notes: Data is from 1996–97 school year, except 1995–96 for Arkansas, Connecticut, Florida, Maryland, Mississippi, Ohio, which did not respond for Fairtest survey.

In the "level" column, use of a slash (/), as in 4/3, indicates that the system is on the border; the first number is the direction in which the state appears to be leaning.

Purposeful Sampling of the Report on the Top Rated State of Vermont
VERMONT

Summary Evaluation

Vermont has nearly a model system. Many of the improvements that should be made to solidify the program are already planned. The assessments are based on state standards, rely very little on multiple-choice items and include portfolios in two subjects. The assessment burden is reasonable, as are the stakes. Sampling is done in re-scoring some locally-scored portfolios in order to obtain state date, but will not be used on exams. Fairness is adequate and improving. Professional development is good and also improving. Public education and parent rights are solid. Reviews are good and are being strengthened. Improving the reliability of the portfolio assessments is an area that will need continued attention. Aside from further progress in the areas already planned, the state should consider using more performance tasks in addition to constructed-response items and using portfolios in additional subjects.

NEBRASKA
The Case of Nebraska

Decisions about whether or not students are learning should not take place in the legislature, the governor's office or the department of education. They should take place in the classroom, because that is where learning occurs.

—Douglas Christensen, Commissioner
Nebraska Department of Education

What is remarkable about the Nebraska case is that:

  a) Nebraska was the forty-ninth state of forty-nine states to adopt standards for K–16 education.
  b) Nebraska students do extremely well on standardized tests all the way around, so they did need to do this.

Now that you have read about Vermont's success with an assessment plan, let us look at the State of Nebraska's plan.

The Nebraska Plan is known as STARS, *S*chool-based *T*eacher-led, *A*ssessment and *R*eporting *S*ystem. The intent of the STARS plan, is to do the best possible schooling for Nebraska's students. This system is very different from other models of "reform." Nebraska does not *mandate* compliance. Nor does Nebraska rely on external approaches or external mandates. Nebraska likes to call their assessment plan, "assessment affirmation." Nebraska rejects the notion that a single test is helpful for students. The Nebraska plan is designed to avoid the pitfalls of high stakes testing. Nebraska emphasizes James Popham's (1999) reminder that standardized achievement tests should not be used as a single measure of quality for the following reasons:

1) Norm-Referenced Standardized Tests do not match what is in the typical school curriculum; the University of Nebraska did a study in 1998 for example. Researchers found that only 35–40 percent of what was on standardized tests matched the Nebraska curriculum.

2) The purpose of norm-referenced standardized tests is to "differentiate scores." In other words, the purpose is to show variance. Thus, those items on which students to very well, are *not* included on the tests.

3) The types of items on standardized tests reflect on information not covered in school. Success on these items either depends on a child's innate ability OR something a student learned elsewhere.

Popham's declaration that "employing standardized achievement tests to ascertain educational quality is like measuring temperature with a tablespoon," says it all.

Nebraska and Assessment Affirmation

The state of Nebraska is one that has not been *FORCED* into assessment. It has 585 school districts. They are performing well. Nebraska schools focus on continuous school improvement. Decisions are *local,* not mandates of the state or federal government. In the spring of 2000, the Nebraska legislature passed L.B. 812. A bill that supports the school-based, teacher-led initiative on assessment. Surely we can learn from this state. Yes, they have teacher-developed criteria. Yes, they strive for high quality assessments. Yes, STARS is designed to assess learning and growth. Yes, the focus is on developing assessment literacy. Thus, Nebraska offers us a good model to emulate.

IOWA

From the Iowa State Board of Education
The Special Case of Iowa

Iowa is the state that has refused to be part of the Standards Movement. Do they have assessment plans? Yes, of course. Although Iowa has four broad state goals, which were developed with public participation, the state has adopted the approach of helping districts improve the capacity to improve themselves. Therefore, the state works with districts to help them develop, "through informed dialogue with its community, a clear set of learning expectations . . . and standards for student performance." The state will provide model standards from professional organizations and other states that districts can adopt or use in developing their own.

Iowa does not have a state test. Instead it has a voluntary testing program in which about 99 percent of the districts use the norm-referenced, multiple-choice Iowa Tests of Basic Skills (ITBS) and the Iowa Tests of Educational Development.

The state expects that districts will use a variety of assessment methods in determining student progress, not just Iowa's. The state has been involved with New Standards, which has assisted local districts in developing alternative assessments. In addition, the state is in the process of identifying multiple assessments to meet the requirements of the federal Title I program of the Improving America's Schools Act.

Evaluation

The focus on improving local and classroom assessments, particularly portfolios, is positive. The state should survey teachers to see if the professional development meets educators' needs for assistance.

FLORIDA

Summary Evaluation

Although Florida did not respond to the Fairtest survey, it appears from other data sources that the state's assessment program needs complete overhaul. The state relies mostly on multiple-choice tests, though a new exam will include constructed-response items in math, has a high-school exit test requirement and mandates that districts use an NRT in two grades and two subjects. The test burden is not very high as only reading, writing and math are assessed. Bias review information was not available, but inclusion efforts need improvement, especially for LEP students. Although the state says that professional development is on its agenda, its reported efforts focus only on writing, and thus it appears this area also needs substantial improvement. Fairtest has little information on reporting, none pertaining to rights and none about review.

In addition, here are examples from five middle range states; Massachusetts, Michigan, Maryland, New York, and Ohio.

MASSACHUSETTS

Summary Evaluation

Massachusetts's new state system, as it is being implemented, needs many major improvements. The system will include mixed multiple-choice and constructed-response criterion-referenced exams, based on state standards. It also will contiue to use a recently introduced multiple-choice NRT in reading in grade 3. The state will require a high school exit exam and high stakes for schools and districts. The state has piloted programs for schools to develop local portfolios. The planned bias review committee needs to be implemented and given adequate authority. Alternative assessments for students with IEPs are needed. It is positive that the state is developing exams in Spanish, but it remains unclear how the state will assess other LEP students. The state's financial support of teacher professional development is substantial, but some elements of a comprehensive approach are lacking. Further work in community education and information, as well as bolstering parental rights, is needed. The review system is still being planned. The state board has shown a proclivity to simply adopt exams without adequate public discussion as to their consequences for or relevance to the state's reform efforts. Key recommendations are to drop the NRT and the graduation requirement and strongly support local assessment development.

Standard 1: Assessment supports important student learning.
Massachusetts has developed content frameworks in math, English language arts, science and technology, history/social studies, world languages, arts and health. All but history/social studies have been approved by the Board of Education. A new state assessment program is being developed based on these standards.

Currently, the state is in a transitional phase. It is ending one program, the Massachusetts Educational Assessment Program (MEAP), last administered in spring 1996, and is beginning a new one, the Massachusetts Comprehensive Assessment Program (MCAP). At this time, the state testing program has three components.

MARYLAND
Summary Evaluation
Though Maryland did not respond to the FairTest survey, it appears from other data sources that the state assessment program needs some significant improvements. Although it has one of the best performance assessment programs in the nation in the elementary schools, it also requires a high school exit exam and uses a norm-referenced test, though on a very light sampling basis. The current high school exit exam soon may be dropped, but it remains uncertain as to whether new high school exams will be used as a graduation requirement. If the current exit exam is dropped and the new exams are predominantly constructed-response and not used as high-stakes hurdles, then Maryland's system will need only modest improvement. However, we have little information on fairness professional development and public reporting, and no information on review of the assessment system.

Standard 1: Assessment supports important student learning.
Maryland has content and performance standards along with curriculum frameworks developed by teachers, school system staff and staff from the Maryland Department of Education. Content standards exist in reading, writing, math, science and social studies for grades 3, 5 and 8. High school standards are being developed.

Maryland's assessment program consists of basic skills high school exit tests, elementary school performance exams, and an NRT. The high school exit test has two components, the Maryland Functional Testing Program (MFTP), a criterion-referenced, multiple-choice test in math, reading and citizenship; and the Maryland Writing Test (MWT), which requires two writing samples, narrative and expository. Students taking the MWT have up to a whole day to complete the exam. Scoring is by a commercial company using a state rubric. The exit tests are administered in grades 7–12, with local school systems determining the appropriate grade level for the first administration. A computer-adaptive version is available. It is used for student diagnosis, curriculum and instructional improvement, school accreditation, and school performance reporting.

MICHIGAN
Summary Evaluation

This program needs some significant improvements. The current program uses multiple-choice and some constructed-response items at three grade levels. The writing assessment provides more flexibility than the usual response to a prompt. Stakes are mostly not too high. Professional development has a good foundation through the pre-service requirements and in-service training. Reporting appears mostly adequate. Reviews are limited. Recommended improvements include significant expansion of constructed-response tasks and portfolios, tests in languages other than English, reports in other major languages, and more systematic review of the assessment program and its impact.

Standard 1: Assessment supports important student learning.
Michigan has "essential goals" and a model core curriculum. It is developing detailed curriculum frameworks that will include content standards, benchmarks, instructional vignettes, performance levels and examples of student work in math, English language arts, science, social studies, arts, foreign language and physical education. The state has completed development of assessment frameworks. A new assessment plan will be developed for 2000–2001.

The Michigan Educational Assessment Program (MEAP) assesses students in grades 4 and 7 in math and reading and grades 5 and 8 in writing and science. Social studies tests are planned for 1998–1999. The High School Proficiency Test (HSPT) is administered to award state-endorsed diplomas in language arts (reading and writing tests), math and science; students who do not achieve a "proficient" score can earn a local diploma. However, the HSPT is quite long, totaling 11.5 hours. Both MEAP and HSPT employ a combination of multiple-choice and open-ended items, plus a writing assessment. HSPT scores were included in student transcripts, but after substantial controversy, that policy has been suspended.

Standard 2: Assessments are fair.
Bias review for MEAP is based on a committee with broad representation that reviews all items. The committee has authority to delete or modify items. Statistical analyses are also used. Reports at the state level include data disaggregation by race and gender.

Standard 4: Public education, reporting, and parents' rights.
A wide range of educators and non-educators have been involved in assessment design for MEAP and HSPT. A parent guide for HSPT is in production, and models of MEAP are available on the World Wide Web.

NEW YORK
Summary Evaluation
The current system needs many major improvements. The state is overhauling its assessment system based on new standards. This will solve some, but not all, of the problems. The new assessments will utilize multiple methods, but the balance of methods is not yet determined. The exams should be predominantly performance and constructed-response. The Regents exams should determine only part of course grades, not whether a student passes the course, as is planned. The effect of requiring passage of these tests for passing courses means

that, added together, the exams determine high school graduation. The testing burden in high school will remain very heavy, as will testing in the two other grades (4 and 8). Expanding assessment in other languages should proceed. More extensive professional development, in line with the new state assessments, the new local assessments and classroom assessment needs, should be supported. Extensive public education will be required. The test burden, the impact of new assessments on curriculum, instruction and high school graduation, as well as the match between assessments and standards, all will need to be carefully evaluated.

Standard 2: Assessments are fair.
The SEA employs a bias review committee that has the power to discard items. Bias review is also part of the charge on content selection committees. The state does not report test results by demographic categories.

Standard 3: Professional development.
The state has no requirements for teacher competence in classroom assessment. It has not examined classroom, school or district assessment practices or surveyed to determine teacher needs for professional development. Print materials for professional development are available. Professional development opportunities are available through regional centers, and through state trainings, particularly for measurement personnel. Training will be required as part of the phase-in on new assessments. Teachers are involved in writing items for state exams, and in scoring writing samples.

Evaluation
Professional development needs to be expanded and made more systematic for pre-and in-service teachers in conjunction with the new assessments. Teacher involvement in assessment development is positive and should continue; teachers also should be involved in scoring performance tasks on assessments.

OHIO
Summary Evaluation
Though Ohio did not respond to the Fairtest survey, it appears from other data sources that the state assessment program needs many major improvements. The tests are mostly multiple-choice, aside from the writing sample, and the state has a mandatory high school exit exam. The burden is moderately heavy, with five subjects tested in each of four grades. The addition of constructed-response items is positive, but they are not a major part of the exams. Bias review information was not available. Inclusion is substantial, but for LEP it is not clear that the assessments are always appropriate. Professional development does not appear to be adequate, though little information was available. We received little information on public reporting, and none on parent rights or on review of the system.

Standard 1: Assessment supports important student learning.
Ohio has standards in English language arts, math, social studies and science.

They are under development for foreign languages, the arts, and health and physical science. The state has content standards. Performance standards exist for designated grades in reading, writing, math, citizenship and science. The state claims its assessments are aligned with the standards.

The state assessment program consists of proficiency testing at grades 4, 6, 9 and 12 in the areas of reading, writing, mathematics, science, and citizenship. All tests are criterion-referenced and primarily multiple-choice, with some gridded-in and constructed-response items on the grade 12 math test and some short- and extended-response items on the various grade 4 and 6 tests. Other alternative assessments are in development, but their use has not been set.

The writing assessment is based on responses to SEA provided prompts twice a year. Each time, students are give 150 minutes to produce a writing sample. Schools are required to give students more time (up to 2.5 hours) as needed.

Standard 2: Assessments are fair.
Print materials are available to prepare students for the exams. Data disaggregated by race and gender are released at the school, district and state levels.

Standard 3: Professional development.
Print and video materials are available to educators for professional development.

We have reviewed the states that are either the most active, the most average, and/or the most in need of help. Here follows the remaining states and their most current status as provided by Fairtest.

IDAHO
Summary Evaluation
Idaho's assessment system needs many major improvements. It is far too reliant to multiple-choice NRTs and tests too often. The state should stop using the NRTs and instead continue on the path it is only now starting: developing constructed-response, criterion-referenced assessment in a limited number of grades. It also will need to substantially strengthen its fairness efforts and professional development. Positively, the state does not attach high stakes to its tests, is developing performance exams, and may have a start on a good review system.

Standard 1: Assessment supports important student learning.
In 1995, the Idaho SEA put on hold its previous frameworks and began development of its *Skill Based Curriculum Guides* in math, science, music, art, social studies, language arts (reading, writing, language, spelling), health and physical education. These include sample methods that districts and schools can use to test at each grade level for each skill in each content standard. Exit standards are being developed.

Evaluation
Despite incorporation of ITBS-based data in the standards, the ITBS, as a multiple-choice test of basic skills, is not an adequate means of assessing all areas of a domain, meaning the assessments are not likely to be adequately

aligned to the standards. Idaho is far too reliant on multiple-choice NRTs, and it tests in too many grades. The new assessments should be a substantial improvement, since they are based on the standards, criterion-referenced and include more constructed-response items. The primary step the state should take is to eliminate the NRT, or use it to sample in a few grades at most, while developing further its own assessments based on the standards.

LOUISIANA
Summary Evaluation
Even with proposed changes that will improve the state's assessment program, the program will need a complete overhaul. New assessments will be a mix of multiple-choice and constructed-response, which will be a positive change. The state should drop its NRTs, which would also bring the test burden closer to the recommended three grades, should drop the use of a test as a high school exit gate, and should increase the proportion of constructed-response items beyond the planned 40 percent. Professional development and public education and information should both be substantially increased. The review process needs only modest improvements.

Standard 1: Assessment supports important student learning.
Louisiana is developing standards/curriculum frameworks to replace existing *Curriculum Guides.* The new standards will be in math, science, English language arts, social studies, the arts, and foreign languages. Standards were reviewed by teachers before board approval.

Evaluation
Positively, the state is adopting new standards and developing new assessments to match them, which will employ mixed methods. However, they will still be somewhat too heavily multiple-choice. Negatively, Louisiana's current CRT is not adequate, it will retain the NRT achievement and readiness tests and it has a high school exit exam. The test burden is somewhat high and could be lightened best by dropping the achievement and readiness NRTs.

Standard 2: Assessments are fair.
A bias review committee, including educators and the public, with specified racial/ethnic composition requirements, reviews test items and has the authority to recommend removal or alteration of items. Item statistics are also analyzed. Gender and race data are reported.

Evaluation
Bias review procedures are solid, and efforts are made at accommodations for IEP and LEP. The graduation requirement is a serious problem, as is the over-reliance on multiple-choice methods.

Standard 3: Professional development.
The state has no requirements for teacher professional knowledge in assessment, either pre- or in-service. It offers information on traditional standardized tests and the state assessment programs, and classroom and performance as-

sessment education is available through the state for teachers in some specific programs. Models for integrating curriculum and assessment are part of the new state curriculum frameworks, and these have been reviewed by outside experts, parents, educators and business people. Professional development based on the standards is expected. The state has not surveyed district or classroom assessment practices, nor teachers for their needs.

MINNESOTA
Summary Evaluation
Minnesota's current program needs many major improvements. The legislature recently adopted some modifications to the current program, but these do not fundamentally alter the state's program.

The Basic Standards Tests (BST) are the only tests currently in place. They are multiple-choice with a writing sample and include a high school graduation test requirement. The high school graduation requirement should be dropped and the BST either dropped or substantially modified, but the legislature affirmed both and allowed the SEA the option of a norm-referenced test.

The planned Profile of Learning assessments, which will be state-developed classroom instruments, could be an interesting development in state assessments, though it is too early to know precisely what they will look like in practice, or whether they will be a successful innovation. The new legislation simply requires district testing and leaves the details to the SEA. The SEA should make certain that they involve performance or portfolio approaches and remain locally flexible. Equity issues will require very close monitoring as the new system develops, as will the curricular and instructional impacts and how the new assessments interact with the high-stakes BST. Extensive professional development and education of the public will be essential for success. If this component develops well, it might make an important contribution to national assessment practices, as well as to education in the state.

Standard 1: Assessment supports important student learning.
Minnesota is developing standards in several categories: Basic Requirements in reading, math and writing; High Standards in the Required Learning Profiles for arts, reading, writing, speaking, listening, math, social studies/history, science, problem solving, inquiry, and use of resources—all to be at a complex or advanced level; and Standards of Distinction.

Evaluation
Positively, the Profiles are to be based on standards, allow for substantial local flexibility, and include multiple methods. As they are under development, it remains to be seen how good they will be, including what proportion of items will be multiple-choice or short-answer rather than extended-response or performance items. It is not clear whether portfolios will be included. Negatively, the state requires a high school exit test, but, unusually and positively, it does allow for alternatives. It is not yet certain how the Profiles will be used for determining high school graduation. Currently, the testing burden is not heavy, but de-

pending on how they are used, the Profiles could be rather overwhelming. The state should develop the Profiles assessments carefully, ensure that there is substantial local control over their use but monitor to prevent misuse, and ensure they include substantial amounts of extended response or performance tasks or a portfolio approach. The state needs also to ensure that the alternative to the BST high school test is readily available and useable for students, though it would be preferable to drop the requirement. It also needs to ensure that curriculum and instruction are not organized toward the BST in ways that undercut the Profiles. Indeed, as the Profiles are developed, the BST should be eliminated.

Standard 2: Assessments are fair.

Representatives of all stakeholder groups are involved in the bias review committee. Items are pre-tested and analyzed before and after testing. The committee can make recommendations about the assessment and has authority to delete or modify items. The new legislation now requires data to be reported by demographic categories.

Evaluation

Bias review for the BST appears adequate. The Profiles could be quite positive in allowing real flexibility and variety based on high level standards. Preventing bias in the local assessments envisioned in the Profiles could be a challenge for the state. Inclusion also needs to be monitored carefully. Although the new law is far more inclusive, it still does not meet the full requirements of the new IDEA for students with IEPs.

Standard 3: Professional development.

The state offers training in most areas of testing and assessment, but has no pre- or in-service requirements. The state has not surveyed assessment practices at the district, school or classroom level. Test information, including descriptions of methods, samples, scoring guides and examples, has been provided to teachers, administrators, students, parents, the community and policymakers.

Evaluation

Substantially more systematic professional development is almost certainly needed if the Profiles are to become a successful, decentralized, high quality, largely-performance assessment program. The kinds of local activities the Profiles seem to seek are likely to require not only professional development but creation of a culture of professional collaboration and substantial restructuring of schools, which in turn will need support and guidance from the state. Educators have played a major role in developing the BST and will need to be similarly involved in developing the Profiles.

MISSOURI
Summary Evaluation

Missouri is undergoing a major shift in its assessment program to one that will only need modest improvement. The shift from multiple-choice to a mixed-method assessment is positive, the ending of sampling is not. However, since most districts used state assessments to test more than the new assessments will require, the shift away from sampling may not result in an actual increase in testing for students. Stakes are moderate. Bias review and inclusion need strengthening. Professional development appears to be quite strong. Public education and reporting are currently adequate but will need strengthening as new assessments are implemented. The review process needs improvement.

Standard 1: Assessment supports important student learning.

Missouri has content standards in communication arts, math, science, social studies, arts, and health/physical education, as well as interdisciplinary process standards. Curriculum frameworks based on the standards that are to be used as models for LEAs also have been adopted. A new assessment system is being developed based on these standards.

Evaluation

The current MMAT appears to be both burdensome (if districts test all the grades) and positive, in that Missouri is the only state to rely exclusively on sampling for state data. The MMAT, however, is all multiple-choice. The new assessments will be an improvement in methodology, and the burden is not heavy for any one grade, but unfortunately sampling has been dropped. The score weights for the different sections have not been determined; the weight of the multiple-choice should not reflect more than its share of testing time. Thus, the changes are generally positive. Stakeholder involvement is strong. The accountability requirements are moderate. Using assessment results longitudinally to measure improvement over time for accountability analysis is positive.

Standard 2: Assessments are fair.

A bias review committee exists and is made up of parents, business people, and community leaders of diverse backgrounds representing different areas of the state. Demographic representation is ensured for these groups. African Americans constitute a larger proportion of the bias committee than their proportion of the state population. The committee proofreads items and makes recommendations, but it has no authority to delete or modify items. Items are also analyzed before and after testing for bias. Reports do not include information by demographic categories.

Evaluation

The review committee appears properly inclusive, but should have more authority. Reports should include demographic-based data. Much more will need to be done for accommodations or alternative assessments for IEP and LEP students. The development of multiple methods should assist equity.

Standard 3: Professional development.

Pre-service teachers are required to receive instruction in testing, observational techniques, and classroom assessment. For in-service, tied to MAP, the state uses a trainer-of-trainers model on developing, scoring and using performance assessments. Nearly half of the districts have been involved thus far. Administrators are surveyed on professional development needs in their schools and districts, including assessment. Annual teacher evaluations done at a local level include competence in assessment. SEA staff visit districts on a five-year cycle, at which time assessment practices are reviewed.

Evaluation
Pre-service requirements are positive, and the model for in-service is systematic and steadily covering the state. The surveys, evaluations, and site visits are also very positive, as is teacher involvement in assessment development.

MISSISSIPPI
Summary Evaluation
Although Mississippi did not respond to the FairTest survey, data from other sources indicate that the state's assessment system needs a complete overhaul. The state relies too heavily on multiple-choice items, uses an NRT in grades 4–9, and has a high-stakes high school exit exam. Data are weak on the other standards, but it appears that while inclusion of IEP and LEP students is similar to many states, it needs improvement. Some professional development in performance assessment is provided, but it is hard to tell how much. Public reporting seems quite minimal. No data were available on system review.

Standard 1: Assessment supports important student learning.
Mississippi has standards in language arts, mathematics, science, social studies, the arts, health and physical education, and business and technology. The standards are embedded in curriculum frameworks.

The Mississippi assessment program currently includes norm-referenced testing (ITBS and TAP), the Functional Literacy Exam (FLE), and the Subject Area Testing Program (SATP). The commercial NRT is administered to students in grades 4–9 in language arts, math, and reading. The test includes some multiple-choice with student explanation and some short-answer items. The language arts and math frameworks are correlated to the norm-referenced test.

Evaluation
Mississippi's use of NRTs, testing in too many grades, over-reliance on multiple-choice, a high school exit exam plus high stakes for schools makes this a program that needs a complete transformation. The use of constructed-response items is a start, but should be greatly expanded. The NRTs should be dropped or reduced to a minimal sample. The end-of-course exams should not be used to determine whether a student passes (if they are so used) and should be primarily constructed-response. The high school exit test should be dropped. The writing to a prompt is too brief to be a good measure of writing capability. Data were not available as to how test results were used in school evaluations and sanctions, but test scores should not be the sole basis for decisions.

Standard 2: Assessments are fair.
Video materials are available to inform students about the tests. No data on bias review was available. The state has an exclusions and accommodations policy

for IEP and LEP students, which is applied individually to determine participation in the various testing components. All students must pass the FLE to graduate. A fairly wide range of accommodations for IEP students is available on the FLE, but few on the NRT or SATP. Exemptions for LEP students on the NRT are determined locally. A modest set of accommodations are available on the FLE and the NRT. No alternate assessments are available.

Evaluation

Based on the available information, the state needs to strengthen both inclusion of IEP and LEP students, including alternate assessments, and to report data by sub-populations as well as the entire tested group. Heavy reliance on multiple-choice items and the high school exit exam also do not meet this standard.

Standard 3: Professional development.

Print and video materials are prepared for professional development. A trainer-of-trainers model was used to prepare teachers for administration of performance assessments.

Evaluation

The trainer-of-trainers model can work well, but no data were available on the extent of the program and little data on the content.

Mississippi did not respond to the FairTest survey. This report relied on CCSSO/NCREL for 1995–96, CCSSO and AFT reports.

MONTANA
Summary evaluation

Montana has a bare-bones state assessment program that needs many major improvements. The state system relies entirely on multiple-choice, norm-referenced tests in three grades. This program should be replaced. Districts are allowed to choose from a list of approved NRTs. They are also required to develop additional assessments. This optional approach should be built upon to help districts implement primarily performance assessments in key subjects. Since the state relies on the NRTs for state-level data, one option would be to continue to do so, but on a sampling basis. A preferable alternative would be to lead a collaborative effort to develop a state rubric that districts may use to score performance assessments or portfolios. This rubric could be the basis for rescoring district samples for state-level information.

Little is done to ensure proper assessment of IEP or LEP students, nor does the state address bias. The state has no professional development program or requirements for teacher competence in assessment. Districts are also responsible for reporting to parents. The state is only now considering a review of the state's program. Since Montana's political culture strongly favors local control, the state has more limited options for promoting reform. In addition to helping districts implement new assessments, establishing requirements for incoming teachers and offering encouragement and guidance in other areas of equity, professional development, public education and reporting would be one route toward strengthening the state's assessment program.

Standard 1: Assessment supports important student learning.
Montana's Standards for Accreditation of Schools includes nine program areas
in which districts develop their own standards and curricula. *Model Learner
Goals* provide guidance in communications arts, math, science, social studies,
fine arts, health enhancement, vocational/practical arts, library media and
guidance, for elementary, intermediate and high school levels.

NORTH CAROLINA
Summary evaluation
North Carolina's assessment program needs a complete overhaul. It relies far too
heavily on multiple-choice tests, tests too often, and has a graduation exam. It
should reduce the grades tested, drop the graduation requirement, ensure districts do not rely on the tests for grade promotion decisions and implement a
performance assessment system based on the state standards. Bias reduction
efforts and inclusion are positive. Professional development should be expanded and focused on classroom performance assessment, parental rights
should be expanded, and the review process should be revised and strengthened.

Standard 1: Assessment supports important student learning.
North Carolina has content standards and curriculum frameworks for all subject areas, including math, English-language arts, science, social studies, arts,
healthful living and foreign languages. The state designs and develops its own
tests, which are all aligned with the frameworks. The state reports that its tests
use authentic reading material and assess mathematics by focusing on problem
solving using real-world information.

Evaluation
North Carolina tests far too frequently, relies far too heavily on multiple-choice
exams and uses tests for high-stakes purposes. The writing samples and small
amounts of constructed-response tasks beginning to be used are positive but
still very limited. Using the NRT only on a sampling basis in a few grades is reasonable. The state should reduce the grades tested, shift to predominantly performance assessments that can more fully match high-quality standards and instruction, and drop the high-stakes tests for individuals. For schools, the new
accountability program appears also to rely too heavily on testing. Districts
must be actively discouraged from using tests as a grade-promotion hurdle.

Standard 2: Assessments are fair.
A bias review committee reflective of the state's demographics reviews test items
and other materials. Statistical analyses are also evaluated. Tests use culturally
diverse materials in the items and prompts. Reports include subgroup performance by gender and ethnicity.

North Carolina's policy is to include students with special needs in the
statewide testing and accountability programs as early as possible. Approximately 15 percent of tested students have IEPs, and approximately 1 percent of
tested students are LEP. Modifications and accommodations are available to

students with disabilities and to students who are LEP. IEP or LEP students may be exempt from testing as dictated by their IEP or written accommodation plan. LEP students may be exempt for a maximum of two years. Students in both of these categories must pass the competency tests in order to receive a state diploma.

Evaluation

Including demographic data in reports is sound, as is the bias review procedure, though the committee should have authority to delete or modify items. Although efforts at inclusion are positive, the over-reliance on multiple-choice testing is a problem for students with IEP and LEP and for equity purposes in general. The high school exit requirement also does not meet this standard.

Standard 3: Professional development.

For licensure, teachers must meet state-established competency standards in assessment. Limited professional development is offered to LEAs on the use of test results. Printed materials about the state testing program; mini-tests in the areas of reading, math, science and social studies (grades 3–8); and an electronic bank with multiple-choice items for reading and math are available for teacher use. Some professional development opportunities in classroom assessment are available upon request. North Carolina no longer surveys educators for their professional development needs because local school districts receive funds and assume responsibility for the professional development of staff.

Evaluation

The over-emphasis on multiple-choice extends to the evaluation of this standard. Too much professional development is focused on this method and on the state tests. Though professional development may be a local responsibility, stronger state guidance and support is warranted, particularly in classroom, performance and portfolio assessment. Teachers are substantially involved in writing items, which is positive, but it would be far better for them to be developing performance tasks.

North Carolina responded by telephone to the short version of the FairTest survey and sent various documents. This report also relied on CCSSO/NCREL, CCSSO and AFT reports. The state responded to a draft descriptive report.

NORTH DAKOTA
Summary evaluation
North Dakota's system needs many major improvements. The state relies on a multiple-choice NRT and administers a "cognitive abilities" norm-referenced test. Both should be dropped. The state tests in four, rather than the recommended three grades. The stakes are relatively low; no required consequences ensue from the test scores. The state is developing new assessments based on its standards that should replace the NRT. Inclusion should be strengthened. Professional development needs substantial improvement. Reporting is currently solid, but public education about the new assessments will be needed. The review process is fairly solid, but can be strengthened in some regards.

Standard 1: Assessment supports important student learning.
North Dakota has voluntary content standards and benchmarks for grades 4, 8 and 12 in English/language arts (ELA), library media, math, science, social studies, arts, business, foreign languages, health and physical education.

The state assessment program consists of testing in grades 3, 6, 8 and 11 in the areas of language arts, math, science, reading and social studies, using both the CTBS/4 NRT and the TCS, a norm-referenced, multiple-choice "cognitive abilities" test. The tests are checked against the curriculum frameworks for alignment, so that what is tested is in the standards. However, the state reports that only about 40 percent of the ELA standards and about 60 percent of the math standards are measured by the CTBS. The state will be looking for a new NRT that better matches the standards.

Evaluation
North Dakota relies almost exclusively on a multiple-choice NRT. Rather than adopt a new one, the state should cease to use it. North Dakota appears to be one of the few states still requiring use of a "cognitive abilities" test. This should be dropped for mass use. The development of performance assessments in language and math is a positive step. When developed, they should replace the NRT. Since "cognitive abilities" tests, like IQ tests, have great potential for misuse, the state should be aware of possible misuse in diagnosis and resulting program placement, particularly for minority-group and low-income students.

Standard 2: Assessments are fair.
Bias studies have been conducted for the English language arts assessment. The bias review committee was selected for racial and gender balance. The contractor, CTB/McGraw-Hill, reviews the CTBS and CTS for bias. Disaggregated data are released by race, but not by gender or SES. The contractor provides test practice materials for schools to use in preparing students for the tests.

Evaluation
We do not know the authority of the bias review committee for ELA, nor how bias review is conducted by the NRT contractor. Inclusion on the NRT appears inadequate. Disaggregated reporting is mostly solid, though data by gender and SES should be released.

Standard 3: Professional development.
North Dakota does not have any pre-service requirements for teachers in assessment, nor does it evaluate teacher competence in assessment. The SEA has surveyed teachers regarding their professional development needs in assessment. The state holds regional test interpretation workshops and uses a workshop evaluation questionnaire for feedback. Voluntary teacher involvement in developing and scoring the new performance assessments in English and math has resulted in professional development. In English, more districts volunteered to participate than had been planned for, creating a shortage of funds.

Evaluation
Professional development needs to be substantially expanded for both pre- and

in-service teachers, particularly in classroom and performance assessment. Educator involvement in developing the new assessments is positive, as is conducting the survey.

North Dakota responded to the short form of the FairTest survey. This report also used CCSSO/NCREL, CCSSO and AFT reports. The state responded to a draft descriptive report.

NEW HAMPSHIRE
Summary evaluation
New Hampshire's state assessment program needs modest improvement, primarily shifting the balance from majority multiple-choice to predominantly constructed-response and performance assessment. The light testing burden and relatively low stakes are positive. The state does well on all other principles, with either minor improvements or expansion of existing efforts advised.

Standard 1: Assessment supports important student learning.
New Hampshire has curriculum and assessment frameworks in math, English language arts, science and social studies, developed by educators, business people, government officials, community representatives and parents.

Results of assessments are used for curriculum improvement and school performance reporting with no high-stakes consequences for either schools or students.

Evaluation
Though the state rates fairly high in comparison with most states, New Hampshire's program still relies too heavily on multiple-choice. The relative balance of methods should at least be reversed. The light testing burden and relatively low stakes are positive, as is permitting extended time for the writing assessment.

Standard 2: Assessments are fair.
Bias review is carried out by the content committee, which can modify or delete items. Statistical analyses are conducted before and after administration. Use of different formats and provision of accommodations are used to respond to different learning styles. Content committees and the contractor review the assessment for developmental appropriateness. The SEA provides sample tests for grade 3, and curriculum frameworks and released items for other grades, to provide test familiarity for students.

Evaluation
The bias reduction efforts are solid, as is the use of multiple methods in the assessments and the reviews for developmental appropriateness. Accommodations appear solid and a higher proportion of students with IEPs are assessed than is the case in most states. Reporting is good.

Standard 3: Professional development.
NH requires preservice knowledge by teachers and administrators about standardized testing, classroom assessments, and the use of test results. Further professional development is offered, but not required, by the state. Samples of

items and scoring guides are used for explaining the state assessments to educators. Training is provided in administering assessment accommodations, understanding reports and using test results. Seventy-five percent of districts have requested training. The state does not evaluate teacher competence in assessment or survey teachers to determine if their professional development needs are being met.

Evaluation

Professional development is decent but can be strengthened with continued in-service education in classroom assessment practices and by surveying for teacher competence and needs. Scoring of writing samples and any extended-response items should be done by teachers.

NEW JERSEY

Summary evaluation

New Jersey's assessment program needs many major improvements, including eliminating the high school exit requirement, shifting the emphasis from multiple-choice.

The New Jersey assessment program tests math, reading and writing through the Grade 8 Early Warning Test (EWT) and the Grade 11 High School Proficiency Test (HSPT), which is a graduation test. Both tests are criterion-referenced and use multiple methods, including multiple-choice, short- and extended-response and open-ended items. All students in designated grades are tested and all students see the same items. Consultants, a commercial firm and committees that included parents, business reps, teachers and administrators were involved in developing the tests and writing items and scoring guides.

Results of the state assessments are used for student diagnosis, placement and remediation, curriculum improvement and program evaluation. Students may take the HSPT a maximum of four times in order to reach a passing score. For schools, test results are used for school performance reporting (school report card) and school accreditation. Consequences for schools may include probation, funding loss, accreditation loss and takeover, but test scores are not the sole criterion. For a district to be certified, 85 percent of eleventh graders must pass the HSPT and 75 percent must pass the EWT. A new law establishes rewards for schools if 90 percent of its students attain the test standards or the school makes unusual progress in raising scores.

Evaluation

New Jersey's assessment program has major problems, some of which may be adequately addressed with the planned changes. The graduation test requirement should be dropped. The balance of items should shift strongly toward open-response. The tests need to be brought into alignment with the standards, and the tests need to adequately assess the standards. The district testing mandate is also a major problem. It is likely to impose far too high a testing burden, even if the requirement is somewhat more flexible. Instead, the state should help districts develop classroom-based assessments, from which sampling can be done, and leave the large-scale tests to the state.

Standard 2: Assessments are fair.

A bias review committee (sensitivity committee), with demographic variety and including members of community groups, reviews tests for language, stereotypes, confusing context, socioeconomic/experiential background bias and gender bias. The committee approves tests and has the power to eliminate items, with input from the content committee. Items are analyzed pre- and post-testing, including statistical review. Equity is evaluated for each test administration. Disaggregated data are reported by SES, but not by race or gender.

Evaluation

Bias review is solid. Reporting should provide further disaggregation, but IEP and LEP should be included in regular reports. Requiring the high school exit test does not meet this principle, but, positively, alternatives do exist for IEP and LEP students. We do not know how many students this actually helps to graduate. When tests are revised to meet the new standards, they should, like grade 4, be built to accommodate IEP and LEP students. The use of open-ended items helps meet the need for assessments that respond to diverse learning styles and cultures, but more open-ended items are needed.

Standard 3: Professional development.

The state requires no professional knowledge of assessment beyond requirements for initial certification. It has not evaluated teacher competence in assessment nor surveyed educators for their professional development needs. Teachers receive training in understanding and using test results. The SEA plans to start professional development when frameworks and revised assessments are ready.

Evaluation

Professional development is currently inadequate for both pre- and in-service beyond the state's revised assessments and includes classroom assessment teachers. Surveys should be done. Professional development should extend. Educator participation in test development is positive, but teachers should be involved in scoring writing and extended-response tasks.

NEW MEXICO

Summary evaluation

New Mexico's assessment program needs a complete overhaul. The key positive steps the state could take are to drop the NRT and the high school exit exam and replace them with a standards-referenced, largely constructed-response state assessment program in three grades. Planned new assessments in grades 4, 6 and 8 could be a step in this direction, but will create an even heavier test burden. It also appears they will remain predominantly multiple-choice and short-answer. Positive attributes, such as teacher involvement in assessment development, assessments in multiple languages, and extensive evaluation should be continued and expanded. Increased professional development is also a must, as is expanded public education. The review process is positive.

Standard 1: Assessment supports important student learning.
New state goals, content and performance standards, and assessment and curriculum frameworks, in language arts, math, languages, arts, science, social studies, math and other subjects, will replace current frameworks. In the next two years, Assessment Blueprint 2000 will start aligning assessment with standards and benchmarks as they are established. Meanwhile, the SEA reports that assessments are aligned to the old frameworks.

The state has released Requests for Proposals for new assessments in grades 4, 6 and 8. These require all items to be aligned with a content standard. Educators in the state will check the alignment. The assessments will include multiple-choice, which will yield some normative comparisons, and constructed-response, criterion-referenced items. As resources become available, the SEA hopes to include extended tasks.

Evaluation
Reliance on a basic skills, multiple-choice NRT as the major basis for accountability and for guiding curriculum and instruction is a major negative. The test may be aligned with the current frameworks, but the frameworks would only be aligned with the test if they were extremely weak and low-level. If the new standards are an improvement, then incompatibility with the NRT will increase. Also negative is the use of a high school exit exam. The use of portfolios for writing assessment is a positive step beyond what most states do, though the concept of the portfolio, with mandated prompts, is limited.

Standard 2: Assessments are fair.
On the state-made assessments, bias review committees are empowered to eliminate flawed items, statistical analysis is employed, and item writing committees deliberately involve educators from diverse cultures. For the grade 1 and 2 reading assessment, LEAs address the issue of bias. The publisher does bias analysis for the NRT. Reporting does not include result breakouts by demographic categories. Print information about assessments is provided to all stakeholders, reaching students through the schools.

Modifications, waivers or exemptions for all testing programs are allowed for IEP and LEP students, as needed, with different assessments using different policies or procedures. Twenty-three percent of the state's students are LEP; data about the proportion of students who have an IEP or percentages tested who have IEP and LEP are not available. The HSCE is available in Spanish, and other languages may be used in the writing portion.

Evaluation
Bias review efforts are positive, as are uses of accommodations, including allowing assessment in languages other than English. Over-reliance on multiple-choice, the NRT, and the HSCE are negative, as is the failure to report data by demographic categories.

Evaluation
Positively, the state encourages substantial teacher involvement in developing

the HSCE, the writing portfolios and possibly the grades 1 and 2 reading assessments. Teachers score the writing samples for the HSCE, but not the writing portfolios, which they also should do. Professional development that can be useful for classroom assessment needs to be expanded and strengthened.

New Mexico responded to the full FairTest survey.

NEVADA
Summary evaluation
Nevada's assessment program needs many major improvements, primarily shifting from multiple-choice to predominantly performance assessments and eliminating the high school exit exam requirement. The state has a rather light assessment burden, testing only a few subjects in three grades. Bias review and inclusion of IEP/LEP students should be strengthened. Professional development needs substantial strengthening. Public reporting appears adequate, but a survey should be done to confirm this. The review process needs improvement. In particular, the state should evaluate the impact of assessment on curriculum, instruction and graduation, and should study the ability of the assessments to measure critical thinking and cognitively complex work.

Standard 1: Assessment supports important student learning.
Nevada has state standards in reading, math, writing, science and social studies. The Nevada state assessment program includes the state-developed Nevada High School Proficiency Examination (NHSPE), first administered in grade 11, in which math and reading are tested with norm-referenced, multiple-choice exams. Writing is assessed with responses to SEA-provided prompts (one hour to answer two prompts). A multiple-choice NRT, the CTBS/5, is used to assess students in grades 4 and 8 in the areas of math and reading and grade 4 in the area of language arts. A grade 8 writing assessment uses an SEA prompt to stimulate production of a writing sample over two 35-minute periods on consecutive days.

In 1997–98, the state introduced criterion-referenced, multiple-choice tests at grade 11 in math and reading to be used as the graduation test. Students will be able to retake the exams through grade 12. These will replace the NRTs that have been in place since 1990.

The purchased NRTs for grades 4 and 8 are aligned with the state's standards according to studies by the publisher. The writing assessment is aligned with content standards through the scoring rubric. The graduation exam contains items written to specific objectives in a state course of study. The SEA recognizes there are areas of the standards within tested subjects that cannot be tested through multiple-choice items and the writing sample.

Standard 2: Assessments are fair.
The state provides preparatory materials on the writing assessments to students. The Terra Nova is reviewed for bias by the publisher. Although the state does not have a standing bias review committee, ad hoc advisory committees are formed by the SEA. The SEA reports that assessment development has at-

tempted to take account of different cultural backgrounds of the students, but not of different learning styles. Disaggregated data are now released by gender, SES and ethnicity.

Evaluation
Bias review appears to be insufficient. Reporting disaggregated data is a positive development. The state will need to make major changes to meet the new federal IDEA requirements for students with IEPs. Reliance on multiple-choice items and the graduation requirement do not meet the fairness standard.

Standard 3: Professional development.
Nevada has no requirements for preservice training in assessment for teachers. It does not evaluate teacher competence in assessment, nor does it survey educators regarding their professional development needs in assessment. The state provides math and reading in-service programs that cover assessment, including scoring writing. Teachers score the writing assessments using rubrics developed by a state advisory committee.

Evaluation
The state needs to address professional development in assessment, which it largely has not done. Teacher involvement in scoring is positive.

Evaluation
Reporting is probably adequate for the limited state program, but a survey would be useful to confirm this. Parents should be able to review tests as this is done with commercial exams in some other states. The rights to appeal and challenge are positive.
Nevada responded to the short form of the FairTest survey.

PENNSYLVANIA
Summary evaluation
Pennsylvania's assessment system needs some significant improvements, primarily a shift away from mostly multiple-choice testing toward performance assessments. Positively, the state does not have higher stakes than public reporting and does not rely on NRTs. The state is emphasizing district standards and assessments, but the SEA should support districts in implementing performance assessments. Bias review and inclusion of students with IEP or LEP seem mostly solid, though reporting by sub-populations should be done. Professional development should be expanded and made more systematic, either directly by the state or with the state supporting the districts. Reporting and public education are currently adequate. The state's review system is not in place as new assessments are being developed, but such a system is needed and should be comprehensive.

Standard 1: Assessment supports important student learning.
Pennsylvania has standards in the form of *Learning Outcomes,* which have been subject to substantial controversy. An advisory committee of educators (with SEA guidance) is developing new content/performance standards and assess-

ment frameworks in reading, writing and math (science is on hold, and others may follow) that are intended to replace the outcomes. The state currently has non-mandatory curriculum frameworks in math, based on the *Outcomes,* and English, not based on the *Outcomes.* The state claims its assessments are aligned to the *Outcomes* but that "alignment has not been checked in a formal study involving content committees independent of the advisory committees that initially evaluated alignment." The assessments are being revised to match the new Pennsylvania standards.

Evaluation

Pennsylvania should shift from mostly-multiple-choice to mostly-performance or constructed-response assessment. The districts should also be encouraged and supported in developing or adopting performance assessments and portfolios. The state seems to be regularly changing its outcomes or standards, making alignment more difficult and creating periods in which the tests will not match the new standards. The absence of high stakes and the light testing load are positive.

Standard 2: Assessments are fair.

The state has had ongoing bias review, mostly statistical analysis. It now has a "Fairness Review Task Force," which plans to look at all aspects and forms of assessment. It will be able to remove or revise items and will attempt to improve tests. The state does not now report data by sub-populations.

Evaluation

With the addition of the fairness task force, bias review seems adequate. Inclusion seems most positive, but development of alternative assessment for those for whom accommodations cannot be used is recommended.

Standard 3: Professional development.

Assessment Handbooks are provided to teachers and administrators for professional development. The state has portfolio projects and other assessment activities that districts can participate in and which provide professional development. Some information about professional development needs comes from local planning reports, which often include assessment training needs. Requirements for pre-service teachers were not reported.

Evaluation

Professional development seems on the right track, but likely needs to be expanded and made more systematic, preferably together with the greater use of performance assessments by the state and districts. More systematic gathering of information regarding training needs, and evaluation of teacher competence in assessment, are recommended.

Pennsylvania responded by telephone to the short form of the FairTest survey.

SOUTH CAROLINA
Summary evaluation

South Carolina's assessment program needs a complete overhaul. The new program now being implemented, which will be based on new state standards, is not a sufficient change. In its old and new systems, the state relies too heavily on multiple-choice testing. Currently, it relies too heavily on an NRT, and it may continue to do so. The state should build some initial work in performance assessments as a starting point for redesigning the system to a largely performance-assessment system. It also should either eliminate or reduce to sampling the NRT and drop the graduation requirement. Bias review and policies for inclusion of IEP and LEP student appear adequate, but as much of this is under LEA control, it is hard to be sure of the extent of inclusion. Current and planned professional development is not adequate for high quality assessment practice by educators. Public education efforts appear solid. Information on review processes was not available.

Standard 1: Assessment supports important student learning.
South Carolina has completed curriculum frameworks along with content and achievement standards in math, English language arts and science. Frameworks with content standards have been developed in foreign languages, and visual and performing arts. They are in development for social studies, health and safety, and physical education. These documents are developed statewide by committees of educators and business people, with broad public review and input.

Current tests are not aligned to the standards. The Basic Skills Assessment Program (BSAP) consists mostly of criterion-referenced, basic skills, multiple-choice tests for students in grades 3 and 8 in the areas of science, reading and math; science at grade 6; and math and reading at grade 10. An off-the-shelf NRT (MAT–7) assesses all students in grades 4, 5, 7, 9 and 11 in the areas of language, reading, and math. The state requires a readiness test in grade 1, a modified version of the individualized, teacher-administered Cognitive Skills Assessment Battery, intended to help teachers identify student capability in reading and math and thus guide instruction.

Over the past five years, teachers in selected schools have been developing performance-based assessments as a pilot program to improve instruction and learning. These are disseminated statewide. Next year, the state also will make training available to K–3 teachers in the use of the Work Sampling System (WSS) or a South Carolina version of the Primary Learning Assessment System (PLAS). This will be a voluntary program.

Evaluation
The state relies far too heavily on multiple-choice exams and on the NRT. The state should either drop the NRT or use it only on a sampling basis in a few grades. The new program will test in at least four grades, one more than the recommended three. The new tests will be disproportionately multiple-choice and should be revised. The graduation requirement should be dropped. The combination of high stakes for schools and individuals with mostly multiple-choice tests is likely to heavily influence curriculum and instruction in a narrow direction. Making performance assessments, the WSS and the PLAS available are

positive steps. They should be made more important parts of the state assessment system while the traditional tests are deemphasized.

Standard 2: Assessments are fair.
Currently, each year's new writing prompts are reviewed for bias. In the new assessments, all items will be reviewed, and items determined by the committee to be flawed will be discarded. Items will be previewed by teachers under secure conditions, including pre-testing on students, as writing prompts now are. Print and video materials are available to students for explanatory information. The state does include reporting by SES and race, but not gender.

Evaluation
Bias review procedures planned for the new assessments appear to be adequate. As LEAs determine inclusion, it is difficult to know the extent of participation by IEP or LEP students. Accommodations appear adequate. The state should also report data by gender. The graduation requirement and the over-reliance on multiple-choice do not meet this standard.

Standard 3: Professional development.
Print and video materials for professional development are available to educators. All the state's professional development efforts focus on the standards, and many will involve using assessments based on the standards. Schools are surveyed about their use of the standards.

Evaluation
Professional development is focused on state standards and the inadequate new state assessments. The support in performance assessment and the planned trainings in using the WSS and PLAS are positive. They should be built on to provide systematic professional development to pre- and in-service teachers in classroom assessment. Educators should be surveyed about their professional development needs.

South Carolina responded by telephone to parts of the short FairTest survey.

SOUTH DAKOTA
Summary evaluation
South Dakota's assessment system needs many major improvements. It relies entirely on multiple-choice NRTs. Unfortunately, legislative action in 1997 has made the situation worse by increasing the amount of testing without improving the instruments used. The legislature should appropriate funding for the state to develop or adopt performance assessments that can assess to the state's standards. It also should not assess in grade 2, as it now plans to do. Issues of equity and adequate system review must also be considered, and professional development expanded. Positively, the stakes remain relatively low.

Standard 1: Assessment supports important student learning.
South Dakota has adopted content standards in math, science, reading, writing,

social studies and the arts. Districts now must either adopt the state standards or develop their own equally challenging standards.

The state's current assessment program includes off-the-shelf, multiple-choice NRTs for grades 4, 8 and 11 in the areas of English, math, science and social studies; and an off-the-shelf, multiple choice NRT for students in grade 9 on aptitudes and career interest (the Career Planning Program from ACT). Private and home-schooled children are required to take the NRT. Pretesting in grade 4 is done for practice on the grade 4 NRT.

The new legislation calls for testing in grades 2, 4, 8 and 11 in reading, math, science and social studies. There will be a writing exam in grades 5 and 9. As no funding was appropriated for new assessments, the state will use an NRT that is supposed to be aligned with the standards. The SEA recognizes, however, that "you can't test standards with an NRT." The SEA hopes to obtain money to develop its own assessments.

Evaluation

Positively, the stakes are low, and introducing a writing assessment will help balance the multiple-choice approach of the NRTs. However, the state is also regressing by initiating large-scale testing in grade 2, which is not developmentally appropriate. As recognized, it will not be assessing its own standards.

Standard 2: Assessments are fair.

Items are pre- and posttested and analyzed by the publisher for bias. Eight percent of students tested have an IEP, and 1 percent of students tested are classified as LEP. Both may be excluded from testing. A few accommodations (Braille, small group administration) exist for IEP on the NRT. Gender and race data are reported at the school level on the current NRTs.

Evaluation

Accommodations for LEP and IEP are not sufficient, and multiple methods of assessment are not used.

Standard 3: Professional development.

The SEA offers professional development in classroom assessment approaches, state assessment programs, and the use of test results, to teachers, school administrators and other school personnel. Professional development in performance assessments is available throughout the state for teachers in a specific program or project. Workshops on pretests and posttests are available each year. The SEA does not survey teachers for needs or evaluate their assessment competence.

Evaluation

The approach and range of content for professional development is positive, though expansion seems warranted to ensure competence in classroom and large-scale assessment by all teachers. Teachers should be involved in both designing and scoring the writing assessments.

TENNESSEE
Summary evaluation

Tennessee's assessment system needs a complete overhaul. It relies almost entirely on multiple-choice items, uses norm-referenced testing, and has a high school exit test. The state tests young children with a multiple-choice NRT, and it tests in too many grades. Bias review may not be satisfactory, and many students with IEPs are not assessed. Some aspects of professional development are progressing, but others are not addressed. Parental rights need expansion in some areas. Public education may be adequate, but the state reporting system is very complex. Reviews have not been adequate and need major strengthening. A few changes made in the 1997 legislative session have not improved the situation.

Standard 1: Assessment supports important student learning.
Tennessee has developed frameworks in all areas if the curriculum. These are periodically revised in conjunction with textbook adoption and now also to align them with national standards.

The Tennessee Comprehensive Assessment Program (TCAP) has three components. The Achievement Test is a customized edition of the CTBS/4 multiple-choice test producing norm- and criterion-referenced results in math, reading, language arts, science and social studies. It has been administered to public school students in grades 2–8 and to home-schooled students in grades 2, 5 and 7. Items are written by teachers, content specialists and outside experts to a design by the test publisher and SEA assessment staff. The legislature recently dropped using TCAP in grade two, but ordered implementation of basic skills tests in grades 1 and 2.

The criterion-referenced, multiple-choice Competency Test in language arts and math is given to public school students beginning in grade 9. It is offered four times annually, and students must pass it to receive a regular diploma. Teachers, administrators, SEA assessment staff and content specialists are involved in all areas of design and implementation.

Writing is assessed in grades 4, 8 and 11 using responses to SEA provided prompts. Teachers, administrators, content specialists and outside experts are involved in all phases, from design to scoring. Students in grades 4 and 8 are given 35 minutes and students in grade 11 are given 25 minutes to produce a writing sample on demand.

Tennessee has begun to implement high school subject matter tests in pre-algebra, algebra I and II, geometry and math for technology. These are customized, multiple-choice tests developed by teachers and the contractor.

The tests are intended to be aligned to state standards (the Competency Test to the grade 8 standards). Alignment is determined by having educators in content areas write items.

Evaluation
Tennessee has developed an assessment system organized around high-stakes multiple-choice tests. Although the tests are intended to be aligned to the standards, multiple-choice is not adequate for measuring to high quality standards and alignment cannot be determined simply by having teachers write items in given content areas. The time allotted for writing is too short for an adequate as-

sessment of writing. Although the state may say that the tests are not intended to guide instruction, it is very likely that the high-stakes tests do have a substantial classroom impact. Controlling schooling through narrow tests runs directly counter to the *Principles* and these Standards. Thus, Tennessee should restructure its assessment system.

Standard 2: Assessments are fair.

Items on all tests are reviewed pre- and post-administration for bias. The contractor for the Achievement tests has a review committee. Bias review for the Competency Test is conducted by the state Testing and Evaluation Center at the University of Tennessee, which can delete items deemed biased. Item selection attempts to take account of the cultural variety in the state. For the writing test, the state's cultural diversity is considered in prompt selection, but no bias review committee exists.

The SEA provides material to familiarize students with test format and typical content. Explanatory information is provided to teachers and administrators, and to students on the competency test. Test reports are only in English and do not report data disaggregated by sub-populations.

Evaluation

Bias review may not be sufficient in that it is not done for the writing prompts and it is contracted out for the competency and achievement tests. Reporting should include data by demographic groups. It appears that many students with IEPs are not tested, though the state's exams may not be appropriate for many students. Heavy reliance on multiple-choice is itself an equity problem, as is the use of high-stakes exams.

Standard 3: Professional development.

The state does not require assessment education for pre-service or in-service teachers. Training is available to educators in a full range of performance and classroom assessment practices and the state exams. Evaluating teacher competence in assessment is one component in the state model for local evaluation of teachers. The SEA has not surveyed educators to determine if their assessment professional development needs have been met.

Evaluation

It is difficult to determine the actual extent of the trainings in classroom assessment; they should be extensively available if they are not. A survey could inform the SEA about unmet needs and interests. Pre-service requirements in classroom assessment should be part of teacher education. Making competence in assessment part of the evaluation of teachers is a good idea; the state should study how well such evaluation is done and whether it has a positive impact.

Tennessee responded to the full FairTest survey and sent various reports.

TEXAS

Summary evaluation

The Texas assessment system needs many major changes. It relies almost entirely on multiple-choice items, except for a writing prompt, and has a high-stakes graduation test. On most of the other standards, however, the state does very well. It has strong bias review procedures, provides solid public information, accords parents substantial rights, and has a thorough and continuing review system. Professional development appears fairly extensive.

Standard 1: Assessment supports important student learning.

State content and performance standards are being revised or developed in English language arts/reading, math, science, social studies, fine arts, health and physical education, languages other than English, technology applications, and other areas. Educators, parents and other stakeholders were involved in drafting the standards. The SEA reported that the assessment frameworks have been completed.

The Texas Assessment of Academic Skills (TAAS) is a CRT that assesses reading and math in grades 3 through 8, writing in grades 4 and 8, and science and social studies in grade 8. TAAS reading, writing and math tests are also used as a high school graduation requirement, with administration beginning in grade 10. End of course exams exist for Algebra I and Biology I, and others are in development. Other than the writing assessment, the exams are all machine-scorable, mostly multiple-choice. New end-of-course tests in English II and US History will include constructed-response items. Writing assessments require responses to commercially-developed, SEA-approved prompts. Papers not meeting the minimum standard receive more detailed scoring to provide feedback to the students. All TAAS tests are untimed.

Texas now has Spanish versions of the TAAS in reading and math in grades 3–6 and in writing in grade 4. The SEA also recently developed a reading inventory to be used in the classroom at local discretion at grades K–2. The results will not be reported to the state. The state also provides for voluntary assessment of students in private schools and home schools. Results of assessments are used for student diagnosis or placement, instruction and curriculum improvement and program evaluation. Students, with some exceptions, must pass the TAAS high school exit exam to receive a diploma. The state contracted for development of a proposal for an alternative assessment system for students who did not pass the TAAS high school exam. However, the proposal concluded that other than individually administering the TAAS exams (which is currently available to all students), an alternative system probably would not make a significant difference in pass rates. Districts can use TAAS tests as grade promotion gates if they choose. Consequences for schools include exemption from regulations, monetary rewards, warnings, probation, funding/accreditation loss, takeover and dissolution.

Evaluation

The heavy reliance on multiple-choice and use of a high-stakes test for graduation are the serious flaws in this assessment system. The state should shift toward performance assessments and drop the high school exit exam. The Spanish-language exams are a very positive development.

Standard 2: Assessments are fair.

Print materials of various kinds are provided to students to prepare them for the exams.

Two levels of bias review committees exist, a general content committee and a specific bias committee that includes only members of minority groups. The committees have authority to delete or modify items. Statistical analyses are done pre- and post-test.

Disaggregated data are reported at school, district and state levels by race, gender, free or reduced lunch eligibility, LEP and IEP status. IEP students' scores are only reported separately.

Seven percent of students tested are classified IEP or LEP. Extensive accommodations are available for IEP students. Procedures for alternate assessments for IEP students are under development. IEP students may be exempt from TAAS by their IEP committees, including the exit exam. If exempted, they can earn a regular diploma. Some LEP students also are exempt, but they must pass the English language arts and other high school exit tests in order to obtain a diploma. A modest range of accommodations are available for LEP students, and tests are available in Spanish in some subject areas.

Evaluation

The bias review procedures, reporting of disaggregated data and provision of accommodations are all solid. IEP students should be included in the full reports. The development of alternatives for IEP and LEP students will be positive. The use of a high-stakes test and over-reliance of multiple-choice items are not in line with this standard.

Standard 3: Professional development.

The state does have general requirements for education in assessment for colleges of education, but the colleges vary in implementation. The assessment division of the SEA does not survey teachers as to their professional development needs in assessment, but that may be done by other divisions. The assessment division does provide a variety of materials, including technical digests, test interpretation guides, videos, and a television series on assessment. Regional service centers meet monthly on professional development issues. The state has a voluntary teacher evaluation, including knowledge in assessment. LEAs can develop their own evaluations, which are not regulated by the state and may or may not include knowledge in assessment.

Evaluation

As the assessment division has only limited information about professional development in assessment, it is possible that more is occurring at both pre- and in-service levels. The efforts of the assessment division and the regional service centers seems solid. The SEA should determine teacher capability in classroom assessment and take any needed steps to improve their skills.

The state has done some evaluation of the impact of the exit exams on high school graduation rates. They conclude that of those who do not graduate, about half are affected by the exam requirement (though many of these students might not graduate anyway). The data are inexact because some districts do not have good records on their students.

Evaluation

Texas extensively reviews its assessments system and its impact on education. State officials are aware of problems, such as some teachers teaching too narrowly to the test. The state has concluded that despite the problems, the overall impact is positive and that the heavy reliance on multiple-choice is a reasonable measurement procedure, a conclusion that is not shared by those who endorsed the Forum's *Principles.*

Texas responded to the short FairTest survey by telephone.

UTAH

Summary evaluation

Utah's student assessment system needs a complete overhaul. It tests far too often, relies too heavily on multiple-choice and uses NRTs. Equity concerns seem to be inadequately addressed, and professional development is insufficient. System review needs improvement. It may be that the SEA's new efforts in performance and portfolio assessment can be the basis for redesigning the system. Positively, the stakes are moderate.

Standard 1: Assessment supports important student learning.

Utah has curriculum frameworks, including standards and achievement indicators, in English language arts, math, science, social studies, arts, information technology, and health and physical education. They were developed on a collaborative basis with state and district personnel, including teachers and parents.

Utah administers the Stanford 9 NRT in grades 5, 8 and 11 in the areas of language arts, math, reading, science, and social studies. The Core Curriculum Testing program in grades 1–12 is required of districts by the state. Although districts may choose instruments they will use, all use the state's Core Curriculum Assessment Program (CCAP), which includes criterion-referenced multiple-choice tests for grades 1–6 in reading, math and science; and end-of-course tests in science and math in grades 7–12. Under recently passed legislation, starting in the fall of 1997, entering kindergartners will be assessed on early reading and counting skills.

Evaluation

Utah relies too heavily on NRTs and much too heavily on multiple-choice. Testing young children with multiple-choice instruments exacerbates the problem. The NRTs should be dropped, particularly since the state uses NAEP as a basis for reporting student achievement in light of national standards. The state should shift toward constructed-response, performance and portfolio assessments based on the standards and away from multiple-choice testing. The testing burden should be substantially reduced. Positively, the stakes are not high, though the SEA should review how heavily districts rely on results from one test to place students or to determine high school grades.

Standard 2: Assessments are fair.

The state does not have a bias review committee or procedure for the CCAP or performance assessments. Data reporting does not include demographic categories.

Students with IEPs can be excluded from the NRTs. Decisions on the CCAP are made locally, but the tendency is to test a student if meaningful results can be obtained. LEP students can be excluded from the statewide testing if they have been taught in English for less than three years and they cannot participate meaningfully. Results for IEP and LEP students who are tested are included in regular state NRT reports.

Evaluation

Bias reduction efforts are weak and reporting should include demographic data. Testing many students with the NRT may be inappropriate. More data on actual LEA practices is needed, but the reported tendency is positive.

Standard 3: Professional development.

Professional development is recognized as a major challenge. Pre-service teachers have no specific course requirements. The state has not surveyed teachers' competence in assessment or their professional development needs. Print and video materials are provided to educators and parents for professional development purposes. Training materials for scoring the writing assessment were provided to districts.

Evaluation

Professional development needs to be substantially strengthened for pre-service and in-service teachers. The SEA should encourage districts to have the writing samples scored by teachers. We did not receive information regarding who scores performance assessments. Teachers also should be involved in the development of performance assessment items. Both scoring and writing can be avenues for enhancing professional development.

Utah responded by telephone to the short form of the FairTest survey.

VIRGINIA

Summary evaluation

Virginia's system needs a complete overhaul, but the revisions the state is making are not positive. The state tests too often and will soon test more, relies entirely on multiple-choice except for writing to prompts, mandates use of an NRT, and has a high school graduation test requirement. The state needs to drop these and its new multiple-choice tests, and develop an assessment system for a few grades using a mix of methods. Bias reduction is borderline adequate and inclusion of IEP and LEP students is being worked on. Professional development is thoroughly inadequate. Public education is acceptable for the kinds of tests used, and reporting is adequate, with surveys of parents and the public a positive point. Reviews are extensive, but apparently fail to address basic issues surrounding the limitations of relying on multiple-choice tests.

Standard 1: Assessment supports important student learning.
Virginia has content standards and student expectations developed by local educators, the state board of education and other stakeholders, in math, science, English, history, and technology. The state is in the process of developing assessments to measure its content standards.

The state is currently field-testing a new Standards of Learning (SOL) assessment, developed by a contractor based on the 1995 standards. The SOL will be administered in grades 3, 5, 8 and 11 in English, math, history and science, as well as technology in grades 5 and 8. The tests will be multiple-choice with writing to a prompt, similar to the current LPT, in grades 5, 8 and 11. The tests may become part of the state's graduation requirements.

Parents of home-schooled children must provide evidence of achievement, which usually means the results of a standardized test.

Evaluation
Virginia fails to meet this standard since it tests too often, relies on multiple-choice on both current and prospective tests (except for writing samples), administers an NRT, and has high stakes. The current high school exit exam is based on now-outdated standards, which means students will be tested to two different sets of standards.

Standard 2: Assessments are fair.
A bias/equity review committee that represents racial/ethnic and gender interests reviews all items on state-made tests. The committee may recommend that an item be modified or removed from the bank. Test results are disaggregated by gender, ethnicity, disability status and English-speaking status.

About 14 percent of students tested are classified with an IEP; 1 percent are LEP. All students must pass the LPT to receive a standard diploma, there are no exceptions. However, IEP students are not required to pass the LPT to be classified as high school students, and accommodations or postponing test-taking are allowed for IEP students. LEP students who have not been in a Virginia public school for three years can be classified as a high school student without passing the LPT, but must pass the test after being in school for three years. LEP and IEP students who are tested are included in regular state reports. Accommodations on the NRT are available for both LEP and IEP students, but their scores are excluded from regular reports if an accommodation that does not maintain standard conditions is used. Further accommodations for IEP and LEP students on the NRT and accommodations on the SOL are being developed.

Evaluation
The bias review committee could be strengthened. Reporting by demographic groups is positive. The extent and quality of accommodations are still being developed. Reliance on multiple-choice does not meet this standard as it does not allow for variations in learning styles or cultures. The graduation exit test also fails this standard.

Standard 3: Professional development.
Pre-service teachers are required to learn about standardized tests and use of test results. Other assessment training is available in the state for in-service teachers. The state does not evaluate teacher competence in assessment or survey to determine teacher training needs.

Evaluation
Professional development is inadequate. Pre-service requirements should be expanded to include classroom and performance assessments. Training in these areas should be systematically provided to in-service teachers.
Virginia responded to the full FairTest survey and sent various documents.

WASHINGTON
Summary evaluation
Washington's current system needs many major improvements, particularly discontinuing its use of an NRT. Many of its problems currently are being addressed. The state is developing a far more positive system that will use multiple assessment methods. Among the goals are to minimize the amount of testing, keep the stakes relatively low, emphasize development of classroom-based assessments, provide a strong commitment to professional development and include strong plans for system review. Continuing concerns include ensuring that an NRT is not used, multiple-choice items are a minor part of the exams, teachers are heavily involved in developing and scoring assessments, parents and the public are educated about and involved in the new assessments, and exams do not become single, high-stakes hurdles for the planned Certificate of Mastery.

Standard 1: Assessment supports important student learning.
Washington is developing *Essential Academic Learning Requirements,* content standards in reading, writing, communications, math, science, social studies, art, and health. The state is planning to align new assessments to these emerging standards and expects the new assessments to guide curriculum and instruction.

The state's current Basic Assessment Program includes an NRT battery, the CTBS/4, in grades 4 and 8, and the customized off-the-shelf criterion referenced Curriculum Frameworks Assessment System (CFAS), in grade 11 in math, English/language arts, science, and social studies.

The new assessment system is in the second year of a planned 5-year development program. The system will include state-level exams, with multiple-choice, short-answer and extended, constructed-response items. They will be administered in grades 4, 7 and 10. Currently the grade 4 math and communications (reading, writing, listening) state exam is operational and voluntary for districts. The grade 7 tests in the same subjects are in pilot stage, to be operational next year, and the grade 10 tests are in planning, to be piloted next year. A science assessment will soon be under development. The writing portion of the communication exam requires two pieces, one longer with revisions and one shorter. For cost reasons, scoring will be done by a contracted company, not by state teachers. Three-point rubrics for short responses and 4-point scales for extended responses are being developed.

A second part of the new system will be classroom-based evidence, which is in the planning stage and is closely related to extensive new professional development activities.

Results of current assessments are used for student diagnosis or placement, curriculum improvement, program evaluation and school performance reporting. Consequences include funding gains for schools.

Evaluation
The current system relies too heavily on multiple-choice items and the NRT. The shift toward a mixed-method system is positive, though it is not clear what the proportions will be (multiple-choice should be a minor part). The state should drop the NRT, both to focus assessments on the standards and to prevent the testing load from becoming excessive. Performance tasks and the writing samples should be scored by teachers. The uses of the new assessments also remain unclear. The exam should be only a part of determining receipt of the certificate, as is now planned. The classroom-based part of the new system, linked to professional development, appears promising.

Standard 2: Assessments are fair.
Bias review, including an item-review committee and technical analysis of items, will be used in the new assessments. Flawed items will be discarded. An item data bank large enough for five years of exams will be reviewed. Gender, race and SES data already is collected and reported for schools, districts and the state.

Currently, 3 percent of students tested are classified with LEP, 5 percent have IEPs. Some students with IEPs or LEP are not tested. Limited accommodations are available for those with IEPs. Results for those tested are included in regular reports. The intent of the new system is to assess almost every student, with all accommodations used in the classroom allowed on the assessment. A statewide committee is working to develop guidelines for LEP and IEP accommodations. The state is attempting to design a reporting system with no incentives to exclude students.

Evaluation
The state has a strong approach to fairness planned for its new assessment program, ranging from the bias review committee to reporting demographic-based data to very strong inclusion efforts (though the new federal IDEA legislation will require even more). The use of multiple-methods in the assessment and the focus on developing classroom-based assessments should also bolster equity. The state should consider developing assessments in languages other than English.

Standard 3: Professional development.
Washington requires testing, assessment and evaluation knowledge of all prospective teachers. The SEA has an extensive professional development

program consisting of 16 regional training centers where teachers learn new assessment techniques and then train others in their districts. Training focuses on teachers' understanding of statewide assessment, mastery of standards and ability to choose and use appropriate classroom assessments. Professional development and the new assessments are seen as complementary.

Evaluation

The state has a strong and commendable commitment to professional development. Teacher involvement in scoring would strengthen this. Whether the professional development efforts will prove sufficient for the new programs remains to be seen. The state should survey teachers and administrators periodically, perhaps as part of the student assessment or as continuing surveys on teacher competence in assessment, to ascertain educator needs.

Washington responded by telephone to parts of the short form of the FairTest survey.

WISCONSIN

Summary evaluation

Wisconsin's assessment program needs many major improvements. The state relies primarily on a 60-percent multiple-choice NRT that is not aligned with the standards. The state should shift to a primarily performance assessment based on the state new content standards. The state does not have a high testing burden and the stakes are moderate. Professional development needs major attention. Some fairness concerns are well addressed, others, particularly inclusion of IEP and LEP students, less so. Public reporting and system review appear to be adequate.

Standard 1: Assessment supports important student learning.

Wisconsin is in the process of developing content standards. It has curriculum guides that are also used to help districts develop standards.

The purposes of the WSAS are to provide expectations for students and obtain data based on the expectations, promote high-quality curriculum and instruction, assist educational planning for students and identify low-performing schools. The RCT also is intended specifically to allow early evaluation of the effectiveness of school reading programs. The assessments are used for identification of pupils needing remediation, public reporting, and to prompt the development of remediation plans for any district in which fewer than 80 percent of the students score above the performance standard on the RCT.

Standard 2: Assessments are fair.

Bias analysis is conducted on the KCE by the contractor. For the RCT, a bias review committee composed of representatives of minority groups in the state participates in selecting reading passages and items. It has the authority to delete or revise items. Scores on WSAS and RCT tests are released by race and gender at the state, district and school levels. RCT test scores are also disaggregated by the percentage of families in the district receiving AFDC and by district size.

IEP and LEP students may be excluded or may receive accommodations to take the exams. About 10 percent of third graders are excluded from the RCT. On the KCE, scores of IEP and LEP students are not reported with other students. Approximately one-half (in grade 4) and one-quarter (in grade 8) IEP and LEP students do not take the test, and those exempted comprise 3–8 percent of the student population.

Evaluation

Bias review and reporting of data are solid. The exclusion of too many students should be addressed by providing further accommodations or alternative assessments. Including more methods of assessment could enhance fairness.

Standard 3: Professional development.

The state provides professional development in assessment to teachers and administrators about the KCE and the RCT through informational workshops for district staff. The state has not attempted to evaluate district school or classroom assessment practices. Educators are involved in developing the RCT assessments, but not in scoring assessments.

Evaluation

Professional development appears inadequate for pre- and in-service teachers. The only positive is teacher involvement in developing the RCT.

Standard 5: System review and improvement.

The state assessment is reviewed every three years. The RCT is reviewed annually by an advisory committee, which includes local educators. The tests' impact on curriculum and instruction is part of the review. On the RCT, the reading passages are reviewed for developmental appropriateness.

Evaluation

The review seems adequate. The developmental appropriateness of the grade 3 test, which is mostly multiple-choice, and the grade 4 test, which is a long exam for students of that age, should be considered more thoroughly. Item review is not the same as review of the format of the assessment. As the new state standards come into effect, the alignment between standards and the exams, and the impact of the exams on instruction toward the standards, will need to be carefully studied.

Wisconsin responded to the full FairTest survey and sent various documents.

WEST VIRGINIA

Summary evaluation

The state assessment system needs a complete overhaul. The state testing burden is far too heavy and relies on multiple-choice NRTs. The number of grades tested should be drastically reduced and the state should shift away from using an NRT. The state should develop an assessment system that more fully matches the standards and that relies on a variety of methods of assessment. An NRT that only partially matches the state standards should not be the basis for mandated reteaching or the awarding of "warranties" on diplomas. Bias review and inclusion are insufficient, professional development needs to be strengthened and reporting is not sufficient. The assessment review process is inadequate, though the on-site visits are a positive approach.

Standard 1: Assessment supports important student learning.
West Virginia has new, revised standards in language arts, math, and science and social studies and is developing performance standards in language arts and math. The state plans to "fine tune" the assessments to better match the new standards.

By law, students are tested in every grade—with a readiness test in kindergarten; an assessment in grades 1 and 2 for reporting to parents and in-school use; and an off-the-shelf, multiple-choice NRT (Stanford 9) in grades 3–11 using the full battery (reading, language, mathematics, science and social studies). The Stanford 9 has a 60 percent match to the curriculum frameworks. The SEA administers the ACT Explorer in grade 8 and the ACT Work Keys in grade 12, both related to career interest and academics. The state also has a criterion-referenced test it makes available to districts to use in grades 1–8.

Evaluation
West Virginia tests students too often, a problem that is compounded by reliance on a multiple-choice NRT that only partly assesses to the state standards. Such a test should not be the basis for mandated re-teaching or the award of warranties on diplomas. Teacher involvement in the writing assessment is positive.

Standard 2: Assessments are fair.
A bias review committee does not exist for writing assessments because, we were told, "there is not enough cultural diversity in West Virginia." Prompts are not studied for bias. Other tests are commercial and rely on the manufacturer's bias reduction procedures. Reports do not include results by demographic categories.

Nearly 10 percent of test-takers have an IEP. Some exemptions and accommodations are available for students with an IEP. Their scores are excluded from regular reports. No separate report is issued.

Evaluation
It may be that there is little racial diversity in West Virginia, but cultural variations rooted in socio-economic class should be considered. Different learning styles are not addressed due to reliance on multiple-choice items. Inclusion for IEP appears weak, and no information was provided about LEP students.

Standard 3: Professional development.
The state provides courses and in-services on a wide range of assessment issues for teachers and administrators, but has no particular requirements. It does not evaluate or survey teacher competence in assessment or teacher training needs.

Evaluation

Professional development needs to be strengthened. Teacher involvement in writing is positive.

West Virginia responded to the full FairTest survey.

WYOMING

Summary evaluation

Wyoming currently does not have a state assessment system that can be evaluated. It only has a vocational test administered to a sample of students. Beginning in 1998, districts will be required to assess students on the state's common core of knowledge and skills. The approach to the vocational exam seems reasonable. A district-based approach is reasonable, but the state should then evaluate the quality of the district assessments. No equity data are available, but should be. Professional development should in any event be strengthened. Public reporting is adequate for the vocational test, and the review process seems reasonable.

Legislation has just passed to create a state exam program that would assess in grades 4, 8 and 11. The SEA and an appointed committee are to report on what the SEA intends to do and the cost. In the same legislation, the SEA is ordered to study whether the state should have a high-stakes "competency test," and the logistics of implementing it. The state should utilize the *Principles and Indicators for Student Assessment Systems* to help guide the creation of the new program. A high-stakes "competency test" should be strongly resisted.

Standard 1: Assessment supports important student learning.

Wyoming is developing "student expectations" in reading, math, writing, science and social studies. They are being developed by local and state study groups with assistance from the Mid-Continent Regional Education Laboratory. State accreditation standards require school districts to develop standards and assessments by the 1997 school year in the common core of knowledge and skills.

Wyoming currently does not have a state assessment program, but it does have a vocational assessment. Legislation is pending to adopt a state assessment for all students in grades 4, 8 and 11 in reading and language arts. It will be standards-based and include multiple-choice and constructed-response items and some performance tasks.

Evaluation

The vocational assessment appears reasonable. As there is no other state assessment, the basic questions are what do districts do and what will the new assessments be like?

Standard 2: Assessments are fair.

There is no bias review of the vocational assessment.

Evaluation

Bias review should be done, and data on LEP and IEP students should be compiled for the vocational assessment. These issues should be addressed in a new state assessment system.

Standard 3: Professional development.

The state requires no assessment expertise for pre-service teachers, nor does it evaluate teacher competence. It has a mandatory in-service on the vocational assessment for vocational teachers that is also offered to administrators. Education in various forms of assessment are available in the state, but the SEA itself only offers sessions on the use of test results.

An annual survey about education needs includes questions about professional development in assessment. The state reports high interest in help with assessment. The state does not survey classroom or district practices.

Evaluation

Professional development should be substantially strengthened, with or without a new state exam. The survey should be a helpful starting point. Teacher involvement in the vocational assessment is positive.

Wyoming responded to the full FairTest survey.

❧ A Glossary of Assessment Terms

Academic standards: These are clearly written expectations of what every learner must learn at a specific grade level.

Authentic assessment: This type of assessment requires authentic tasks of students that show what they can do. It assumes feedback and redirection for student growth. It shows what a student "can do."

Criterion-referenced test (CRT): This type of test is designed to measure how well a person has learned a specific body of knowledge and skills. A multiple-choice test for a driver's license is an example of a CRT.

Computerized testing: This refers to tests taken on a computer. For example, the Graduate Record Exam (GRE) has a format that allows a person to test on the computer. However, critics point out that computerized tests constrain test takers. If a student enters an incorrect answer, they cannot go back and redo the answers on the computer. In addition, computers may worsen test bias because schools with diverse and low-income populations are less likely to have computers. Also, research shows that girls are adversely affected by computerized testing because they statistically use computers less than boys.

Freedom of Information Act (FOIA): The Freedom of Information Act (FOIA) law, passed by Congress and signed by the president in 1966, gives citizens the right to obtain certain government records. The law was written to contribute to an informed citizenry so that they could better participate in democratic decision making. States have their own FOIA laws and regulations that pertain to state and often local government agencies.

Depending on the state FOIA laws, some or all of the following may be public information subject to FOIA or may be "exempt" from disclosure: the state's request for proposals for test creation and scoring and criteria for choosing the contracted company; test validity and reliability studies; test answer scoring procedures; cut-score or level-setting procedures (such as how a failing score is determined); expenditures for certain tests or assessments overall; the type and cost of training provided for teachers to learn alternative assessment practices; the cost of rewards to high-scoring schools; the cost of retaining students in grade an extra year; a breakdown in test scores by race, gender, and socioeconomic class. In some states, the contract with the test manufacturer may also be a public document.

In order to use the FOIA, a letter detailing the information sought must be sent to the appropriate record-keeping department. If you are not sure where to begin, consult your secretary of state or state legislator's office for guidance.

Gender gap: This term usually refers to the gap reflected on test scores between boys and girls. A gender gap favors boys across all demographics including family income, parents education level, grade point average, rank in school, size of high school, size of district, etc.

High-stakes testing: This is a term referring to standardized tests that are used for high stakes such as withdrawing money and support from a school or retaining a student in a grade level.

Multiple intelligences: This refers to the theory of multiple intelligences formulated by Howard Gardner. This broadens the view of intelligence and how the mind works to include musical, bodily kinesthetic, logical-mathematical, spatial, interpersonal, intrapersonal, and linguistic intelligences.

Multiple-choice test (MCT): An MCT usually has many test items. For each question a person selects one best answer from a given list of usually four or more choices. Many of the choices are distractors. Most standardized tests are made up of multiple-choice items.

Norm-referenced test (NRT): This type of test compares a person's score against the scores of a group of people called the "norm group." They are most often multiple-choice tests. Some examples of NRTs are the California Achievement Test (CAT), the Iowa Test of Basic Skills (ITBS), and intelligence quotient (IQ) tests.

Performance-based assessment: This term is often used interchangeably with *authentic assessment*. It is assessment based on performance tasks to show what a student can do.

Proficiency level: This is a cut-off level that indicates that a student's performance is at a minimal, basic, proficient, or advanced level. These levels are set against an absolute standard.

Retention: This term refers to nonpromotion of a student from one grade to another—in other words, holding a student back in a grade. The decision to do so is often made on the basis of standardized test scores.

Rubric: This is a set of scoring guidelines for evaluating a student's work. Rubrics provide criteria for judgements on performance. Usually there is a scale, or range of possible points, assigned to a rubric. Each level of performance on the rubric must have specific descriptors that indicate what a student must do to achieve that level. Rubrics are often associated with standards and how those standards are met.

Standards-referenced test (SRT): This is a type of criterion-referenced test (CRT). Many states have adopted content standards for subjects such as reading, math, and social studies. They have performance standards for the content standards. Students must reach "base," "proficient," or "advanced" levels in the subject area. Tests are based on the standards and are judged by teachers or groups of teachers.

✎ Sample Letter for Exercising Your Right to Information on Testing in Your State

DATE
Mr/Ms.
Title
Department
Agency
Address
City, State, Zip
Mr/Ms. _____,

I would like to request copies of the following information under the Freedom of Information Act and as a request as an Ohio citizen. Could you and the Ohio Department of Education (DOE) please provide me with copies of any and all documents that discuss, evaluate or state the appropriate and validated uses or the inappropriate and invalidated uses of the data resulting from all of the Ohio Proficiency Tests (fourth grade, sixth grade and ninth grade). Examples of this type of information could be discussions and evaluations of using the 4th grade test to determine grade promotion or the appropriate use of the data to compare academic quality between school districts. I would also like to request copies of any documents stating or referring to test takers rights.

It is likely that some of the types of documents that may include this information are (but are not limited to):

1. The initial request for bid/proposal documents that were submitted to test writers/contractors stating what the tests are to measure. In other terms, the scope of work and objectives for developing the tests.
2. Contractual documents where the test contractor put in disclaimers or other statements related to the appropriate and validated (inappropriate and invalidated) use of the test results and test takers rights.
3. Technical manuals written both externally and internally detailing the appropriate and valid (inappropriate and invalid) use of the test results and test takers rights.

4. Technical evaluation documents discussing and evaluating resultant data in terms of overall appropriate use of the data and validated uses of the data. These may be internal or external (outside contractor) documents.
5. Internal memos within the ODE of other State Offices discussing these subjects or letters to legislators or other politically important people discussing these subjects.

Pursuant to [your own local FOIA law], we request a waiver of any and all fees for searching for and copying materials that respond to this request. Disclosure of the requested information is in the public interest, will greatly benefit the general public and is not in the commercial interests of the undersigned or any other person.

    It would be helpful if a time estimate could be given for submission of these documents to me. They are needed as soon as possible.

    Please feel free to contact my anytime with questions. A hard copy of this request will follow this facsimile in the mail.

    Source: www.fairtest.org

●● Index

AACTE. *See* American Association of Colleges for Teacher Education

About Alternative Assessments (website), 150

Accountability, 85, 97–98

ACT. *See* American College Testing (ACT) assessment

Administrators, 140

AERA. *See* American Educational Research Association

AFT. *See* American Federation of Teachers

Alternative Assessment for Adult Learners (website), 150

American Association for Higher Education (website), 150–151

American Association of Colleges for Teacher Education (AACTE), 155

American College Testing (ACT) assessment, 104, 105

American Education Research Association, 104

American Educational Research Association (AERA), 141–145, 168–169

American Evaluation Association, 169

American Federation of Teachers (AFT), 155–156

American pragmatism, 81

American Psychological Association (APA), 141

American Standards: Quality Education in a Complex World, The Texas Case (Horn and Kincheloe), 99

APA. *See* American Psychological Association

Army, testing in, 89, 91

ASCD 1998 Assessment Conference on Teaching and Learning Set (video), 146

Assessment
alternative forms of, 127–128, 130
assessment movement described, 1
characteristics of authentic and meaningful assessment, 121–122
chronology of the assessment movement, 91–94
fair and equitable means of, 110–111
the value of, 83–84

Assessment (website), 151

Assessment, Accountability, and Standards (website), 151

Assessment and Accountability (website), 149

Assessment in Math and Science— What's the Point? (video), 146–147

Assessment Interactive Training Multimedia Package (video), 147

Assessment-related sites, index (website), 151

Association for Supervision and Curriculum Development (ASCD), 146, 170–171

Auden, W. H., 123

Authentic assessment, 1–4
current politics of, 79–81
implementation of, 128

Authentic assessment, *continued*
principles of, 87
versus typical tests, 81–87
See also Authentic assessment,
examples of; Standardized tests
Authentic assessment, examples of,
7–12, 85–87
assessing writing, 132
case studies of personalized
assessment, 130
versus standard tests, 81–87
yoga practice, 120–122
Authentic Assessment Samples
(website), 149–150
Authentic Portfolio Assessment
(website), 151–152
Autobiography
assessment of writing, 86–87
education autobiography, 60
example of student portfolio,
37–49, 62–66, 71–79
Automating Authentic Assessment
with Rubrics (website), 152

Berliner, David, 4, 93, 109
Bias, in norm-referenced tests,
104–105
Biddle, Bruce, 4, 93, 109
Bilingual Education Clearinghouse,
156
Binet, Alfred, 89, 91
Bloom's Taxonomy, 132
Book reviews, 66–67
Bush, George W., 113
Business orientation, of testing,
97–98, 130–131

California Achievement Test, 103
California Senate Bill 662, 15
Campbell, David, 138–139
Characteristics
of authentic and meaningful
assessment, 1–4, 121–122
of standard tests, 1–4, 90, 114
Chicago: high-stakes testing, 112

Chicago Principal Assessment Center,
157
Civil rights movements, 92
Class differences, 90
Classroom assessment, 127, 146
Community involvement, in
assessment, 128
The Contradictions of School Reform
(McNeil), 97
CRESST. *See* National Center for
Research on Evaluation,
Standards, and Student Testing

Defense spending, 93
Department of Education, 92–93
Dewey, John, 81, 98
Disabilities, students with, 134, 144
The Disciplined Mind (Gardner), 108
Discrimination, 101–102
racial differences, 90, 100,
103–106
in testing and scoring, 103–106
Doctoral student portfolio, 36–53
Dynamic assessment, 131

ECS. *See* Education Commission of
the States
Education: Wiggins's theory of
teaching versus learning, 83–85
Education Commission of the States
(ECS), 157
Education Publications Center, 157
Education Research Office, 158
Educational Resources Information
Center (ERIC), 158
Educators for Social Responsibility
(ESR), 159
Electronic portfolio, 14–15
Elementary school years, educational
autobiography of, 72–73
ERIC. *See also* Educational Resources
Information Center
ERIC Clearinghouse on Assessment
and Evaluation (website), 152,
159–160

ERIC Clearinghouse on Information and Technology, 160–161
ERIC Clearinghouse on Teaching and Teacher Education, 161
ERIC Clearinghouse on Urban Education, 161–162
ESR. *See* Educators for Social Responsibility
Essay exam questions, analytic and holistic rubrics for, 10–12
Ethical issues
    multiple intelligences, 106–108
    norm-referenced tests, 102–106
    standards movement, 96–102
Examples, of authentic assessment, 7–12, 85–87
    assessing writing, 132
    case studies of personalized assessment, 130
    versus standard tests, 81–87
    yoga practice, 120–122
Examples, of portfolios
    doctoral student portfolio, 36–53
    middle school student portfolio, 54–58
    teacher portfolio, 17–35
    university undergraduate student, 58–70
Exemptions, from testing, 145

Fairness, of assessment, 80
FairTest organization, 93, 104, 105, 113–114, 165
Feedback: student, parent, and teacher
    electronic portfolio, 15
    middle school student portfolio, 55
    parent and teacher feedback on assessment, 137–138
    for teacher portfolio, 26–35
    on teacher quality, 63–66
    undergraduate student portfolio, 60, 67–69
Florida: high-stakes testing, 112
Frames of Mind (Gardner), 106

Galecka, Michele, 54–58
The Galef Institute, 162
Galton, Francis, 89, 91
Gardner, Howard, 5–7, 92, 106–108, 125, 128–129
Gender differences, 90, 106
GI Forum v. TEA, 100
Goal assessments, for portfolio, 55–58, 140
Government involvement in education, 92–93, 95, 113
Group projects, 69–70

Haney, Walter, 101
High-stakes testing
    history of standardized testing, 113–115
    NCTE resolutions, 174–176
    opposition to, 145
    problems with, 112–113
    resource materials, 137, 141–145
History, of assessment, 4–7, 113–114

IMMEX home page (website), 152
Inequalities, in testing, 98–99
Influence of Performance-Based and Authentic Assessment (website), 152–153
Intelligence quotient (IQ) testing, 89, 91
International Reading Association, 145, 169–170
Introduction to Science Portfolios (website), 152

Journal writing, 134

Language, use of in testing, 112
Learning, versus teaching, 83–85
Legal issues, 99, 106
Lund, Jacalyn, 83–84

"Manufactured crisis," 108–110
The Manufactured Crisis (Berliner and Biddle), 93

Maryland Assessment Consortium, 162–163
McNeil, Linda, 97–98
Method, 95–96
Middle school
  educational autobiography example, 73–74
  middle school student portfolio, 54–58
  resource materials, 135, 148, 166
  support for standards in, 139–140
Minorities, rising test scores for, 119. *See also* Discrimination
Multiple Intelligences: The Theory and Practice (Gardner), 106
Multiple intelligences, theory of
  authentic assessment movement and, 5–7
  early beginnings of theory, 92
  ethical issues, 106–108
  maintaining academic rigor, 135
  resource materials, 125, 128–129
Myths, about student achievement, 4–5, 108–110

NAASP. *See* National Association of Secondary School Principals
NABSE. *See* National Alliance of Black School Educators
NASBE. *See* National Association of State Boards of Education
"A Nation at Risk" report, 93, 95
National Alliance of Black School Educators (NABSE), 163
National Assessment of Educational Progress (NAEP), 157
National Association of Secondary School Principals (NAASP), 163
National Association of State Boards of Education (NASBE), 163–164
National Board for Professional Teaching Standards, 164
National Center for Education Statistics (NCES), 165

National Center for Fair and Open Testing. *See* FairTest organization
National Center for Research on Evaluation, Standards, and Student Testing (CRESST), 150, 153, 171–172
National Center on Educational Outcomes, 165
National Collegiate Athletic Association (NCAA), 106
National Council for Accreditation of Teacher Education (NCATE), 165–166
National Council for the Social Studies (NCSS), 172–173, 172–174
National Council of Teachers of English (NCTE), 174–176
National Council on Measurement in Education (NCME), 141
National Education Association (NEA), 176
National Forum on Assessment, 114
National Middle School Association (NMSA), 166
National School Boards Association (NSBA), 166–167
National Science Teachers Association (NSTA), 176–177
National Staff Development Council (NSDC), 167
NCATE. *See* National Council for Accreditation of Teacher Education
NCES. *See* National Center for Education Statistics
NCME. *See* National Council on Measurement in Education
NCSS. *See* National Council for the Social Studies
NCTE. *See* National Council of Teachers of English
NEA. *See* National Education Association

Neill, Monty, 113
Nixon, Richard, 92
NMSA. *See* National Middle School
    Association
NSBA. *See* National School Boards
    Association
NSDC. *See* National Staff
    Development Council
NSTA. *See* National Science Teachers
    Association

Parent and teacher feedback on
    assessment, 137–138
Parent organizations, 93
PDK. *See* Phi Delta Kappa
    International
Performance, defined, 84–85
*Performance Assessment in the
    Classroom: A Video Journal of
    Education* (video), 147–148
*Performance-Based Assessment in
    Quality Elementary and Middle
    Schools* (video), 148
Perot, Ross, 97, 98
Phi Delta Kappa International (PDK),
    170
Politics, of assessment
    authentic assessment versus
        standardized tests, 79–81
    the manufactured crisis in
        education, 109
    resource materials, 130–131
    social and political effects of
        language, 112
    source material for, 126
Portfolio development, 7–12, 94, 127
Portfolios
    Authentic Portfolio Assessment
        (website), 152
    contents and examples, 16–35
    doctoral student, 36–53
    educational autobiography, 71–79
    elementary level student, 133
    individualization of, 134

middle school student, 54–58
school portfolio, 126–127
science portfolios website, 153
teacher portfolio, 17–35
types of, 12–14
university undergraduate student,
    58–70
Postmodernism, 89–90, 92, 94
Pragmatism, American, 81
"Principles and Indicators for
    Student Assessment Systems,"
    113–114
Professional teacher organizations,
    93
Psychological testing, 89, 91

Racial differences, 90, 100, 103–106
Reagan administration, 92–93
Record-keeping portfolio, 13
Redesigning Assessment (video),
    148–149
Reform, educational, 4–7
    general characteristics of, 95–96
    Reagan administration, 92–93
    Texas standards case, 97–102
Relearning by Design, 167–168
"A Report Card on Assessment," 113
Research, on assessment, 81–87
    cognitive and biological research,
        129
    multiple intelligences, 119–120

San Diego Unified School District, 15
Scholastic Aptitude Test (SAT) scores,
    119
Science portfolio, 153
Showcase portfolio, 14
Simon, Theodore, 91
Site-based management, 99–100
Socioeconomic status, 90, 105–106
Software, for electronic portfolios,
    14–15
Southern states: high-stakes testing,
    113

Soviet Union, 92
Sputnik satellite, 92
Standard scales, 89
Standardized tests, 3–4, 93–94,
    102–106
  adverse impact on learning,
    130–131
  alternatives to, 129
  versus authentic assessment,
    81–87, 136
  norm-referenced tests, 102–106
  parent and teacher feedback on,
    137–138
  practicing for tests, 100–101
  problems with high-stakes tests,
    115
  racial discrimination, 101–102
  relabeling as assessments, 114
  resource materials, 134–135
  support for standards at middle
    school level, 139–140
*Standards for Educational and
    Psychological Testing,* 141
Standards movement, 95–96, 96–102
Student portfolios
  doctoral student, 36–53
  middle school student portfolio,
    54–58
  students with disabilities, 134
  university undergraduate student,
    58–70
Sztam, Saul, 37–53

TAAS. *See* Texas Assessment of
    Academic Skills
TABS. *See* Texas Assessment of Basic
    Skills
Tanner, David E., 6
Teacher portfolio, example of, 17–35

Teachers
  assessment examples and
    resources, 132–133
  impact of TAAS on, 98–99
  student critiques of, 63–66, 72–75
  teaching strategies, 134
Teaching, versus learning, 83–85
Testing, versus assessment, 136
Texas: school reform case, 97–102
Texas Assessment of Academic Skills
    (TAAS), 97–98, 100, 101
Texas Assessment of Basic Skills
    (TABS), 99, 100
Thorndike, Edward L., 89

Undergraduate student portfolio,
    58–70, 74–75
Unions, 92

Vietnam War, 92

Watergate, 92
*What's New in Schools: A Parent's
    Guide to Performance Assessment*
    (video), 149
Wiggins, Grant, 6, 83–85, 93, 110–111,
    120, 167–168
Wilson Academy for International
    Studies, 15
Working portfolio, 13
World War I, 89
World War II, 89–90
Writing, evaluating, 132
  assessing autobiography, 86–87
  journal writings, 134
  portfolio development, 8–10

Yoga practice, as authentic
    assessment example, 120–122

❖ About the Author

Valerie Janesick is professor of educational leadership and organizational change and chair of the Department of Education at Roosevelt University in Chicago.